The House of Islam

THE RELIGIOUS LIFE OF MAN
Frederick J. Streng, Series Editor

The House of Islam

Second Edition

KENNETH CRAGG
University of Sussex, England

DICKENSON PUBLISHING COMPANY, INC.

Encino, California and Belmont, California

ISBN-0-8221-0139-4
Library of Congress Catalog Card Number: 74-83949

Printed in the United States of America
Printing (last digit): 9 8 7 6 5 4 3 2 1

Table of Contents

Foreword

THE RELIGIOUS LIFE OF MAN series is intended as an introduction to a large, complex field of inquiry—man's religious experience. It seeks to present the depth and richness of religious concepts, forms of worship, spiritual practices, and social institutions found in the major religious traditions throughout the world.

As a specialist in the language and culture in which a religion is found, each author is able to illuminate the meanings of a religious perspective and practice as other human beings have experienced it. To communicate this meaning to readers who have had no special training in these cultures and religions, the authors have attempted to provide clear, nontechnical descriptions and interpretations of religious life.

Different interpretive approaches have been used, depending upon the nature of the religious data; some religious expressions, for instance, lend themselves more to developmental, others more to topical studies. But this lack of a single interpretation may itself be instructive, for the experiences and practices regarded as religious in one culture may not be the most important in another.

THE RELIGIOUS LIFE OF MAN is concerned with, on the one hand, the variety of religious expressions found in different traditions and, on the other, the similarities in the structures of religious life. The various forms are interpreted in terms of their cultural context and historical continuity, demonstrating both the diverse expressions and commonalities of religious traditions. Besides the single volumes on different religions, the series offers a core book on the study of religious meaning, which describes different study approaches and examines several modes and structures of religious awareness. In addition, each book presents a list of materials for further reading, including translations of religious texts and detailed examinations of specific topics.

We hope the reader will find these volumes "introductory" in the most significant sense: an introduction to a new perspective for understanding himself and others.

Frederick J. Streng
Series Editor

Preface

"France," George Bernard Shaw once observed, "is such a great country. What a pity to waste it on the French." The sentiment, of course, might equally well be set down about every land and its people. How much more, then, about religions. "Christianity is so rich a faith: what a tragedy it is held by Christians." In any study, such as this of Islam and Muslims, it is imperative to keep a balance between a true and worthy appreciation of the essential faith, and an honest open realism about its fortunes in the tumult of the world. The doctrinal and the actual, the ideal and the empirical, must always judge and address each other. To keep them in related focus is no easy task.

To attempt it, and be confined to an "introduction," is to encounter sharpened problems. There are few general statements that do not require qualification and reserve. But one cannot take in fourteen centuries with a microscope. So all that follows here is no more than an essay in interpretation. It aims to be as adequate as its limitations admit, for purposes of initial acquaintance with Islam, and in preliminary elucidation of its central themes, and for use—within these limitations—as a single text. But it will have failed if it does not leave the strong impression of the need to look further—a hope which the brief, annotated bibliography is intended to suggest and inform. The final entries there may be excused and explained, on the plea that, writing in this way about a theme which an author knows in his heart deserves so much more and better, he may be allowed to indicate what that more should be. Beyond all bibliography are the occasions of human exchange and community within and across the frontiers of faiths.

This second edition embodies suggestions made by users of the first edition, whose comments are gratefully acknowledged. Opportunity has also been taken to enlarge on some aspects of Islamic history which found no place in the earlier treatment. It is hoped that these emendations and additions will provide a fuller perspective, without displacing the essential and continuing concern with "religious life."

K.C.

Table of Dates

The Muslim dating A.H. (*Anno Hegirae:* "in the year of the Hijrah") begins from July 16, 622 A.D., when Muḥammad emigrated from Mecca to establish his cause in Medina. A Muslim year consists of 12 *lunar* months and each, therefore, recedes approximately 11 days each *solar* year. The Muslim calendar thus gains about three years every century on the Christian calendar. The fifteenth Hijrī century is due in 1979 A.D. on November 21.

It was considered tedious to insert both A.H. and A.D. dates in the text. The following table may assist an appreciation of chronology in relation to Islamic beginnings.

A.H.		A.D.
52 years before H.	Birth of the Prophet	570
27 years before H.	Marriage with Khadījah	c. 595
12/13 years before H.	First experience of the Qur'ān	609/10
7 years before H.	First Muslims find refuge in Ethiopia	615
3 years before H.	Death of Khadījah and of Abū Tālib, Muḥammad's protector	619
-	The Hijrah	622
2	Muḥammad's victory at Badr	624
3	Muḥammad's reverse at Uḥud	625
8	Conquest of Mecca and consolidation of Islam	630
11	Death of Muḥammad	632
13	Death of Abū Bakr, the first Caliph	634
14/15	Capture of Damascus and Jerusalem	636/37
18/19	Conquest of Egypt and Persia	639/40
23	Murder of 'Umar, the second Caliph	644
28	Muslim seizure of Cyprus	649
29	Canon of the Qur'ān established	c. 650
35	Murder of 'Uthmān, the third Caliph	656
40	Assassination of 'Alī, the fourth Caliph	661
41/132	The Umayyad Caliphate	661/750
50	Foundation of Qairawān, Tunisia	670
61	Massacre of Karbalā' and death of Ḥusain	680
71/72	Construction of the Dome of the Rock, Jerusalem, and of the Al-Aqṣā Mosque	690/91
92	Construction of the Great Mosque at Damascus	710
92	Muslim conquest, under Ṭāriq, crosses from Morocco into Spain	711
94	Entry into Indus Valley, capture of Multan	713
94	Taking of Cordoba, Spain	713
95	Capture of Samarqand	714
110	Death of Ḥasan al-Baṣrī, earliest Sūfi	728
114	Battle of Tours: turn of the tide of Islam in France	732
132	Rise of the 'Abbāsid Caliphate	750
145	Foundation of Baghdad by Caliph Al-Manṣūr	762

A.H.　　　　　　　　　　　　　　　　　　　　　　　　　　　　　A.D.

148	Imām of the Seveners goes into "hiddenness"	765
150	Death of Abū Ḥanīfah, great early legist	767
179	Death of Mālik Ibn Anas, founder of the second School of Law	795
193	Death of Hārūn al-Rashīd of the 'Abbāsid "golden age"	809
204	Death of Abū 'Abdallāh al-Shāfi'ī, founder of the third School of Law	820
212	Caliph Al-Ma'mūn's official proclamation of the Mu'tazilite doctrine of the Qur'ān	827
221	Building of the Great Mosque of Qairawān, Tunis	836
241	Death of Aḥmad ibn Ḥanbal, founder of the fourth School of Law	855
256	Death of Al-Bukhārī, the great traditionalist	870
259	Death of Ḥunain ibn Isḥāq, scholar and translator	873
264	Imām of the Twelvers goes into "hiddenness"	878
265	Building of Mosque of Ibn Ṭulūn, Cairo	879
297	Rise of the Fāṭimids in North Africa	909
311	Death of Abū Ja'far al-Ṭabarī, great annalist and commentator	923
313	Death of Abū Bakr al-Rāzī, greatest of Muslim physicians	925
324	Death of Al-Ash'arī, leading theologian	935
339	Death of Al-Fārābī, the Islamic Aristotle	950
345	Seljūq Turks Islamicize	956
356	Fāṭimids in Egypt: Cairo founded	966
358	Foundation of Al-Azhar, Cairo	969
426	Death of Ibn Sīnā (Avicenna)	1036
442	Death of Al-Bīrūnī, natural scientist and linguist	1050
449	Death of Abū-l-'Alā al-Ma'arī, poet and sceptic	1057
456	Death of Ibn Ḥazm	1064
463	Seljūq Turks occupy Damascus	1071
492	Crusaders capture Jerusalem	1099
505	Death of Abū Ḥamīd al-Ghazālī, great architect of Islamic spirituality	1111
561	Death of 'Abd al-Qādir al-Jīlānī, founder of the Qādiriyyah Order of Sufis	1166
564	Accession to power of Salāḥ al-Dīn (Saladin)	1169
616/621	Mongol devastation of Transoxiana and Khurasan	1219/24
638	Death of Ibn al-'Arabī, Spanish-Arabic mystical philosopher	1240
657	Sack of Baghdad by the Mongols and fall of the 'Abbasid Caliphate	1258
657	Death of Al-Shādhilī, founder of the Shādhiliyyah Order	1258
659	Mamlūks halt the Mongols in Palestine	1260
672	Death of Jalāl al-Dīn Rūmī, founder of the Maulawiyyah Order	1273
715	Death of Raymond Lull, Christian apostle to Islam, at Bougie, Tunis	1315
728	Death of Ibn-Taimiyya of Damascus, great Ḥanbalī theologian	1328
807	Death of Tīmūr-lang, Mongol conqueror	1404
808	Death of Ibn Khaldūn, philosopher of history and sociologist	1406
859	Ottoman Turks capture Constantinople	1453
897	Fall of Granada: end of Muslim Spain	1492
923	Salīm I conquers Egypt and carries the last titular 'Abbāsid Caliph to Istanbul	1517

Introduction

"When my mind travels to the eighty million Muslims of Indonesia, the fifty million in China, and the several other millions in Malaya, Siam and Burma, and the hundred million in Pakistan, the hundred or more in the Middle East and the forty million in Russia, as well as the other millions in the distant parts of the world, when I visualize these millions united in one faith, I have a great conscious-ness of the tremendous potentialities that co-operation amongst them can achieve."[1]

The figures are obviously rounded and the locations broad and incomplete. What matters is the sentiment, whether in the lowliest of those multitudes or in the exalted station of the writer, the late President of Egypt, reflecting on Islam in his book, *The Philosophy of the Revolution.* There was controversy even in the context. For Jamāl 'Abd al-Nāṣir (Nasser) was suggesting the use of the annual pilgrimage to Mecca as a ready, and proper, occasion for political consultation among heads of state—a plan which other opinion finds quite inconsistent with the sole devotional business of the pilgrim rites and season. It is also to be noted that, for all its sincerity, his plea for Islamic solidarity stood only third in his priorities, after the paramount claims of Arab unity and the Egyptian obligations with Africa. Arabic and the Nile, national feeling and geography, took prece-dence over faith and the universal.

Even so there was an emotion in the words which finds an echo through all the territories of which they speak. Not for half a century at least has Pan-Islam been a viable political program, still less a reality of power. But it is no less, for that reason, a passion and a bond, a community of experience and shared identity, extending through a segment of the human family large enough to constitute at least one seventh of mankind.

The aim of the chapters that follow is to study the religious life of this great *Dār al-Islām*—the name, meaning "House of Islam," current among Muslims from a very early date to describe themselves. By Muslim measure, any such isolation of religious life is uncongenial. For Islam, by its own showing, is a unity in which culture, society, and the political realm, no less than devotion and cultic forms, partake. It is, for Muslims, a western and deplorable notion to think of religion as separable from the totality of the human context. All must be claimed for the sacred loyalty. Yet this needs the ritual focus and the dogmatic structure. It is these, with their kindred elements of social feeling and allegiance, which must here do duty for the larger whole.

The *Dār,* simply understood, is the place where things circulate in their own habitat, the abode of persons moving where they belong. The term is much more than geographical, though Islam takes in every continent. There are Muslims in the Americas, as well as in Asia where they originated, and in Africa and Europe where they conquered and increased. In and beyond the territorial meaning of the phrase there belongs a whole sociological and cultural complex, with a bewildering variety of form and temper, yet all somehow self-aware and participant in one identity. The concept is often defined by reference to its antonym, *Dār al-Ḥarb*, "the House of non-Islam," "the unpeaced abode," which in the days of *Jihād*, or so-called "holy war," was yet to be brought into conformity and concord with Islam. In its old rigorous sense the distinction between Islam and non-Islam no longer holds. Face to face with secular pressures and modern conditions, the two *Dārs* might be said to co-exist within every Muslim community and within every Muslim struggling for a worthy discipline of his duties and desires. No simple division of humanity into two camps, with a militancy poised and pledged to subdue the enemies of truth across a single delineated boundary, whether of map, creed, or code, any longer possesses either exterior occasion or interior validity.

While the sense of mission persists, as the obligation inherent in being Muslim, the caliphal expression of *Dār al-Islām* ceased this last half century. There seems no prospect of its renewal. The Arab revolt against the Ottoman Caliphate in the First World War was a remarkable assertion of the principle of nationalism at the price of Muslim against Muslim, though it is true that the excesses of the Caliphate itself in its nineteenth century Ottoman shape had themselves provoked that cleavage within Islam. After the war the Turks themselves took up the same principle; they vigorously abandoned their empire and the Caliphate, and moved under Atatürk's leadership into a militantly laïc, secular state, in which Islam itself was deprived. This was indeed a rare venture for Muslims, even though the sequel has demonstrated that history must see this assertion of Turkism, subduing religion to a merely sociological function, as nevertheless an event *within* Islam.

Freed from the Turks, the Arabs found themselves delayed and frustrated by continuing western imperialism in the form of mandates and by the oddly parallel, but deeply provocative, principle of Zionism, with its pursuit of statehood for Jewry. That tragedy apart, Arab nationalism is everywhere outwardly accomplished throughout the Middle East and North Africa—but accomplished in the form of fragmented territories whose boundaries, though hard to merge, represent more the competitions within the departed imperialisms than the realities of the Arab spirit. "Our frontiers," said Shukrī al-Quwaitlī, once President of Syria, "are not our limits but our wounds."

In further Asia the same problem obtains, for vastly more numerous populations. Islam in the Indian subcontinent was divided into separate political territories by the partition that gave being to the state of Pakistan. Islamic statehood for the majority people in the territory where they were a majority, could only be at the cost of separating them from their own religious kindred. These have to subsist as a minority people in areas where they are fewer. As the necessary consequence of statehood, this was seen as a valid price for the preservation and expression of Islam, as conceived by Pakistan. The paradox was that it entailed a situation beyond its frontiers in which some fifty million Muslims in (political) India have to achieve their Islam without statehood of their own, in a multireligious society where they will never predominate. This is the very fate—or vocation (depending on how you take it)—which Pakistan was conceived to deny and created to avoid. The problem has been more severe for India's Muslims, by the existence of Pakistan, than it would have been for the Muslims of the whole subcontinent in a conceivable all-India federal unity. This does not, however, disqualify Pakistan, either in fact or theory. It merely measures the complexity of the issues provoking Islamic nationalism and the consequences of its pursuit. Certainly the Muslims of India on their side of the partition have a destiny quite novel, in its dimensions and character, in the whole history of Islam: that of existing "just as a religion" without benefit of political hegemony—a condition so far from ever being congenial or normal that the phrase itself has no acceptance. Soviet Muslims share this circumstance, as do Muslim minorities in the west, but in sharply special form.

Though everywhere fragmented into nations, the house of Islam is, nevertheless, alive and alert. Imperialism had a deadening effect upon the inward ideology of peoples. By contrast, counterimperialism means a great stimulus to self-sufficiency in every sphere, and a recovery, even if sometimes oversanguine, of the inner dynamic of religion. The resulting sense of competence gives a lively incentive to the tasks of apologists, to the theorists, evangelists and counsellors of the faith with which nationalism is allied. The stimulus is mutual; there are at once new opportunities and new occasions and, with them, new aspirations and energies. The Islam we have to study can only be known by a willingness to move with the pace and the ambition of its own temper.

But the pace in contemporary affairs, after independence, has sorely taxed the resources of the religious will and the traditional dogma. New nationalisms have come to their own concurrently with the burgeoning populations, industrial pressures, economic disequilibrium of nations, rapid urbanization and other chronic stresses of the time. There is disenchantment as well as exuberance. The intractability of many problems of nationhood, and the sense that solutions which are vital turn on factors that are beyond local control, mean a hope/despair and a love/hate relationship vis-à-vis technology and all its ways. Under these burdens it is natural that the house of Islam presents to the observer a whole variety of attitudes and a diverse chorus of voices, conserving, defending, reforming, advising, disputing, and commending, as interpretations allow and tensions dictate. Our main business with them all, aside from a lively feeling for the struggles and the strains, is to understand religious meaning. It is to see Islam "housing" Muslims, in experience under God, as heirs to a long past of monotheistic assurance and a singularly inclusive, emphatic system of religious allegiance and observance.

What does it mean to be a Muslim today? What did it mean to be one in the first days of the Qur'ān and the immediate "companionship" (to use a technical word) of Muḥammad? What did it mean in the succeeding centuries of traditional identity and institutional continuity? Why are there Sunnis and Shī'ahs as abiding segments within the one house? Who are the Sufis, the mystics, and what was the secret of their origin and of their persistent role in Islam? And, within all these enquiries, the question: Who is the Muslim?

That question is not as easy as it seems. We might answer, One who accepts Islam. But what, in turn, is Islam unless it be what Muslims acknowledge?

Other religions have the same interdependence of definition between believers and belief, between the faithful and the faith. "Whatever the disciple is destined to discover in the Law was given to Moses on Sinai," says a tradition of Judaism. It seems almost to validate anything, until we notice the safeguard in the word "disciple." The conservative, fearing the dictum for its threatening liberties, can still, for his comfort, disqualify from "discipleship" the interpreter of whom he disapproves. But, in the end, Sinai is what Sinai means to those who belong at Sinai. The collective is the clue to the identity that makes it. From this circularity there is no escape. There has to be a parallel saying for Islam, though it is not traditional. "Islam is what Muslims hold it to be." But they are Muslims because Islam holds them, and there will be continuing debate among them about who, and how, they properly are.

The chapters that follow are concerned with both sides of this equation—with the Islam of Muslims and with Muslims in their Islam. We proceed to it by first pondering the Lordship of God, the primal reality and the source of all. From the transcendent rule of God all else follows—Muḥammad, the Qur'ān, Law, Liturgy and *Ummah,* the Prophet, the Scripture, the *Sharī'ah,* the rites of *Dīn* and the fact of the community or "household." After studying all these in their interrelation, we turn, in the final chapter, to glance at what the will to fulfill itself universally has meant in the more recent history of Islam.

1.
"Lord of the Worlds"

To enter into Islam it is better to go to the mosque than to reach for the dictionary. But where there is no physical opportunity for the one, we must begin from the admitted inadequacy of the other. Encyclopedias, it is true, all too readily turn the mystery and livingness of things into terms and technicalities, and this destroys them. Truly to know the Muslim in his faith we must somehow linger in the precincts of his prayer, kindle to the accents of the Qur'ān reciter, and feel the pulse of the fast of Ramaḍān. But, outsiders as we are, we need for these interior ventures the discipline of academic statement. Sympathy and scholarship must excite and complete each other. Only by their partnership are religions understood. The hope in these chapters is to seek and to sense the poetry of Islamic religion through the prose of Muslim doctrine, law, and community.

The great Arab-born monotheism of Asia and Africa is unique among faiths in being denoted by a term that is also a common noun. Hinduism takes its name from a land and a river, Buddhism from the meaning of a founder figure, Judaism from a people, Christianity from the concept and achievement of "the Messiah." Islam, which is never properly called "Muhammadanism," differs from all these. The name "Islam" could just as well be *islām*.[1] The Arabic language has no capital letters and, therefore, no means of indicating the significant distinction between proper names and common nouns. It uses one term inclusively for both the simple action and the historical incorporation. The distinction between *islām* and Islam may be seen as comparable to such familiar usages as labor and Labor or public health and Public Health. There is the general and the specific; there is the idea and its definitive expression, the thing in itself and the thing in its "institution." Islam organizes *islām,* enshrines and defines it. It makes Muslims of *muslims.* The active noun—what Arabic grammar calls "the name of the doer" —has the same double quality as the verbal noun. Islam is the thing and Muslims are the doers, both from a single root. Abraham, for example, was a *muslim* centuries before the Prophet Muḥammad and the Scripture, or Qur'ān, that inaugurates Muslims as history finally knows them.

This situation needs to be kept steadily in view. The faith that stems from seventh century Arabia believes itself to be continuous with all true religion and to perfect what right worship everywhere intends. It gives final, institutional form to the proper religious temper of mankind. It is the dimension by which all other relationships are to be subdued. It is ultimate religion in unambiguous definition and in true balance. The role of Islam in relation to all other faiths is to prune,

5

correct, purge, and complete them. In the finality of the Qur'ān, God's worship-fulness and man's worship come into authentic and ultimate relation.

The fact of God, One, All-Powerful, Sovereign, Eternal, "the Lord of the worlds," is the all-embracing reality. Islam means the steady duty of the Godward reckoning, the habit of obligation under God as the central and inclusive meaning of existence. Man in Islam is firmly and vigilantly set in the Divine milieu, not by election in distinction from others, but by dint of natural human worth, universally shared, born under the Divine mercy, destined for immortality and judgment, and meanwhile guided, exhorted, habituated, and disciplined by Islam into that conformity with the will of God which is the whole *raison d'être* of humanity.

The documentation of this theology is the Qur'ān (Koran). The means to its enunciation in the world is Muḥammad. The shape of its reception is the sacred law. The pattern of the human response is in the ritual and social duties of the faithful. By these, *islām* becomes Islam. Each of them calls for detailed exposition in the chapters that follow. But the prior duty is with the Divine. We elude the whole nature of Islamic faith if we propose to give it time or attention only because we are interested in orientalism, or archaeology, or psychology, or comparison of creeds. God, by Muslim criteria of worship, cannot be the end of an argument, nor an object of discourse. The notion that other peoples' religions may be "interesting" is not the temper likeliest to do justice to the inner meaning of Muslim prostration in prayer.

But if, with this in mind, we begin with "the Lord of the worlds," the reader who is first concerned with the instrumental things may well go at once to the succeeding chapters. What they take up is here presupposed.

Ashhadu anna lā ilāha illā-llāh: Muḥammadan rasūl Allāh—such is the Islamic creed, or *Shahādah,* sometimes also called the *Kalimah,* the word that witnesses to the sole reality of God and the apostolate of Muḥammad on behalf of God. "There is no god but God and Muḥammad is the apostle of God," to which each believer prefaces the word: "I bear witness that . . ." It begins with the absolute negation of the pseudo-deities. The great struggle of the Prophet was against idolatry and tribal superstition, against belief in a variety of pagan powers thought to dwell in wells and winds and hills. His mission was to give the lie to these fictions and fears by proclaiming against them the indubitable Lordship of God. It was not that the Divine sovereignty needed this defense. It was the misguided and perverse distortions of men that required its reiteration. It is only as notions that idols need to be denied, for they have no other existence.

So "there is none but He." The word *Allāh* is incapable of a plural. There is no reluctance to pronounce its fluent syllables, such as Judaism feels over pronouncing *Yahweh.* On the contrary: let those flowing "l"'s of the *Shahādah* be perpetually heard. For the very mention of God is beneficent, protective, and devout. This is the most repeated word in Muslim vocabulary, whether it be to greet a friend or to comprehend the universe. There is none save *Allāh,* whether we acknowledge a salutation or invoke the heavens. The grammarians suggest at least a score of derivations for the word. But their ingenuity is dubious. It suffices that God *is,* uniquely, unassailably, overwhelmingly. As the Hebrew New Year liturgy has it:

God high exalted, Dynast of endlessness,
Timeless transcendency
Worshipped eternally,
Lord of infinity.

Islam stands squarely in the Judeo-Christian tradition of insistent and urgent monotheism and does so all the more vehemently for its desperate polytheistic environment in pre-Islamic Arabia and the sharp, strenuous iconoclasm for which, and as which, it was born.

That original alertness against all false theologies accompanies the whole elaboration of Muslim religion. It is, as it were, a supreme "protestantism" in its very genesis, a cry of heart and a mission of will against all that violated the Divine unity or distracted men from the single direction of their love, their loyalty, and their obedience. Hence the ringing shout of praise that echoes through all Islamic ritual and dogma: *Allāhu akbar,* "Greater is God," which, grammatically, is a comparative form made all the more striking by its refusal, indeed its inability, to enter any stated comparison. "God is greater" than all that could conceivably be set in any clause after "than." The idea of framing such a clause is itself unthinkable. Yet the superlative ("God is the greatest") is not preferred, for this could imply approximate equality and would, as such, be open to ambiguity, as the psalm is which declares: "He is a great king above all gods." Are we to understand that the gods exist, if only as underlings? Or do we mean that the Lord reigns in utter majesty alone? Islam has no truck with such double possibility of intention. It was not the existence of *Allāh* that Muḥammad proclaimed. The tribes knew Him by His Name. It was His *sole* existence, negating all pluralism. God is, exalted above all that might—though always impossibly—compare with Him.

The crowning purpose of the Quranic affirmation of God is worship and submissiveness. Though capable of meticulous argumentation and sometimes busy with scholastic subtleties, Islamic dogma is essentially the handmaid of religious duty and not a pursuit in its own right. It is theology in the imperative, with the accent on law, rather than on ontology, on the will of God rather than on His being. Its genius has always been in the realm of response to the Divine claim rather than with disquisition into the Divine character. It has an instinctive sympathy with the rabbinic tradition that has God saying: "Would that they left Me alone and did My Torah." There is no merit in excessive curiosity. Direction is more important than conjecture. Religion has to do with action rather than analysis. *Ḥasbunā Allāh* runs a frequent Quranic phrase: "God is our enough." Though it may be invoked for the mystic's "unfathomable mystery," for the average Muslim it means rather that the end of all debate is the reality of the Divine, that God suffices, both for present life and future destiny, both for fidelity

and for faith. It is characteristic of Islamic thought and Muslim habit to terminate, if not to foreshorten, all enquiry with the words: "God knows."

And we know all that is religiously necessary to know about God by revelation. Islam might be described as the practice of unreserving reserve. There is a
reverence which draws back from the mystery of God, for there is a mastery about
all knowledge which can never be proper for men in respect of God. But this
"reserve" about the veiled wonder and otherness of God is, by that quality, all
the more total and entire in its surrender. Islam sees itself more authentic as
religion, by the very diffidence of its theology.

The Names of God

This attitude is well illustrated in the Ninety-nine Names of God, which
figure so prominently in Muslim doctrine and devotion. These *Asmā' al-Ḥusnā,*
"the Excellent Names" of God, are so numbered symbolically, the hundredth
Name being hidden. With a rosary, or string of beads, the worshipper tells the
Divine titles as he runs the beads through his fingers. In tradition well over five
hundred Names have been current. Some seventy are Quranic. Many are near
duplicates of each other, being alternative derivatives from a smaller number of
root verbs or concepts. Some are active participles, referring to creation, sustenance, providence, direction, and decree. Others are adjectival. It is with the latter
that the significant theological tensions arise. Some short account of these may
serve to underline the quality of Islamic divinity.

Adjectives, of course, take their significance in human speech from human
situations. It is from human reference that they derive their content. Only so are
language and literature possible, only so is it feasible to pray, to theologize, or
even to speak of God at all. Yet to apply human descriptives, relevantly, to God
seemed to involve religion in a situation where the Divine was being made to
participate in the human, the eternal to be characterized by the temporal. This,
for Muslim instinct, was intolerable, since God is wholly other than man. The
Divine majesty is immune from such "identifiability" in terms of the human.
"God," as John Donne used to say, "is only and Divinely like Himself."

Yet prayer, not to speak of theology, requires, and requires urgently, that
we be able to say what He is "like." If, out of fear of demeaning the Divine
otherness, we veto all theological description and opt for utter silence, we also
silence worship. This some mystics and negative theologians may be ready to
allow. But it does not do for common men. Theological silence equals religious
futility. A God we cannot "name" is a God we cannot acknowledge. We cannot
pray unless, in measure, we can conceive. All address is description. The Arabic
verb here, *da'ā,* like the English "to call" has a double sense which enshrines the
whole problem. It means to name and so to invoke, to identify and so to summon,
to call and to call upon. Authentic prayer means feasible theology, even though
we may readily concede that beyond both, worship goes out into mystery.

This is, plainly, the familiar theme of "anthropomorphism," or speaking of

God in human categories. It applies also to phrases such as "the face of God," "the hand of God," "the arm of the Lord," as well as to adjectival Names. The issue is familiar in many creeds. But nowhere has the paradox been so uncongenial as for Islam. Nowhere has there been a greater reluctance to concede relationality toward man on the part of God, lest this should endanger the sovereignty of God and somehow open the way again for the renewal of idolatry. The classical theologians have remained loyal to the anti-idolatrous urgency of the historic genesis of their Islam. In the other monotheisms, especially in Christianity, there is a much more relaxed dogmatism of unity, no less uncompromising, but readier for "the Word" in relation with the "flesh."

Islamic reluctance here does not, of course, mean that *Allāh* is not involved with man. On the contrary, the Divine giving of the law means that there is no Divine indifference to the world. No lawgiver can be immune from concern about the reception of His commands. By enjoining *islām* and expecting it from men God stakes something of Himself on their response. If deafness or rebellion are a matter of indifference, then there is a fundamental unreality, either in the commands themselves, or in the option they summon. Such an unreality would make nonsense of the legislative will and vacuity of the Divine reign. Through law unto *islām,* God in Islam is crucially involved in human situations.

Nevertheless, to return to the Excellent Names, there is a rooted, and honorable, uneasiness for Islam about all such thoughts. Muslims prefer to believe that God's Lordship is beyond all human damage, indeed, beyond all human import. Whatever damnation they may mean for man, broken law and flouted sovereignty are somehow unharming to God. The Divine inviolability abides. All the more, then, those other involvements of the Divine with the human, namely the terms of invocation, are also outside His inaccessible character. They can still, however, be used. For they are religiously indispensable, despite their theological untenability.

This conclusion was the consensus of traditional theology in the tenth and eleventh centuries, after prolonged controversy. It was embodied in the neat formulas *bilā kaif* and *bilā tashbīh.* The worshipper uses the Names of God "without implying 'how' " and "without representational intention." Sovereignty and sublimity are conserved by these conclusions, at the price of imaginative warmth and confidence. Islam considers that deference here is a truer theological virtue than assurance. This theme is the Islamic form of a recurrent perplexity and tension about all religion and belongs with a large contemporary discussion on the feasibility of religious language.

Understanding this large reservation in its true temper, we have to ask, briefly, about the Names themselves. The most notable are the two that stand in the *Bismillāh,* or invocation, at the head of every Quranic chapter (except the ninth): *al-Raḥmān al-Raḥīm.* "The merciful Lord of mercy" seems the best translation, though "the compassionate, the merciful" is more familiar. The root word in both words is the same, and it seems odd to translate with two different English terms. The difference in sense between them is progressive, moving from "mercy" as an essential quality, to "mercy" in actual bestowal. What God is, to use an old fashioned word, in "His property," He is also in His activity. In both senses, He is benign, beneficent, good, forgiving, compassionate.

Classifiers have tried to arrange the whole sequence of Names, according to frequency, emphases, affinity and context. Within the intellectual reticence already noted, they give religious confession to the sense of Divine authority, power, eternity, majesty, omniscience, decisiveness, tremendousness, and kindly forbearance. They are Names, not treatises. Their meaning withdraws into their Lord, Who wills to be so celebrated. In the words of Surah 7:180: "To God belong the Excellent Names, so call upon Him by them."

Divine Lordship

There is one dominant phrase in this theme which stands as the head of this chapter, namely *Rabb-al-'Ālamīn*, "the Lord of the worlds," and which opens up other vistas of our duty with the Islamic sense of God. The term *Rabb* responds to *'abd*, which is the most characteristic descriptive of man. He is "servant" to his "Master," God. God is the Lord of all spheres and realms. The word *Rabb*, as some modern commentators are eager to claim, may have connotations belonging to "nurture" as well as to "rule." On that ground it has been fitted into an evolutionary understanding of the world, within a loyal theism. God, so to speak, presides over all the processes and developments by which things are, and by which they move. The plural "worlds" here fits the same idea of diversity and interdependence belonging to the universe as science knows it. All that is, from planets to atoms, from the infinities of space to the intimacies of the soul, derives from the creative *fiat* of God, Who originates and undergirds them all. The word *'ālamīn* belongs with a root having the sense of "to know." The clear implication is that the physical and material and sentient worlds are means whereby the creating power of God may be traced and discerned.

Our earlier insistence on the impenetrable transcendence of God and the Islamic reliance on revelation, not reason, as the foundation of faith, does not imply any reluctance to esteem reason in the mundane sphere. On the contrary, Islam encourages empirical observation and scientific intelligence. It argues these from the recurrent Quranic exhortation to note with gratitude and attentiveness "the signs of God" in the natural order. These are everywhere present in the open countenance of nature, where they are amenable to human interrogation and provoke to rational investigation as well as religious wonder. It is the Creator in Himself, not in His works, to Whom we have no rational access, and where even revelation brings only intimations of guidance for our actions, not of disclosure for our curiosity.

This "scientific" access to the nature of the worlds is implicit in calling them *'ālamīn*. God's presiding and ordering Lordship comprehends all that men do in culture and civilization, the whole drama of their history on the stage of nature. Man under that Lordship is a servant with a tributary authority of his own. This indeed provides the substance of his *islām*. For if he had nothing about which to be obedient, there could be no point in his obligation. Thus the Divine rule presupposes man's dignity. It is on both counts that it denies and vetoes the nature-gods and the pseudo-deities, which tyrannize over men in their ignorance and pretend against God.

Divine Lordship over the worlds is sometimes interpreted so as to make the whole of nature, as well as humanity, in some sense *muslim*. There is the concept of a natural, cosmic *islām,* in which stars and molecules, species and elements, plants and creatures, all "worship" by their very conformity to the laws of their being. This *islām* has to be understood as involving many diversities, the inert and the mobile, the material and the animal, the mineral and the living. Surah 3:83 is sometimes quoted in this connection. "Freely or otherwise, the denizens of the heavens and of the earth submit to Him." The "unwilled" submission here may well refer, however, not to inanimate nature but to obstinate humanity. In that case the passage would have to do with persons only. But whatever may be true of the rest of creation, man's is certainly the arena of the Divine will, of volitional surrender to the one Lordship. Only man is capable of this ultimate *islām* of mind and soul, and only he, by the same token, is possessed of the option of defiance.

Yet that very option is also the crux of man's high calling, his responsible creaturehood. That God is, over man, and that man is, under God, is a belief that dignifies the human dimension in safeguarding the Divine worth. The command of God hallows and exalts man as hearer and doer. His submission is his liberation. His status is realised in being religiously accepted. Islam means that man is invited to will his true being by heeding the Divine will as that which conditions and describes it.

The human calling turns on the dethroning and disowning of the false gods. "There is none save He." Men are enslaved, degraded, undone, defiled, and damned by their false worships. *Islām* does not truly happen except before the worthy God. *"Shirk"* says the Qur'ān, using two of its profoundest terms, "is great *Zulm"* (Surah 31:13). *Shirk* is this allowance of other gods beside God, this chronic idolatry, which denies to God alone the worship, trust, honor, and gratitude, due to Him. Such denial, precisely, is *Zulm,* wrong in its utmost form, the refusal of the truth of things. It is *Zulm* against God. But it is also *Zulm* against man, against ourselves. The idolater is his own worst enemy, in that he corrupts and distorts his own being in the untruth of his gods. The right surrender emancipates from the pride of evil.

One of the most familiar themes of the Divine Lordship is that which relates to human destiny in time and history. It is a common view that Muslims are traditionally "fatalistic," because of the strong emphasis of their doctrine on the power and unquestioned will of God. The opinion could be substantiated from much in Muslim attitudes, as popularly held, and also from classical Islamic theology. But western critics have often misconstrued the matter. The sense of God over all, omniscient, omnicompetent, and omnipotent, certainly dominates, even oppressively, in orthodox thinking and assumption. Some have readily identified history with God's will, in an iron grip of celestial necessity, inflexible and inescapable, to the point of denying to natural and historical causation any genuine place. All is seen, without mediating causes, as God's decree and God's deed. When puzzled about the moral accountability of men, if God is the sole author of all their deeds, the theologians found refuge in a verbal solution, by which God willed the deed *in* the will of the doer. This was held to make the action at once reprehensible and responsible, inescapable and yet accountable.

Al-Ash'arī (d. 935 A.D.), notable among the authors of *Kalām,* or scholastic theology, set the matter down as adamantly as any in his refutation of the *Qadariyyah* and the *Mu'tazilah,* the contemporary "deviationists" and "libertarians." Asked about *kasb,* or "acquisition" (this doctrine that the doer "acquires" each deed, in his history, from God's willing it *in* him), he replied:

> It has no agent, who makes it as it really is, save God, and no one with power over it so that it will be as it really is, in the sense that he creates it, save God.[2]

In a further passage, the same author goes on to state the untrammelled will of God in terms that capture with typical blandness this aspect of Islamic faith.

> The proof that God is free to do whatever He does is that He is the supreme Lord, subject to no one, with no superior over Him who can permit, command, chide, forbid, or prescribe what He shall do and fix bounds for Him. This being so, nothing can be evil on the part of God. For a thing is evil on our part only because we transgress the limit and bound set for us and do what we have no right to do. But since the Creator is subject to no one and bound by no command, nothing can be evil on His part.[3]

All such thinkers were loathe to think their way beyond this impasse to a sense of there being a law within the Divine nature. For this, somehow, seemed disloyal to His unconditionedness.

These attitudes, however, need to be set in somewhat different focus by reference to the Qur'ān itself. It is easy enough to substantiate from it a total Divine predestination. But there are some passages clearly pointing in the other direction. There is the reiterated cry (more than a hundred times): "Perhaps ye (or they) may . . . ," linked with all the major themes of human decision—faith, perception, gratitude, and submission, and seeming to set them squarely within the province of personal will. True, there are other contexts which place belief and unbelief, goodness and evil-doing, heaven and hell, all irresistibly within the Divine dictation and irreversible decree or *qadar*. But "the grand perhaps," to borrow Browning's line, is still a deep element in the Quranic picture and, in a sense, it takes a free human being to be a Muslim. For if his *islām* is utterly arbitrary, it is to that extent either meaningless or unnecessary. Self-help is certainly commended to believers. As we shall see in Chapter 2, "providence" in the early story of Islam is far from being something to wait for in passivity. Muhammad gave robust evidence of the legitimacy and effectiveness of personal resourcefulness. There is the oft-quoted comment of Surah 13:12 that "God does not change a people's state until they change their own hearts' thoughts." The force of this, however, is blunted, though not belied, by the succeeding words: "Whensover God desires evil for a people, there is no averting it." While it is true that there is nothing which would not have been different had God willed it otherwise, the conviction (Surah 13:18) that God is the creator of everything need not be taken in a crudely fatalistic sense.

The wisest course in this vexed theme of Islamic doctrine is not blindly to insist on the centuries old traditions of determinism, whether theoretical or popular, nor yet to fall uncritically for the free dynamism of such modern interpreters as Muḥammed Iqbāl (d. 1938 A.D.) who taught that God Himself awaited the "ego" of the human genius. Both of these incur different liabilities with the Qur'ān. It lies rather in seeing the Islamic view of events and wills as enveloped, positively, in this totality of the Divine rule. All things are to be related directly and, as it were, jealously, to the will of God. But such a zeal that no other than He be accredited the determinator did not, in Islam's genesis, and does not now preclude the vigorous role of human action.

When Islamic understanding of the Lordship of the worlds turned from these more concrete issues of destiny and will, of faith and works, to the still more metaphysical problems of the Divine unity or the status of the Qur'ān as the Divine word, it was even more inclined to leave the basic questions to silence, or to formulate the problems themselves into dogmatic "answers." This is not to say that Islamic history lacks profound philosophical curiosity and speculation. There were thinkers of the stamp of Al-Fārābī (d. 950 A.D.) and Ibn Sīnā (d. 1037 A.D.), who rank with the greatest in the western medieval world, and ambitious mystical systems with their complex formulations of Divine knowledge. Islam expanded into a world of Christian theological intellectualism and Greek rational heritage. It could hardly escape, in its first centuries, the onus of these relationships, their habits of disquisition and reflection. It shares with the west in an ancestry that includes Aristotle as well as Abraham.

There were, moreover, many implicit questions deferred, of necessity, to later times, in the initial fervor and urgency of the Islamic task under Muḥammad. These came into their own in the succeeding centuries—questions about the eternity of the Qur'ān, the role of reason in revelation, the mystery of the Divine attributes, the ontological status of prophethood, and the like. The broad consensus of the centuries, after unhappy ventures into lively controversy, was that authoritarian dogmatism was the proper posture. One of its most typical representatives was the theologian Al-Nasafī, author of '*Aqā'id,* (d. 1142), a treatise on the dogma of Islam, part of which runs as follows:

> God Most High, the One, the Eternal, the Decreeing, the Knowing, the Seeing, the Hearing, the Willing: He is not an attribute, nor a body, nor an essence, nor a thing formed, nor a thing bounded, nor a thing numbered, nor a thing divided, nor a thing compounded, nor a thing limited. He is not described by *māhiya* [what-ness], nor by *kaifiyyah* [how-ness], and He does not exist in place or time. There is nothing that

resembles Him . . . He has qualities from all eternity existing in His essence. They
are not He nor are they other than He . . . [His] Word is a quality from all eternity,
not belonging to the genus of sounds and letters, a quality that is incompatible with
coming to silence.[4]

In similar vein was the commentary on the first half of the *Shahādah,* contained
in Al-Ghazālī's celebrated *magnum opus, The Renewal of the Sciences of Religion,*
Book 2, in a series of paragraphs intended for memorizing by children.

> He in His essence is one without any partner, Single without any similar, Eternal
> without any opposite, Separate without any like. He is One: Prior with nothing before
> Him, from eternity, without any beginning, abiding in existence with none after Him,
> to eternity without an end, subsisting without ending, abiding without termination.
> . . . Measure does not bind Him and boundaries do not contain Him.[5]

On the vexed and much debated question of God's seatedness on the Throne,
Al-Ghazālī wrote:

> He is seated firmly on His Throne after the manner which He has said and in the
> sense in which He willed a being seated firmly, which is far removed from contact
> and fixity of location and being established and being enveloped and being removed.
> The Throne does not carry Him but the Throne and those that carry it are carried
> by the grace of His power and mastered by His grasp. He is above the Throne and
> the heavens and above everything unto the limit of the Pleiades with an aboveness
> that does not bring Him nearer to the Throne and the heavens, just as it does not
> make Him further from the earth and the Pleiades . . .[6]

In each of the other themes of traditional dogma, omniscience, determining,
unconditionality, Al-Ghazālī's "instructor" is equally scholastic, erudite,
guarded, and prone to careful negation as a means of at once defining God and
reserving Him from definition.

> Events have no place in Him and mishaps do not befall Him. He does not cease,
> through His various epithets, to be far removed from changing and through His
> perfect qualities to be independent of perfecting . . . He knows the creeping of a black
> ant upon the rough rock in the dark night . . . What He wills is, and what He wills
> not is not . . . There is no analogy between His justice and the justice of creatures,
> since tyranny is inconceivable in the case of God, though conceivable in the case of
> a creature dealing with property of some other than himself. He never encounters
> any rights in another beside Himself so that His dealing with it might be a doing of
> any wrong . . . No particular action toward any one is incumbent upon Him . . . and
> no one possesses any right against Him.[7]

The length of these extracts is justified by the cumulative effect of their insistent
exoneration of the Divine, their instinct to eliminate the relationality of God and
man except in the most arbitrary terms. Al-Ghazālī, and those whose orthodoxy
he did so much to solidify and establish by dint of his profound intelligence and
his immense prestige, embody the gathered verdict of the Islamic mind about the
reality of God.

Despite its uncompromising severity, however, it is throughout an understanding about mercy and compassion. Somehow these elements were less exposed to the issues which needed such vigilance from the theologians in respect of sovereignty and will. As befits its emphasis, the classic theology of Islam is less concerned about the "comfort" of man than it is about the majesty and immunity of God, since these must be seen as, in every event, a prerequisite of the mercy. In its own urgent way, the Qur'ān is warmer, kindlier, more compassionate than the theologians. While the Book of Islam underwrites and prompts the latter in many of their concerns and something of their temper, its vitality and fervor, its mission and movement, bring the reader into a different world from the aridity and calculation of the dogmatists.

God in Human Awareness

There remain, in general terms, three fundamental questions belonging to the Islamic sense of God. They have to do with superstition, suffering, and secularity, and they relate the unity of God to the diversity, the tragedy, and the autonomy of the human situation. How does this Lordship of the worlds contain, as it were, the pluralisms of existence, its sorrows and its arguable self-sufficiency?

The first of these is the religious problem of the emotional love of the natural order and all its ways and wonders, the problem of the imagination in worship. The world of phenomena is irreducibly plural and manifold. Our context of human experience, of love and sense awareness, is endlessly rich and diverse. This manifoldness, of course, lies at the root of superstition. It inspires the creation of images, to capture its delights or allay its fears. It is the source of nature worships, and of the language, the metaphors, the myths, by which men respond to it.

The doctrine of the unity of God is not meant to exclude this manifold. Rather the Qur'ān embraces it in the concept of "the signs of God," evocative of gratitude and wonder. All things may be celebrated, but only God is to be adored. Yet it is supremely difficult not to depreciate, or even atrophy, the register of cognizance of nature and of life in its fullness, if the doctrine of unity is stern and sharply hostile to the imagination. Conversely, there is a danger of idolatry implicit in all alertness to the external manifold. There is the temptation to stop at things and not pass through them to God. Do we not need myths and imagination, mind-pictures, word-pictures, if we are to possess the wonder? Yet may not these, by their very efficacy, divert the mind and heart from the God they affirm?

The Islamic doctrine of the unity of God, and its correlative, the menace of *Shirk,* or deification, have demanded the prohibition of all representational art. In the realm of worship Islam enforces, often with a puritan severity, a total veto on artistic joy in shape and image, music and iconography. Color, design, the craftsman's skill—these had to be reserved only for "religious" objects in the mosque, for lamps and tiles, for the margins of Qur'āns and for calligraphy. There could be no reproduction of the delightsomeness of flesh and blood, or form and

body. This is the more notable in that, on the social plane, Islam is not, traditionally, ascetic, but rejoices in the physical benedictions of life.

The reason, of course, lies in the intense anti-idolatry necessary in the context
of its genesis. Yet the problem remains. How is the worship of God alone properly
to harness and reflect the endlessly plural benisons of His world and His creation?
Nature cults, fertility rites, plural shrines—in a word, idols—are all rightly
anathema. They arrogate from God the glory due to Him alone. But how, in a
proper jealousy for that glory, do we conserve and articulate the love, the glad-
ness, the wistfulness, the intimacy of dependence, the nearness of soul, which
breathe in ignorant and "primitive" idolatries? How do we feel and move, as
"unitarians," within the plural world, keeping the poetry of nature, but excluding
the partializing superstition? How do we come by a worship that no longer
suspects art, and by a love of the manifold which is not tempted to idolatry?

In all this Islam is close to a deep and perennial problem in the religious life
of man. It is no less so in the second problem of the compatibility with Divine
unity of the mystery of evil and suffering in the experience of man. If we affirm
a sovereignty that is all-knowing, all-powerful, all-merciful and unrivalled, what
are we to say of the burden of tragedy and wrong that weighs upon our whole
history?

We have already heard the theologians insisting that there are no obligations
in God, no laws of His nature by which He is bound. Yet the Qur'ān declares
that "he has written down for Himself mercy." (Surah 6:12). Faith in the rule
of God surely involves what is sometimes called a "theodicy," a justification of
God in face of the reality of evil. The Islamic notion of *Ẓulm*, to which earlier
reference has been made, includes the theme of "things which ought not so to be."
The root idea in the term is out-of-placeness, insubordination, defiance of right,
or things—in a notable New Testament phrase—"standing where they ought
not." What then are we to say about the reign of God in the light of the
pretensions, the challenge to it, of the wrongs in life?

In the main, because of its emphasis on the transcendent, Islam ignores or
neglects or does not hear these questions. It simply sustains its affirmation of God,
of His unity and power, and its belief in His sublime immunity. It does not find
a theodicy necessary either for its theology or its worship. On the practical and
social level, wrong is to be identified, disowned and reversed by dint of the
education and the discipline of the human community in a true *islām*. The
ultimate mystery must not be understood to trouble heaven or the theologian.

What, then, finally, is the ultimate significance of the Islamic sense of "the
Lord of the worlds"? It is a passion against all usurpation. It is the conviction
that wrong worship is the sum of evil, that power, or race, or state, or creed,
improperly exalted above God, spell the human wasteland. It is a perpetual
warfare against all false absolutes. Only in the truly worthy truly recognized can
human benediction lie. In the negative, it is a constant warning: "There is no
god . . ."; in the positive a supreme assurance: ". . . except God."

In the deepest ways, therefore, it bears the full brunt of the contemporary secular challenge to the religious view of man and the world. As the most insistent and uncomplicated Divine charter for human life, its forthright theism means "theonomy," not autonomy, for humanity. Revelation Divinely given, law Divinely ordained, duty Divinely ordered, bring the sovereignty of heaven directly into all human business. The structure of obligation is authoritarian, statutory and inclusive. Every issue, every situation, returns to God and leads back to an obligation theologically constituted. Islam, in these ways, might be said to be programmatic religion *par excellence.*

What, then, of present assertions of human self-sufficiency, for which theism is no longer philosophically feasible, morally tolerable, or religiously desirable? What of man's alleged ability to dispense with the Divine hypothesis, in the adequacy of his own management of the world? What of his contrasted mood of futility and misgiving, prompting him to opt out of an existence with whose pointlessness and disorder he will have nothing to do?

For these disqualifications of its surest conviction about God Islam has answering resources. It is true that on the ordinary level Islamic thought has not yet squarely met these current secular pleas either of arrogance or despair. It is also true that in practice much secularity has invaded Muslim law and society, and that some conformity is sustained more by political and cultural emotion than by spiritual confidence. Nevertheless it teaches man both the boldness and the humility of the true iconoclast. It sees man as called to identify and dethrone the false gods, and able to do so. This, in the ultimate sense, *is* the meaning of the only proper autonomy. Insofar as current "religionlessness" is such a dethroning, Islam, implicitly, is with it. It has always made idols its central negation.

But, immense tribute as this freedom to be idolatrous and this duty to be anti-idolatrous are to the dignity of man, the evident corollary of both is that he is called to, and fulfilled in, the true worship. There *is* an autonomy, but only for the sake, and in the way, of the ultimate submission. To cope with both the validities and the pretensions of secularity we can find all that we need in the single truth of the dual Islamic conviction: "There is no god . . . except God."

This chapter has set in review the main themes of the religion of the rule of God. God is "Lord of the worlds," Creator, Ordainer, Sustainer, and Disposer. "The excellent Names" serve a religious temper by also deterring a theological presumption. Whether in nature, or history, or aesthetics, or ethics, we find the same dominating concern for God over all, and the same tension, actual or potential, with the tumultuous factors in human affairs. The indictment against *Shirk* defends the sovereignty of God from all competitive challenge. Within the whole, there is the unresolved issue of how the Divine majesty and authority relate to the actualities of sin and wrong.

All these, the last most of all, must now be studied in the shape and in the policy of original and traditional Islam as history knows them. The *Shahādah* has its second clause: "Muḥammad is the apostle of God."

2.
Muḥammad and the Rasūliyyah

The formidable looking title word is simply the abstract noun from *Rasūl,* the credal description of the status role of Muḥammad, for which there is no precise or satisfactory English equivalent. The center of interest in this chapter is the vocation of Muḥammad in its personal and religious aspects, as a focal point of profound themes of truth and power, of revelation and response, of the word and the deed, leaving to the following chapter the scriptural corollary of that vocation, the Qur'ān, as the source book of law and theology, the textbook of faith and the manual of devotion.

When we search for a word to convey either the "doer" or the "doing" within the root verb about "sentness" we are in a difficulty. "Prophet" translates another and different word, denoting what is in general taken to be a relatively inferior station. Moreover, prophets, at least in the highest Biblical tradition are politically powerless as the necessary condition of their ministry and their integrity. They face establishments without displacing them, as Jeremiah so heroically exemplified. "Messenger" may do, but in popular English it is rather a minimal word, suggesting a negligible errand. "Apostle" also works, but is associated too much with Christian notions. New Testament apostles are always in relation to Jesus, as teacher and savior. They are only "apostles" for God by their relation to Christ. Muḥammad has no such derived ministry through a master: he is directly and immediately "apostled" to God Himself. The Qur'ān as Scripture comes only to him: it has scribes other than himself who write it down but it is not *their* composition. "Herald," "emissary," even "commissioner," would all possibly serve, were they not encumbered by associations that are too sentimental or too mundane.

Rasūliyyah, the state of being sent, is essentially a juncture of message and mission, an affirmation with an imperative, a meaning that is to be declared, not a private awareness of truth, nor a publicity that has no roots in duty and urgency. It is communication acting by the energy of what it tells, and it is this event proceeding in and by a human personality instrumental to it. Muḥammad, says the creed, is *Rasūl Allāh:* the *Rasūliyyah,* we may safest say, is what it confesses. If this seems enigmatic, we go on to explore it on several levels: empirical, psychic and spiritual. But first it must be acknowledged as the central historical element in the genesis and the significance of Islam.

There are in fact in Islam no paradigmatic events other than this one, no corporate and communal happenings that take their place in the definition and imagination of the faithful as constitutive of their religious being. The Old Testament turns on the pivot of the Exodus as the formative event, as memory takes it in the mythic expression of history—the Exodus, with Sinai and the Covenant and the Law. Christianity takes definition from the Cross and the Resurrection, highly singular events to be sure, yet embodying in their reception a deep, collective experience of newness of life and of salvation through suffering, incorporating the society of faith. Both these, and other, related faith events like the Exile, make the paradigm, or representative crisis, from which the character of the religion is determined. The *Rasūliyyah* of Muḥammad is the one such event in Islam, or, in different language, the Qur'ān is the only miracle. We must find the religious clue to Islam in the mystery of Muḥammad, recognizing that it is singular and unique. Revelation, as an experience, belonged to him alone. But the Scripture he received communicates the message, and this in turn may be taken to oneself by memorizing and recital. From the page it may live in one's lips and heart. What it meant, in the receiving, was the private awareness of Muḥammad. There is continuity, in some sense, between what happened to Muḥammad and the role of earlier prophets, back to Abraham. But these kinships are not projected into the future and there is no vicarious participation in their essence. Muḥammad is "the seal of the prophets" with whom revelation ends in climax.

The Man Muḥammad and the Qur'ān

There are several different levels on which the historian may tell the story of the man and the Qur'ān. In its barest terms, a man named Muḥammad, son of 'Abdallāh, born around 570 A.D., within a minor branch of the Quraish of Mecca, a pilgrim center of the Hijāz in western Arabia, began near the age of forty to preach in the city of his birth about the unity of God and judgment on idolatry, prompted, he said, by Divine commission so to do. After initial misgivings, he developed a vigorous crusade in this cause, but recruited relatively few followers and little influential response. The opposition he encountered from the majority of his fellow citizens deepened from mild irritation to sharp antagonism. Whereupon he seized a favorable opportunity, migrated with his community to the city of Yathrib, to the north, later called Medina, which he brought increasingly under his control, involving its resources and people in armed struggle in the cause of Islam, until after several skirmishes and by wise manipulation of alliances and interests, he was able to bring the former capital to heel and establish a religio-political state under his complete authority through most of the Arabian peninsula. Throughout this whole activity, the revelations which had initiated his apostleship continued in intermittent sequence, directing his words and policies and giving dogmatic and legal patterns for the community. These ended just before his death in 632, when his achievement was complete and his work poised for perhaps the most dramatic eruption into general history that obscure beginnings ever attained.

It is important to measure the political dimensions of this concise and factual narrative, for they dominate the history and temper of Islam. Islamic origins did not take place in a time of rigorous military imperialism, like that of Rome in the first Christian century. On the contrary, the place and time of their first history still awaited effective unification of its chronic tribalism and its tradition of divisiveness. Efforts after unity, it is true, had been proceeding within Arab society in the decades immediately prior to Muḥammad's call. But the vital principle was still lacking, with the necessary quality of thrust and assurance to turn yearning into fact.

It was just this which the Prophet supplied. Tribal rivalries belonged with religious pluralism. To preach the unity of God against all territorial gods and nature-powers was to disclose the clue to human unity. But the victory of the message necessitated the overthrow of the *political* sanctions which sustained the pagan cults. Meccan idolatry had powerful vested interests, relating to the commerce and prestige of the city as guardian of the pagan pilgrim shrines. Hence the antagonism of their city-state to the person and word of Muḥammad—an antagonism sustained through thirteen weary years in ridicule, calumny and plot against him. The *Hijrah,* that is, "the emigration," by which he broke out of that impasse, involved the important, and new, principle of the priority of faith-allegiance over blood relationship. This revolutionary step gave clear warning to tribalism. Muḥammad saw himself immune from the obligations of nonbelligerence in the months of tribal truce and reaped the benefit of the resultant surprise in his campaigns, shrugging off the opprobrium as merely incidental to the new order. After capitulation came magnanimity. It seemed right in retrospect to have broken truces which belonged to a system itself under repudiation, rather than to have failed effective unity. For, as the Qur'ān observes: "Sedition is more grievous than killing." (Surah 2:191). But then peace is better than chaos.

This story, however, with its emphasis on the political service of Islam is seriously incomplete, if the religious thrust is seen only as a gift-horse to the goal of unified rule. There has to be a third narrative to do larger justice to an honest whole. Islam could not have served these ends had it not been an end in itself. As such its crux in Muḥammad's story is vastly more profound than the foregoing.

As prophet-statesman, Muḥammad emerges as the exemplification of the deepest tension in religion. His vocation, as already narrated, was first puzzled, then thwarted, then burdened, by the mystery of antagonism. The inner conviction of prophethood by which he was energized and held to his course, in the ongoing revelation of Divine direction, ran into this reception of ridicule, scorn, rejection and conspiracy. How could this be borne? How should he resolve or even explain the enmity, without reneging on the vocation that aroused it? How might he maintain, still more vindicate, the commission in face of its public vilification, its cruel nonsuccess? Truth is great and prevails—but how? by what means and sinews? Does the business of witness enlarge to take in the duty of reckoning? At one stage the Qur'ān says explicitly: "Yours is the communicating: *(al-balāgh),* Ours [God speaking] is the issue, *(al-ḥisāb)."* (See Surahs 29:17; 24:53; 36:16; 42:47 and 13:40.) The patriarchal stories figure largely at this stage of the Qur'ān to reinforce the staying power of a sadly pressed Muhammad. Yet fortitude under adversity was not their only quality. Did not the patriarchs come to outward and evident triumph over their antagonists? Noah was certainly vindicated in the flood that drowned the taunting world, while Moses and David wielded supreme powers. The conviction steadily grew upon Muḥammad that he, too, should expect a similar vindication and enjoy authority as the means to it.

So, through the vicissitudes in Mecca, between 609 and 622, A.D., between his initial call and the climax of the *Hijrah,* he pondered the shape of prophetic duty and concluded it must involve statehood and warfare in the service of its truth and in the interests of its success. It did not suffice to send followers into the safety of Ethiopia, as he did in 615 A.D. He must seek an establishment where he might himself be master and whence he might bring to submission the stubbornness of his Meccan foes. The vision on Mount Ḥirā', it is true, had said only: "Arise and warn . . . recite in the name of thy Lord." But wrestling by words for that mission in the markets of Mecca had kindled the assurance that rule and strength of arm must be invoked, if the cause was not to fail. Religion must not evade the political realm: it needs its forces and by force must take it.

This task was the burden of Muḥammad's years in Medina. It hinged on two critical battles and the pacification which garnered their results. The Battle of Badr (624 A.D.) and the Battle of Uḥud (625 A.D.) were fought with the Meccan enemies. In the first Muḥammad gained a resounding success and his purpose gathered momentum. The Qur'ān calls it "the day of the sign of favor." Uḥud was a more ambiguous encounter. But success crowned both Muḥammad's arms and his diplomacy, and eight years after his exile Mecca received him as its conqueror.

But this third narrative still does not suffice us. The historian has still not done justly by the Prophet. To say that a man began to preach, and all else followed by an inner logic, is to tell a fact and conceal the truth by so barely telling it. Where was that *Rasūliyyah* born? To answer: "In the will of God" is theological; "in the genius of Muḥammad" interpretative; "in the core of mystery" evasive. We are bound to seek the spiritual answer, by which "God" and "genius" and "mystery" may be related. If Muḥammad's vocation reacted in the ways we have described in sequel, to what was his vocation itself responding in its genesis?

It is customary to dub the pre-Islamic times "the *Jāhiliyyah,*" or "the days of ignorance." Tradition's later picture of them is piously overdrawn and conflicts with immediate evidence from the Qur'ān itself and, indeed, from the pre-Islamic poets with their Arab virtues of manliness and courage. The term *Jāhiliyyah* is not simply "ignorance," in the sense of utter benightedness, but rather that stubborn unruliness we have already noted—a kind of insubordination that defies both single worship and a peaceful society. Even so, it was not an altogether unrelieved condition. There were already the *Ḥanīfs,* to whom the Qur'ān refers, men of the mold of Abraham, discontented with disunity and reaching after purer faith. Their apparent revulsion from idols may have stemmed from Jewish and Christian influences. These were certainly considerable in various parts of Arabia, though probably slightest in the immediate environs of Mecca. In the north and south of the peninsula and in parts of the Medinan region, their traditions were familiar. The Ghassānids and the Lakhmids—tribes in the border areas to the north—were Christian peoples and there were churches in Najrān. These communities of Biblical monotheism, however compromised from its fullness, in circumstances we need not here explore, were probably accessible to Muḥammad.

Among their characteristics, the most impressive was the possession of Scriptures. "People of the Book" is a recurrent Quranic phrase. If Muḥammad was yearning for a source of unity here was the proof of one. To have Scriptures, to be "scriptuaries," was to constitute a people. For some reason the existing Scriptures did not suffice, had not sufficed, to fulfill the need within the Arab soul and Arab society. Perhaps it was that their communities were too possessive of them, or, in the case of the Jews, too insistently distinctive. Neither in fact, nor in intention, nor yet—it would seem—in translation, were they Arabic Scriptures. A book for the Arabs would have to be a new departure, extending, indeed finalizing, the principle, but in independence and distinction.

Hence, it would appear, came the germinal idea of "an Arabic Qur'ān"—the phrase with which the Scripture of Islam carefully describes itself. (See Surahs 12:2; 20:113; 41:3; 42:7; and 43:3 and pp. 30 f. below.) With the need came the instrumentality. Muḥammad seems to have come to vocation by this road. The initial summons to recite grew into a conviction that, by his obedience, a Scriptural *corpus* of heavenly deliverances would steadily achieve a book on earth in the tongue of his own people.

Already before his fortieth year he had formed the habit of withdrawal to mountain retreats, to a cave or hillside, to brood and pray, away from Mecca's pagan confusion, its idol shrine and milling pilgrims, its busy merchants and rhyming poets—though these last, with their subtle skills and pleasing arts seem to have both fascinated and repelled him.

At an early point the Qur'ān refers to him as the "enmantled one" "enwrapped in robes," and the terms become in fact the titles of two of its chapters (Surahs 73 and 74). These are certainly not, at that point, the mantles of power it has in mind. Could they be, simply, the garments of a discipline of contemplation, the technique even of a mystic's search for illumination? Can we assume, in Muḥammad's own experience, something at least of the patterns later followed by Islamic mysticism, known as Sufism, in the centuries beyond? Such patterns of self-abstraction require, and serve, a cutting off of the sense world so that, undistracted, the spirit may await the visitation of the word. A cloak over the head makes a kind of tented abeyance of sight and sound, and the silence—to vary the imagery—spreads a sail for the wind of the Spirit. Was this the "enmantled" condition the Qur'ān means us to understand?

"Technique" is no doubt an alien word in this whole context, suiting more the instincts of an inquisitive science than the imponderables of a religious genesis. But when the initiation happened, when the words that were to become the earthly Qur'ān began to be heard and uttered by Muḥammad, what more fitting than that it should excel in native eloquence and be "an Arabic Qur'ān"? The authority of language and the rhythm of words—these were the joy and genius of Muḥammad's people, only that lyrical beauty deserved a better cause than loves and feuds. By the different inspiration of heaven, the native tongue should be the medium of their saving oracles: hence, it would seem, the careful insistence with which the Qur'ān repudiated the charge of mere poetry and imitation, yet claimed a surpassing eloquence.

The sense of vocation, then, and the genesis of a Scripture came in one event and moved together in parallel progression—Muḥammad, the recipient soul and voice of a Divine revelation, and the Qur'ān, the book of that recipience, gathering towards a whole in the movement of his prophetic action. "Recite in the Name of thy Lord . . ." runs the opening of Surah 96, which may well be also the opening of the entire book. The imperative verb *iqrā'* means to utter the given word, not extempore preaching, not private perusing of a silent text. "The voice said 'Cry.' " To the question: "What shall I cry?" came, for Muḥammad, the answer of a steady, if intermittent, sequence of deliverances, moving with the vicissitudes of his own career, with guidance, direction, vindication, illumination, and instruction, through the successive events by which Islam was launched and achieved. The documentary aspects await the next chapter.

Is the picture of Muḥammad now complete? The careful historian will probably ponder one further enquiry. Within this factual, political, social, and religious event in its composite unity, what manner of man was Muḥammad himself?

The answer depends upon the criteria the historian brings. There are many unfavorable assessments of Muḥammad from western writers impressed by military ruthlessness, strong egoism, marital excess, political opportunism and religious belligerence, and his toleration of the massacre of the Banū Qurayẓah and the disposession of the Jews of Khaibar.

It does not blunt these criticisms to say they were the faults of time and place. For sensitive Muslim thought sees Muḥammad as the paragon of all the eras.

The right conclusion would seem to be a verdict more ultimate than these critics attain and more rigorous than the sentimentalists allow. More than any other religious leader, Muḥammad symbolizes the alliance of power and religious ends. For all the subsequent appropriation of the Prophet by the Muslim centuries as paragon and hero the essential factors belong with the immediate history. They are not the formulation of a later reverence. The shape of his place in history was fashioned in his lifetime. Traditions, as we shall shortly see, grew voluminously around his legacy. But it was as a living presence, not as a legacy, that the achievement of Muḥammad abides in history. "Charisma" seems the right word even if it hides what it also tells. By some mystery of personal quality or authority of soul and force of will, he became that to which all else is commentary. In the Meccan/Medinan milieu of many gods and of wistful, turbulent men, Muḥammad toiled and strove in a single politico-religious vocation, inwardly assured and at length outwardly triumphant as the *Rasūl* of God.

Uncompromising as was its inner confidence and its use of power, that *Rasūliyyah* stays within its own bounds. The dignity did not need or receive the doubtful support of lavish manners or gratuitous pretension. Nor did it proceed by cringing adulation. And it resolutely precluded all notions of divinization. There was a radical way with hostility and a quite unhesitating assurance of the paramountcy of the cause over traditional mores or tribal conventions if these obstructed its path. Though in a spiritually perilous way, as we must observe, the office and the person were identical, the latter was wholly subdued to its understanding of the former. It is notable that the Qur'ān uses the personal name, Muhammad, on only four occasions. One (33:40) has to do with the fact that he had no male heir, and another (3:138) is in the context of the general mortality of all prophets.

The same concern to have only the status which revelation gave made him eager to disavow all literary competences. It was a matter of importance that he be clearly dissociated from all professional versifiers, and when such connections became a taunting accusation they were vigorously denied. He was "the unlettered prophet," *al-nabī al-ummī*—apostle to those who had no Scriptures, but himself pretending to no prior skill in verse or oratory. The Qur'ān is to be seen as more certainly God's for being manifestly not his own.

Muhammad in History

There is a posthumous Muhammad, the apostle in later tradition, the axis of mystical devotion. There were, broadly, three consequences for posterity in the *Rasūliyyah*. They were the political, the cultural or traditional, and the emotional.

The political is the Caliphate. When death claimed the *Rasūl,* in 632 A.D., his community was already a state and was about to become an empire. His demise had consummated the Scriptures of Islam: it might well have undone the state, for Muhammad had been everything within it. The answer, prompt and timely, was the Caliphate, the office and dignity of successor to Muhammad. The word *khilāfah* means simply following after and so filling the room of another. It did not include revelation, for the Qur'ān was now ended and could have no other instrument. But the springs of authority, the tasks of public leadership—these were committed to the successor, first Abū Bakr, then 'Umar, both fathers-in-law of Muhammad, beginning an institution which continued, through many toils, down to 1924. It was a practical answer to a practical need. The theory developed after the fact. It has no explicit authority from the Qur'ān. But necessity and tradition sustained it for thirteen centuries as the legal, juridical form in which Muhammad's rulership, his administrative, military, judicial, and other functions in the community, were given into other hands. We shall meet it again in discussing the community *(Ummah)* of which, until the last half century, it was an indispensable symbol.

But the gap at the Prophet's departing was not merely governmental. The Qur'ān, it is true, was complete. His death did not abruptly cut it off, for he had received its final sentences to crown his life. But that fact, so to speak, sacramentalized the heavenly silence. It was now over to the memorizers, the keepers by heart, the copyists. But they were serving a Book which was itself the seal of books of God. Men have to live beyond the last chapter of revelation, and what may be dogmatically complete is emotionally daunting. In these circumstances what was more natural than that they should turn to the memory of their mentor. What sounder reliance than the man upon whom God had relied?

So there came about in the sequel to the Qur'ān's finality the birth of tradition. All the areas of life for which the Scripture provided no guidance must be subdued to the exemplariness, the recollected habits, the preferences and anticipations of the Prophet. Let him be the criterion. That word, in Arabic form, *furqān,* was one of the titles of the Qur'ān itself. In Muḥammad's legacy of character and wisdom, as devout posterity remembered or conceived it, would be found its surest commentary and enlargement.

The growth in this way of a vast body of traditional lore about Muḥammad is one of the most remarkable phenomena in religious history. There is nothing quite like it outside Islam. Much of its content, as criticism of tradition readily allows, is extraneous to the real Muḥammad and comes into Islam from custom, law and sentiment encountered by the new religion in its rapid expansion in the two centuries after his death. But the important thing is that it came that way, with that imprint. Islam was not merely hospitable to accretions from without. It claimed them as the Prophet's own. And what was originally his own it enlarged, interpreted and applied, with meticulous concern for his approval. Thus Muḥammad reigned from the grave over the imaginations, the legislation, the daily life and personal habits of his community. Tradition became the second source of law, complementing the Quranic and extending its scope.

The impulse to find new law made legists the main group in the task and science of tradition-collecting. Given the religious authority over the whole of life, their search covered an immense territory of material down to the minutiae of personal hygiene and social behavior. It also covered a wide territory of travel. For such was the devotion to authenticity in traditions that their recorders across the lands of Islamic empire required themselves to join their own citations of example to the testimony of the last reporter in person, and thus backward to the immediate contemporary, or "companion," of Muḥammad, whose eye or ear had noted the original action or opinion. Attestation was primarily by the soundness of this chain *(isnād)* of reporting, rather than by the content or inherent credibility of the substance *(matn)* of the tradition. The science of biographies and movements relating to these bearers of traditions in their sequence became one of the major items of Islamic erudition. The canonical editors of the third Muslim century (800 A.D.) are among the most esteemed figures in its history.

It must be clear that the "virtue" by which Muḥammad filled this role was carefully distinguished from his Qur'ān recipience. That state of revelation *(waḥy),* usually denoted by certain external symptoms which became habitual, was one thing. The residual authority by which his *obiter dicta,* his example, came to be held as inspired and law-affording was another thing. Tradition did not confuse the unique status of the Quranic transactions that had occurred under the special aegis of the Divine. The tradition-yielding was a more general and diffused quality of his person, accruing, as it were, from the immense honor of his prophetic vocation. For its legal and religious role God had left ample occasion in the areas where the Qur'ān itself had been silent. Both the needs and the piety of the community saw that it was filled.

It was natural that ensuing time and widening spheres should make heavy demands upon the Prophet's posthumous directives thus recounted. But the lengthening years, of necessity, shifted the onus for new directions on to a communal consensus *(ijmā')* beyond fields which could ever, even by deference, be linked historically with his person. Even then, however, consensus was complementary to tradition and relied heavily upon it for precedent and argument.

While tradition-finding continued up to the time of the great sifters and editors of the ninth century, Al-Bukhārī, Muslim, Ibn Mājā, Al-Tirmidhī and others, there was, already, in some measure, this element of interaction between the Prophet *(Rasūl)* and the community *(Ummah),* between the repute and the pride that cherished it. It was not simply that Muḥammad shaped their patterns; it was also that their ideals shaped his image. He was the focus of their possessive satisfaction, the epitome of their ideology. Muḥammad's role in Islamic history thus exemplifies the religious necessity of concreteness, and the urge to find ideology embodied superlatively in a figure who is then corporately, even aggressively, possessed and set beyond all other comparison. It might perhaps be called in this Islamic form "religious mentorship." Its sanction lies in its holding all values in terms uniquely proprietory to one's own community. "Where we like, we liken" is a rule not only for language in the making of metaphors, but for faiths in the making of their souls.

This consideration merges into the third aspect of Muḥammad's role in history, earlier described as the axis of devotion. Muslims as legists had the stake we have described in the Prophet's memory. But as well as lawyers there were saints and seekers. Muḥammad had sternly forbidden all veneration. Together with the Jesus of the Qur'ān, and all the prophets, he was strictly and only a servant. The battle he had for Divine unity was at all times preoccupied with the menace of Divine "association"—partners with God, deifications, and divinization—all deadly dangers to the purity of faith and the proprieties of truth. Of no such travesty could Muḥammad ever be guilty. This fidelity was never in doubt.

Yet, in his vocation, he had been, operatively, very close to God. Allāh and the *Rasūl* were bracketed, inseparably, in the *Shahādah* or witness of faith. Throughout the Qur'ān there is a steady reiteration of the juncture between the concerns of God and of the Prophet. The range and frequency of this has a quite terrifying quality for those to whom it is not axiomatic. It far outdoes any temper the reader meets and shrinks from in the Psalms, where the psalmist's interests —and enemies—are assumed to coincide with God's. "Your patron is God and his apostle" (Surah 5:60). "We believe in God and his messenger and we obey" (24:40). "God and his messenger spoke the truth" (33:22). "Obey God and obey his apostle and dispute not with one another lest your power departs" (8:45),— an allegiance about which there is no room for debate. The converse is equally adamant. "Those who disobey God and his messenger, theirs is the fire of hell" (72:24). The bounty that enriches is both God's and Muḥammad's (9:75). Throughout, there is this close, intimate linking of both, in respect of claims to loyalty, threats against treachery, rewards, and promises. All alike come from the twin source. Here is one of the sharpest religious problems of the whole Qur'ān. For it seems to jeopardize the very sovereignty, undivided and singular, for which Islam stands. Yet *islām* is its justification. The absolute tends to absolutize whatever serves it and so endows the service with its own absolutism. All the Joshuas, the inquisitors, the Divine-righters of history, pass this way.

The Quranic situation certainly intends only instrumentality, and argues that it is precisely instrumentality which makes it what it is. The dilemma is deep and it is there symbolically when the worshipper enters the mosque and notes the two large circles or discs, of equal size, high on the walls, where the single words Allāh and Muḥammad are set, in clear script, as the foci of his thought. That context of the mosque and spirituality is where this third dimension of Muḥammad's meaning for Muslims must be understood.

It is, emphatically, association without *Shirk*. In orthodox Islam, Muḥammad has no mediatorship and no suprahuman status. The *Rasūliyyah* confers great dignity, but no divinity. Popular devotion, however, acclaims it with its own emotions and instincts, which strict theology has been unable to repress. Early in the sequence of traditions, stories multiplied of the Prophet's infancy and youth, of prenatal signs and portents and of miraculous elements in his biography. The Qur'ān lends some limited support to the last—though the passage may be taken figuratively—in the allusion to the night ascent to heaven via the "farthest mosque" in Jerusalem. (Surah 17:2 f.) But it was overwhelmingly tradition and pious instinct, not the Qur'ān, which developed this Muḥammad of miracle and wonder.

Of greater significance was the spiritual cult of Muḥammad's person and character as bridging, so to speak, the divide between the awful majesty on high and the struggling frailty below. There grew in Shī'ah Islam[1] an intense devotion to the Prophet's family, to 'Alī—cousin and son-in-law, to Ḥasan and Ḥusain— grandsons, and the line which so precariously survived the massacre of Karbalā'. Out of political failure, the Shī'ah cause became the ground of a passionate devotion to the lineal family of the Prophet, the *Āl* of Muḥammad, hallowed by the bitter tragedy of martyrdom and emotionally sharpened by the suffering of external failure. Sunnī Islam, with its accent on the community of believers, its external success and its dogmatic rigorism, rejected these Shī'ah emotions as disloyal and perverse.

To reject them, however, was not to escape the religious yearnings to which they related. For all their emphasis on solidarity, on law and sound tradition, on realism and nondeviation, Sunnis also needed to possess Muḥammad in terms

satisfying to the springs of personal religion. From one angle, their very antipathy
to Shī'ah positions accentuated cultic trends in their own Sunnī direction. Muḥammad's legacy, however well entrusted to tradition and to law, could not live
in a devotional silence. It could not be left only with pundits. Alongside the ritual
prayer, or *Salāt,* to which all Muslims were bound, went a popular incorporation
of Muḥammad into acts of devotion. With the help of ambiguity in a pivotal verse,
his intercession was sought and believed. (Surah 2:255 asked: "Who is there that
will intercede with Him save by his leave?" and it was argued that leave would
be given to Muḥammad.) Petition, eulogy, celebration all came to be offered in
his name. The position his example enjoyed with the moralists, his person filled
for the worshippers. The *Rasūliyyah* that had been the highway of the word from
God to men became the highway of many words from men to God.

This development owed much to the encouragement it received from a single
verse in the Qur'ān. Surah 33:56 reads: "God and his angels celebrate the
Prophet. O ye who believe celebrate him and greet him with peace." The word
here translated "celebrate" means "to pray" and is so used in respect of the ritual
"praying" or *Ṣalāt,* to be studied in Chapter 5. God cannot, of course, be said
to "pray." The word, in origin meaning "to bow," has then the sense of recognition or commendation. "Send down, or invoke, blessing upon" is a frequent
rendering. Help can be had from the converse in 33:57. "Those who speak evil
of the prophet . . ." where the sense is to "malign."

God, then, "blesses" Muḥammad and the believers do likewise. This is
known as *Taṣliyah,* a technical noun derived from the verb. It is closely linked
with *Taslīm,* or the invocation of peace: "Greet him with peace," and this lends
support to the idea that the whole phrase may have to do with an inviolability
of the Prophet, a sort of Hosanna: "God save Muḥammad" which is at once fact
and invocation. There *may* in this context be a purely practical sense, namely
vindication against detractors; so say some modern exegetes. But it is much more
likely to be, as it is popularly taken, a kind of reverent, celestial Hurrah!

Heaven rejoices in Muḥammad, and the faithful echo Divine approval. Men
salute him whom God perpetually attests. Here devotion found abundant opportunity. Mysticism took ready incentive, as we will see in the chapter on Liturgy,
not only from the Prophet's example of meditation, but from the idea of his
oneness with the Divine mind. He was the Aḥmad (a variant of Muḥammad)
without the "m"—meaning he was *Aḥad* or the One, a title of Allāh. Or he was
"the 'Arab" without the "A" that is, *Rabb* or Lord. He was the very Divine *Ṣalāt*
in the *miḥrāb,* or niche, of the Divine being, the eternal joy of God in the reality
of His revelation—a concept perhaps loosely comparable with that of personified
wisdom in the Book of Proverbs: "I was daily His delight . . ." The obvious
tension of these mystical ideas, and the practices they sanctioned, in conflict with
the orthodox dogma, did not prevent them from playing a prolonged and major
role in the religious prosperity of Islam.

Popular faith possessed Muḥammad with less subtlety but no less fervor.
Poems on his birthday, *Maulid* songs and processions, invocations of his name,

and celebrations of the episodes of his life diffused through the centuries a sense of participation in heavenly things, a vicarious proximity to God in the supreme intermediary, the Prophet after God's own heart. The mention of his name and office in all pious writing or speaking is immediately followed by the formula: "Let the blessing and peace of God be upon him."

It must conclude this brief venture into the fact of Muḥammad within the house of Islam. There is much else to which a fuller study should give heed and some aspects will emerge under other themes that follow. It is, however, remote and academic to call it a formula. For those within it is a salutation of the heart, a greeting to the proven ways of God.

3.
Qur'ān

Our best point of departure in a study of the Qur'ān is from the fact of its being Arabic. In reflection on the career of Muḥammed, we have noted the twin elements of Scripture possession as the clue to a people's cohesion or solidarity, and the fascination of poetic forms and freedom for Arab society. On both counts the Prophet's revelation is "an Arabic Qur'ān," responding both to the Arab love of language and to the Arab yearning for the unity a proper Scripture might bestow. "Had We made it a Qur'ān in an alien speech," observes an interesting conjecture in Surah 41:44, the foes of the preacher would have said: "If only its verses had been made plain to understand. Fancy! an uncouth tongue, and he an Arab!" Clearly pride of language, comprehension, and propriety all required that the Scripture should address its first and "native" people in the music of their own tongue.

But, by the same token, it is "an alien speech" to all those multitudes who come to it in the worldwide dispersion of its fame and mission. For them the obstacles are formidable indeed. They meet us at once in the simple but bothersome business of transliteration. Why not "Koran," which is a generally recognizable designation? The vowel "o," however, does not exist in Arabic and "k" is another consonant not used in this word. We have to make a choice between a distortion that happens to be current and a correctness that may be puzzling. Again, why "Qur'ān," and not "the Qur'ān" in the heading? A good enough reason, better clarified subsequently, namely that there is a concept here as well as a book, something akin to "history" and "the history," or "news" and "the news." The Qur'ān by its own showing is also a Qur'ān: it finalizes an entity (revelation and recital) of which there are other examples.

The Qur'ān's Arabic Form

But far more vexing than these elementary matters are the exacting ventures of translation proper. Let it be said at once that the difficulties are not insuperable. There are, after all, vastly more Muslims than Arabs. Persians, Turks, Pakistanis, Indians, Indonesians, Hausas, Malays, and scores of others have the Qur'ān at the center of their religious existence, with only a tiny fraction of their numbers, pundits and experts, able to reach it in the original Arabic. But, heartening as this thought is, the daunting and sober truth is that the Qur'ān is, in fact, untranslatable. The exasperation to which endless readers, Carlyle and Gibbon outspokenly among them, have been reduced in their struggle to appreciate the Qur'ān without

Arabic, is no idle thing. It is honest fact and all the more teasing for the very sympathy that wanted to surmount it. The frustrations of patience are more disconcerting, faced with the obscurities that foreign translations often involve, than are the complaints of hostility. Resourcefulness and assurance over this problem can only grow from a frank and intelligent appreciation of its nature.

The Qur'ān's being untranslatable must be assessed from two angles, the dogmatic and the literary. The former is the more easily handled. It arises from the traditional and long-standing exegesis of the several passages, noted in Chapter 2, which insist: "We have sent it down an Arabic Qur'ān." The simple case here is that if God willed the Holy Book should be Arabic, it is no part of obedience or submission to turn it into any other tongue. There is a dogma, therefore, about the form as well as about the substance, and these are not separable. Revelation, we may say, is a linguistic as well as a spiritual phenomenon. The Scripture is a miracle of eloquence and diction, as well as the repository of final truth. Meaning cannot be assured in such sacred and crucial fields of truth unless language is also verbally inspired and given. Once given, in the revelatory particular, which is Arabic, it cannot be undone or transposed. Translation, even if successful in respect of content, deliberately destroys form, so that the result is, at best, only half of the original. It was for this reason that Marmaduke Pickthall, for example, as an English Muslim, in 1928 entitled his translation: "*The Meaning of* the Glorious Koran." For the title: "The Glorious Koran" could not rightly be given to any non-Arabic version. Others get over the difficulty by printing Arabic and the other language in parallel columns. The duty of the faithful is to honor the Divine mind that decreed the Arabicity and not seek to change either the one or the other.

However, there is one overriding consideration which, in our present context, suffices to terminate the long and often meticulous debate on this theme and to sustain the enterprise of translation as both loyal and desirable. It is the simple observation that in almost all the passages that refer to "an Arabic Qur'ān" intelligibility for the Arabs is the reason, explicit or implied, why it is so. "Perhaps you will understand," or "for a people who know . . ." or ". . . that you may warn the mother of the villages," namely, the metropolis of Mecca with its Arabic-speaking populace. The same note is sounded in the conjecture with which we began. An *'ajamī* Qur'ān, a Scripture other than Arabic, would not be decipherable. Such a "revelation" would be pure folly and empty mockery, being only a jingle of sound, a "barbarous thing."

But if the Arabic language of the Qur'ān is for its intelligibility to Arabs, then translation, where non-Arabs are involved, becomes imperative. Seen in this sense, the very passages, which justified orthodox persistence in the belief that only Arabic could be "Qur'ān," in fact imply a duty of translation, since otherwise the central intention, namely understanding, would be thwarted. Many other practical and rational factors have tended powerfully in the same direction, and the old reluctance now has a diehard and archaic kind of look. Translation, in fact, if not in unanimous theory, is everywhere conceded and undertaken. Many Muslims today urge that believers should not let this task go by default to unbelievers.[1]

The literary problem still remains. Translation is not merely a theme for debate among dogmatists. It is a strenuous enterprise for a painstaking scholarship, and one that can never be wholly satisfactory. The form and substance question just noted is greater as a concrete issue for translators than as a theoretical matter for theologians. Sense is closely wedded to words, and meaning to shape. The Arabic of the Qur'ān has its vocabulary subtleties, its cadences and rhymes, its metaphors and poetry. All these tax the ingenuity of the translator. It is almost impossible, in many passages, to avoid interpretation in translating. Hence the otherwise misleading title of much the best English version, A. J. Arberry's *The Koran Interpreted,* where the introduction may usefully be consulted for many of the technical problems incurred.[2] This translation is not, as its title might suggest, a commentary. But it concedes that there is a subtle quality which makes the Qur'ān outside Arabic no longer itself. All that English, or German, or any other language can do is to interpret that quality in another key.

This matter is, no doubt, common to all great literature. Shakespeare in French is as deplorable to an Englishman as Dante in another tongue is to the Italian. The indefinable quality of the native utterance becomes tame and flat in the new guise. The non-Arab, whether Muslim or westerner, has to keep always in view the impoverishment represented by his, albeit intelligible, version, as contrasted with the feel, the emotive power, the warm thrill, of the original for its own heirs.

There are inviting vistas of poetry. Consider Surah 94, in Arberry's rendering —less inspired than usual:

> Did We not expand thy breast for thee
>   and lift from thee thy burden,
> the burden that weighed down thy back?
>   Did We not exalt thy fame?
>
> So truly with hardship comes ease; (repeat)
>   So when thou art empty, labour,
> And let thy Lord be thy Quest.[3]

Dawood's version, *The Koran,* runs as follows:

> Have We not lifted up your heart and relieved you of
>   the burden that weighed down your back?
> Have We not given you high renown?
> Every hardship is followed by ease. (repeat)
> When your task is ended, resume your toil, and
>   seek your Lord with all fervour.[4]

The English, in neither case, betrays the fact that there are here four and two terminal rhymes, two and two interior rhymes, as well as the refrain. But it would

take freer paraphrase to attempt them in English and at best it could only be
remote.

> Have We not lightened your heart,
> Your shoulders now sparing,
> The load you were bearing,
> And lauding with honour your part?
> For pain of grief there's gain of peace (repeat)
> When steadied, be readied anew,
> And all your desire be your Lord's.[5]

The Arabic refrain *ma' al-'usri yusran* yields no such neat, sweet equal, and our
feeble attempts at interior and final rhymes are still far away from the lilt and
the metre of the original. We had better regret to be prosaic than strain to be
poetic. For from that kind of hardship there is no ease.

The reader may multiply this sort of situation scores of times. Poetry aside,
there are perplexities of grammar. For example, take the vital passage denying
the actuality of the crucifixion of Jesus in Surah 4:157. "They did not kill him,
they did not crucify him, but he (or it) was resembled to them." Translators have
said the antecedent to the (hidden) pronoun "they" is "the Jews." Others suggest
(with much less ground) that there is an intention of discrimination—not "these"
but "those"; namely, it was the Romans who did it. Or it may be that the pronoun
is left intentionally imprecise. Further, is the second (also hidden) pronoun "he"
or "it"? Was Jesus made to be resembled by some other person—crucified, by this
mistaken identity, instead of him? Or, was "it," namely crucifixion, only apparently accomplished, only seemingly done? It is impossible to decide these questions in an equivalent English sentence without implicit exegesis as well as actual
translation.

Or again, there are elastic terms which themselves undergo development
within the Qur'ān. The term, *fitnah,* for example, when it first occurs means a
trial or test—the dangers of military service for a family man (see Surah 64:15).
It later comes very close to "sedition," the menace that intrigue is to the established cause. In the latter case *fitnah* is the archenemy, which warfare has to
liquidate, "in order that religion may be wholly God's"; in the former it is an
emotion within the ranks which deters the will for the risk of battle.

Examples recur throughout the Qur'ān and they are more readily solved, or
held in solution, when they are left in Arabic, than when, as translation usually
requires, they have to be forced into resolution of their essential ambiguity.

But the other side of these matters is that their very presence is the token
of the Quranic excellence in its original Arabic. We must pause to take this fact
in its technical measure. Muslims believe in what is known as the *I'jāz* or
mu'jizah of the Qur'ān—its matchlessness and incomparability. The terms mean
that it cannot be rivalled in respect either of form or of worth. This superlative
eloquence is regarded in orthodox circles as the crowning evidence of its Divine
origin, the more so as it is found on the lips of a Prophet who disowned all poetic

competence and was understood to be *ummī,* or "illiterate." We have seen earlier the more likely sense of this phrase as "the unscriptured" one. But it is widely understood as indicating actual inability to read or write and so to mean "the scripted" Prophet, that is, one who received what he uttered—just as a spokesman might from a text whispered to him in the wings—a text which is on his lips from a composing source outside himself. So the words and sequences of Quranic recital by Muḥammad follow the content of the book in heaven, "the preserved tablet" whence their phrasing, as well as their meaning, is drawn. Muḥammad is thus the mouthpiece of the preexistent Scripture, given to him in the experience of *waḥy,* or "revelation," which covers both substance and form.

This heavenly composition in the prophetic utterance is, accordingly, *sui generis,* incapable of being imitated. This uniqueness was made the theme in several places of a challenge to Muḥammad's foes and doubters. "Bring a surah like it": "bring ten surahs like it" if you are sincere. (See Surahs 2:23; 10:38 and 11:12). The incapacity of the Arab hearers—the challenge was not to foreigners —to match or better the Quranic eloquence has always been interpreted as attesting its indubitable worth and its heavenly origin. Therefore, eloquence is the only miracle and the sufficient one. The authority of the Qur'ān is religiously bound up with the incomparability of its language. That this aspect of its revelatory credentials is not accessible outside the Arab world does not affect, doctrinally, its universal relevance and its multilanguage destiny as revelation.

The Question of Chronology

The most obvious recourse for the reader in search of the intelligible Qur'ān is the sense of chronology. What Muḥammad received in his claim to *Rasūliyyah* coincided, as we have seen, with a sequence of events through the twenty-three years of his prophetic life. What medieval exegetes called "the occasions of the descent [of the Qur'ān]," *asbāb al-nuzūl,* were the historical circumstances, the corporate or personal episodes, in relation to which the Qur'ān came, and in the light of which it had to be understood. The steady accumulation of the deliverances marched with the narrative evolution of his fortunes, in the developing roles, first of preacher, then of ruler. This accumulation was necessarily an experience which could not be expedited so as to anticipate events which had not yet emerged within the logic of his mission in its environment. The Qur'ān could not have been vouchsafed to him as a whole book at one time (Surah 25:32). In his understandable eagerness to receive more, Muḥammad is warned not to "hurry the recital." This directive could refer to hasty speaking but more likely means the desire to have totally what could only come gradually. The Qur'ān was given by God in installments so that the Prophet may be duly upheld and the people progressively instructed (Surahs 17:106 and 75:16).

For this reason the criterion of chronology is built into the very structure and concept of the Qur'ān as a cumulative revelation. Unhappily, however, it does not dictate its actual arrangement. The Surahs, or chapters, after "the Opener," are arranged, approximately, in order of diminishing length, from the longest (2) to the shortest (the last ten). Within themselves many of the longer Surahs are composite and belong to different points in the time sequence. Some exegetes, in their reluctance for contextual, as opposed to dogmatic, exegesis, hail this non-chronological arrangement of the Quranic canon as Divinely willed, though by this attitude they also deprecate, at least by implication, its historical setting. Others, of surer instinct and less timidity, strive to identify the precise sequence, and even to rearrange the whole accordingly.

The average reader simply has to cope as best he may with the handicap of this situation and might be well advised, in a rough and ready way, to begin at the end and move backwards to the start, knowing that thus he will be proceeding with the general run of the history. Or he may follow one of the several rearrangements ventured by different Muslim and western scholars.

The data for such chronological editions are readily at hand, even if they involve debate and divergence on particular points. The Qur'ān itself incorporates officially in its chapter headings the note *Makkiyyah* or *Madaniyyah* "at Mecca" or "at Medina." The *Hijrah,* on which the story of Muḥammad hinged, occupies, therefore, the same centrality for the Scripture. There are the revelations that are pre-*Hijrah* and those that are post-*Hijrah.* The watershed that gives the calendar its origin divides the book just as it defines the *Rasūliyyah.*

The ninety or so Surahs of the Meccan period (609 to 622 A.D.) and the twenty-four of the Medinan period (622 to 632 A.D.) can be further identified by characteristics belonging, in a fairly obvious way, with their setting in time. The former are often subdivided into early, middle and late Meccan. The early utterances are fervent, ecstatic, intensely poetic, ejaculatory, with their ardent themes of judgment impending and idolatry doomed. The passion and urgency of the first warnings and summons to faith and repentance slowly merge into more measured, argumentative, dialectical style and mood. The initial preaching, as we saw, runs into ridicule, opposition and disdain. Controversy develops. The Meccan hearers make charges of jinn-possession, madness, pretension, or deceit, which Muḥammad is directed to deny and rebuff. The Qur'ān, throughout the middle period, settles into prolonged contention, battling with the gibes. There is frequently the exchange: "They say . . . ," "Say thou . . ."; the charge and the answer. Poetry cannot be quite so vibrant and spontaneous in this setting. Controversy is its necessary second round.

In this general milieu comes, for the most part, the patriarchal material in which the Qur'ān parallels, in broad terms, the Old Testament figures. Their relevance seems to lie in two considerations. They provide patterns of fortitude by which Muḥammad may be encouraged, since most of them had to struggle against similar odds in the same idol-defying cause. But they also emerged to success and vindication. The Qur'ān does not speak of the tragic and broken-hearted prophets, of Hosea or Jeremiah. The bringer of the Arabic Scripture may thus be reassured as well as fortified. These narratives teach other lessons also, of providence and truth. They undergird the Quranic conviction that there is a unity within all Scriptures, however disloyal their preceptors may have been.

But just as intensity of poetry gave way to tenacity of witness, all within the same *preaching,* so, in turn, stouthearted utterance gives way to energetic action. We have already studied this inner decision of Muḥammad for the power structure that the *Hijrah* reaches towards and inaugurates. The *Jāhiliyyah* of resistance is not simply an ignorance to be informed, or a dullness to be illumined. It is also a stubbornness to be overcome, a perversity to be defeated. The Qur'ān naturally registers this fundamental shift from prophet to statesman, from preacher to ruler. Events, skirmishes, deputations, treaties, accessions, become more conspicuous as *asbāb al-nuzūl.* The text marches with the armies and moves with the public affairs of Medina. The legislative element becomes pronounced. The Surahs grow longer, argument recedes and authority dominates. Personal events in the life and entourage of Muḥammad assume an importance they did not have in Mecca. There develops what is apparently a much readier incidence of deliverances, without the anguish and soul-searching which belonged with the outset of the Qur'ān. The text is now involved in the superintendence of the life and order of a whole community, both in war and peace, in the social manifold of birth, marriage, divorce, inheritance, citizenship, taxation, ritual, and community. Some of the content of the Qur'ān in this dimension will meet us in Chapters 4 and 5. The translator's problems are, of course, correspondingly less exacting in this sphere. Prose, especially the lawmaker's, has much less to lose in another tongue than the exaltations of poetic fire. All the commentator needs is a sense of time and place and a legal head.

It is worth observing here that the Qur'ān has little reflection on general history beyond its intense interest in the transitoriness of human communities. It sees men as successors to one another in the flux of history, hastening their sheer mortality by their perversity. Retribution and requital, as well as natural transience, overtake the proud cultures and fabled empires of men. "How many a city have We destroyed for its evil-doing and now it is fallen on its very turrets" (Surah 22:44). There were the glories of south Arabia, nourished by the vast irrigation works around the town of Ma'rib whose collapse left an awesome memory in the tales of Muḥammad's people. There are fleeting references, also, to Alexander the Great in Surah 18:83, with his far-flung conquests, both eastward and westward, "the owner of the two horns" bestriding the earth. Surah 30 opens with a reference to a defeat of the Greeks by the Persians, the reversal of which is promised anon. This no doubt mirrors the protracted rivalries of Byzantium and Persia in the days before Islam.

For the rest, the sweep of universal history does not figure in the Qur'ān. Patriarchal narratives have their bearing on the Meccan scene. But the history that receives and "contextualizes" the revelation is within the single quarter century of the unique apostle and in the orbit of the twin cities that his mission embraced.

The canon of the Qur'ān, arising from the twenty-three years of Muḥammad's *waḥy,* took an even shorter period to receive definitive recension. For it was completed within the reign of 'Uthmān (d. 656). The Prophet's preaching and speaking within the Quranic state was assiduously repeated and loyally memorized by his followers. The very term "Qur'ān" applies equally to this recital of theirs as to his. Scholars generally hold that what he so delivered found its way, without serious loss or impairment or alteration, into the canon, and that extraneous material, lacking this double *imprimatur* of his uttering and theirs, his inspiration and their reception, did not. The things recited were inscribed, no doubt in different ways and places, consistently with their periodic character. It appears that Muḥammad used secretaries. These fragments steadily accumulated but do not seem to have been edited or incorporated into a volume before his death. Abū Bakr in 633 A.D. set the first recension under way. But twenty years later there had come to be diverse, even rival, texts, associated with different local centers and dialects. It was to obviate strife that 'Uthmān finalized and authorized one recension only—a step which in fact engendered deep dissension and contributed to the unrest and revolt which ended his rule. The canonization, however, stood, and the almost complete elimination of other copies foreclosed what might have been bitter controversies. Though many quests and questions remain for academic scholarship, the Qur'ān has a documentary uncomplicatedness akin to its authoritarian directness and simplicity.

The Climactic Scripture

What we have called the concentration of the Qur'ān in time and place needs to be seen in the context of its belief in the long sequence of prophets and their scriptures. It is itself the last, not the solitary, Scripture. From Adam through to Jesus, prophets, teachers, and apostles came and went, bearing their message from God and their witness to men. They came "from God, reading purified pages comprising authentic books," to quote Surah 98:2. Adam gave the creatures names and so inaugurated all knowledge. Moses received the *Taurah* or Torah, David the *Zabūr* or Psalms, Jesus the *Injīl* or Gospel. Almost all the Biblical figures down to Elisha and Jonah are present in the Qur'ān, together with extra-Biblical names, Ṣāliḥ and Hūd and the intriguing Luqmān, or Aesop. These servants of the Divine will differed in the reach of their audience or the range of their message. Some had limited constituencies and only preparatory truths. All comes to its climax in the finalizing Qur'ān, the revelation that ends revelation. Muḥammad is the seal of the prophets, and the consummation of their wisdom.

So it is that in the Muslim view all the Biblical Scriptures should be consistent with the Qur'ān. When they are not so, it means that their custodians have tampered with them and distorted their contents, or that the final revelation has abrogated their provisions as being only a proximate stage on the way to truth. This assumption of corruption or of abrogation has, of course, been a provocative and taxing issue between Islam and the earlier monotheisms. Some of the divergencies in the patriarchal narratives are only slight and concern emphases more than essence. They can readily be studied in the story of Joseph which, unlike the diffuse references, say, to Abraham, or Noah, or Moses, is concentrated in a single, orderly sequence in one Surah, the twelfth. But other aspects involve sharp controversies about the Bible arising within Muḥammad's own career. Notable among these are the covenant-election theme of the Old Testament and the Incarnation and the Cross of Jesus in the New, both of which the Qur'ān energetically denies.

There are, also, more subtle differences and disparities. Scriptures as the Qur'ān sees them, "come down" upon their servants, who recite their contents. They are the human iteration of the words of God. The concept of texts, even "sheets," or papers, *scripta,* is paramount. Revelation does not include human address to God, as in many psalms, nor the personal, autobiographical, travail of prophets. Nor is it the corporate experience of a community at large. Nor, again, is it in any sense the significance *per se* of a personality in a situation. The word is never made flesh to dwell: it is made speech to utter. Nor, again, is it the living commentary of a pastoral spirit on the sharp crises of existence, as these occur, for example, in the epistles of the New Testament. Epistles, on a Quranic view, can never be revelation, since they travel horizontally: they do not "come down."

Yet, for all these strenuous and indeed irreducible differences, there is deep importance in the Quranic idea of scriptural continuity. Some are ready to see, in the Quranic view that every people has its messengers, a possible validation of Hindu and Buddhist Scriptures also. Certainly, within the Judeo/Christian/ Muslim sphere, there are many shared dimensions of faith. It is well not to allow the contentions to obscure how much is assumed in common and contested from common premises. If, to many, the Qur'ān's claim to supercession is distressing, it at least implies affinities that are by no means wholly negated and whose durability may at length affect the harshness of the enmity caused and returned.

One of the most striking of Quranic passages about God is in the Surah of Light (24):

> God is the light of the heavens and the earth.
> The likeness of His light is as a niche,
> Wherein is a lamp, the lamp in a glass, the glass like a glistening star,
>   kindled from a blessed tree,
> An olive neither of the east nor of the west,
> Whose oil would almost shine had no fire touched it.
> Light upon light: God guides to His light whom He will:
> God brings similitudes for men and God has knowledge of all things.

It seems clear that niche and lamp and oil and light belong to a similitude of chapel and rite. For the verse goes on:

> (Light) in temples God has allowed to be raised up,
> Where His Name is commemorated,
> Glorifying Him therein, morning and evening,
> Men whom neither commerce nor trafficking
> Diverts from the remembrance of God.

Exegesis

The discernible, interreligious features of the Qur'ān are not, here, directly, our concern. But our taking Surah 24 this way brings us to the whole question of exegesis in Islam. The centrality and finality of the Qur'ān make commentary a major field of theology and law. What, then, are the criteria to be applied to the understanding of the sacred text? Are exegetes free for the sort of conjecture we have just made, finding and proposing allusions which common sense or history suggest? How, in fact, has commentary proceeded in the long history of scriptural possession by Muslims?

The answers are, in part, implicit in what has been already indicated. The strictly scriptural nature of revelation has made for an extreme reverence for the letter. Grammar, vocabulary, construction, and case receive a meticulous attention. Parsing is the first obligation of the classical commentators. The dogma of "Arabicity" is taken to preclude search for the bearings of loan words from other languages, which might usefully indicate possible sources of Quranic background and provide clues to original meanings. If it is not conceded that there are non-Arabic words this field of enquiry is closed. The habit of continuous memoriter tends to keep devout response to the text close to the adjacent verses, as they stand in the reciter's sequence. It is often assumed that the nonchronological order has a Divine sanction—a belief that can discourage thematic cross-reference and even reduce concern for "the occasions of revelation."

These latter, however, come into their own in exegesis at least for the sake of exhortation or homiletics. Commentary draws heavily upon traditions, seeing that the stories from the Prophet's companions fill out details of events and situations in which Quranic history is involved. Citation of them helps to reinforce the moral guidance of the Qur'ān and is customary in the mosque sermon.

The most important single principle of commentary yielded by the Qur'ān itself is in Surah 3:7, which reads: ". . . the Book, some of whose verses are decisive, being of the essence of the Book, and others which are ambiguous." The following verses go on to suggest that the "ambiguous" verses attract dissidents and pretentious exegetes, who need to remember that finally "interpretation" is known only to God. The two crucial adjectives here, "decisive" and "ambiguous," mean, in the one case, clear, direct, unequivocal, perhaps even legal and precise, and in the other, metaphorical, analogical, figurative, allegorical, and parabolic. There is some doubt about what is intended in describing the former as "the mother of the Book," a phrase which is used elsewhere in the sense of the heavenly original, the celestial Book recited to Muḥammad that, by his recital, it might in turn be the revelation on earth. It is clear, at any rate, that both types of verse are integral to the Qur'ān, that it possesses clear and direct contents and contents needing deference as hidden, subtle, mystically opaque. Shī‘ahs and Sufis, as we shall see, take up the second type vigorously and diversely. Sunnī conservatism tends to be circumspect and awed.

A working relation to this distinction argues that the plain, clear sense, if it manifestly exists, should stand without cavil and foreclose all tedious debate. Such, at any rate, are many of the laws of the Qur'ān. As for the ambiguous, they may be discreetly allowed a latitude of interpretation, and even in some quarters a wide initiative, consistently with loyalty and consensus. They cannot be taken repugnantly to the clear intention of other passages. Given the very extensive use of metaphor in the Qur'ān, the pressures of circumstance and the ingenuity of Muslims, it is safe to see the relation of Scripture to community as, actually and potentially, freer and less predictable than the patterns and instincts of dogma would suggest.

Some contemporary, or near contemporary, commentary makes far-reaching appeal to the metaphorical principle and even enlarges it to involve, in a sense, the whole Quranic situation, interpreted as a seventh century parable of twentieth century concerns, needing to be "transposed," so that Muḥammad's battle against vested interest becomes an incipient socialism where the community controls the means of production; his statehood emerges as the consecration of power in the pursuit of justice; his religious leadership stands as an essential dynamism on behalf of progressive humanism. In some cases, as in that of Muḥammad Iqbāl in Indian Islam, philosophic and linguistic ingenuity comes to the aid of these reinterpretations, to find, for example, in Semitic religious terms like *Rabb* (or Lord) and *Allāh*, new connotations consistent with creative evolution and scientific views. The "ambiguity" concept then develops into a kind of foreknowing by which the Qur'ān is subsequently seen to mean what its first hearers could never have appreciated. In less able hands, this style of commentary proposes easy claims of Quranic anticipation in respect, for example, of the cutting of the Suez Canal, the invention of gunpowder, bacteriology, and the use of metallic alloys.

Such inventiveness, however, wanting to have both worlds, the dogmatic and the contemporary, has been vigorously repudiated in responsible quarters, where it is insisted that the essential message of the Qur'ān must be read in its religious character and derived from its historical setting. The argument for development, it is held, must be consistent with that double test. The crucial questions are: What did the Book mean, and intend, and achieve, in its first human context? Only when they have been loyally and rightly answered, can we properly and constructively develop its arguable relevance in a new situation. When this, the true, obedience to Surah 3:7 is given, the timeless potential of the Qur'ān may be seen to be very great indeed, as Chapter I above has illustrated.

The Qur'ān by Heart

Beyond all these aspects of the Islamic Scripture lies the ultimate question: what does the holy Book mean in the inner religious experience of the loyal Muslim? It is guidance, warning, mercy, reminder, criterion, as its several titles indicate. But how does it effectuate them in his daily life? One may cite in reply its dominance in Islamic art and mosque decoration, where the sacred script receives, and in receiving confirms, a central devotion where art and the spirit combine. The chanting of the Qur'ān is, equally, the primary music of Islam. For the mosque knows no musical instruments and no choral praise. It finds its sole consecration of sound in its recital of the words of revelation. Yet, beyond calligraphy and chant, is the innermost reality by which, for the individual Muslim, the speech of God comes into the storehouse of memory and into the currency of his lips.

Memorizing and recitation, fundamental as they are to traditional Muslim piety and scholarship, are integral to ordinary believing. The Qur'ān is not simply a blueprint for society, nor only a storehouse for theology and law. It is these because it is first and always a Scripture to be confessed, and that not merely by acknowledging its status but by rehearsing its contents. Made audible in the faithful utterance of its verses, as these have been faithfully stored in the heart, it constitutes what may well be called a sacrament of mind and voice, participating in what is God's.

Quranic recital engages the heart and speech of the faithful Muslim in a taking within himself, and an expression from himself, of what he understands to be the "oracles" of God. He is faithfully doing after him what the Prophet did inclusively, for him and all Muslims, on behalf of God. This is the sense of Qur'ān, without the article, for which we were concerned at the head of this chapter. Where the New Testament speaks of "that which we have seen, and heard, and handled . . . ," Islam would speak of "that which we have heard, and remembered, and rehearsed. . . ." Reciting is the appropriate "possession" of a revelation that is taken to be essentially a Book. By *Ḥifẓ al-Qur'ān,* as the term goes, the Scripture is both received and known. For it seeks, not merely listeners, or hearers, or perusers, but receivers who symbolize their identity with its meanings and commands by their consecration to them of memory and tongue.

There is something abiding about this quality of things even where, as is increasingly the case, strict memorizing is no more general or entire. It may still be parabolized in the few phrases of formal prayer, including the first Surah, which figure in Arabic in all Muslim worship. These are the signs of the rest, just as the whole is, verbally, the sign of Divine communication. In the *Shahādah,* or confession, the same idea is central. Silent assent is not witness. The voice and the memory are recruited to be the tokens and the pledge of the rest of discipleship.

This answer admits, then, of a further question: what does this vocal participation in the Quranic Scripture mean in the characteristic preoccupations and emphases of the piety and faith it nurtures? The sense of the Divine authority and claim; the earnest dignity of human existence and the trivial, transitory folly of human perversity; the wistful realities of mercy and the precarious contingencies of life; the intense vividness of the eternal condition both of bliss and doom; and the impending, inescapable judgment and destiny. Relying on other areas of our study to fill out some of these, and much else in the Qur'ān, let us take a single

Surah, almost at random, and ponder its emphases, its directives, its warnings, its passionate quality. For an alert reader, its own impact may be worth a tome of commentary. Choice is bewildering, yet, in a way, also unnecessary. Take Surah 25. It is Meccan, in the middle period. It bears as title one of the names of the whole, namely, "the Criterion." Let us briefly set down its contents.

> Blessed be He Who has sent down upon His servant the criterion [of truth and right] that he may warn humanity.

The Divine mention promptly excludes all associates in the Kingdom, and disowns all the idols, powerless, profitless, futile, as they are. Controversy is at once joined. The unbelievers want some extraordinary messenger, some angel, some lordling. Muḥammad is too commonplace, a forger, an upstart. But all other prophets knew these calumnies and history records the overthrow of their adversaries. So it will be again. The rejected Qur'ān is vindicated in the doom of the gainsayers.

> It shall be a Day harsh for the unbelievers. Upon that Day the evil-doer shall bite his hands and say: Would that I had walked in the way of the messenger.

The very idols, questioned in the judgment, disown their worshippers, who thus find no alibi for their misdeeds and no release from their misery.

In the living world, the signs of God abide, the measuring sun and the garment of the night, the flowing winds and the reviving showers, and after them the devastating comment that most men belie the grace in them. Each new day is a kind of resurrection. But men do not rise with it into thankfulness. "The unbeliever is always a partisan against his Lord." A brief note about the making of the creature and the angelic demur about acknowledging him is followed by the familiar, reiterated characterization of the true Muslim.

> The servants of the ever-Merciful are those who walk modestly in the earth, and who say: Peace to the ignorant when they accost them; who pass the night standing and kneeling in reverence to their Lord; and who say: Lord, ward off from us the punishment of Hell, for it is a fearful chastisement, and an evil abode and a vile resting-place; who are neither extravagant nor niggardly and observe the golden mean; who call upon no other god except God, nor slay the soul God has forbidden, except it be rightfully; who do not commit adultery, for the adulterer shall meet with evil and a double chastisement on the day of resurrection, abiding forever in disgrace, unless he repents and believes, and does righteously. For God changes the evil doings of such into good deeds, for God is the ever-merciful, the compassionate. Whosoever repents and does rightly he turns indeed to God penitently. [The servants] are those who do not bear false witness; and when involved in profanity around them retain their honor; who when they are reminded of the signs of their Lord do not turn a blind eye and a deaf ear; who say: Lord, give us joy of our wives and children and make us examples to those who fear Thee. These will be rewarded for their patient endurance with the heavenly mansion and shall be received there with greeting and peace. They shall dwell there forever, a blessed and sure abiding place.

Here, in epitome, are the great themes of Quranic religion, and its authentic atmosphere, urgent, forceful, confident, and decisive, "a book in which there is no dubiety," holding in its reach time and eternity, angels and men, truth and error, nature and signs, the piety of the good and the doom of the evil, and all within the immediacy of a strenuous prophetic encounter with a vexing and recalcitrant people. With the final verses we are already in the themes of ethics to which we must now turn, not overlooking the sting in the closing warning to the unbelieving:

> Say: My Lord cares little that you do not call upon Him. The die is cast in that you have belied [His signs].

For this is the downrightness and the simplicity of the issue in itself.

4.
Law

"A transcendence rigged up to slander mortal existence" was Nietzsche's verdict on Christianity. He proposed "a radical counter-doctrine," to denounce theistic moralism as a libel on life, and to restore human living to its due hilarity and liberty.[1] The esthetical, he insisted, had to replace the ethical, as the only concern of man. God himself was a reckless artist, reflecting His own tensions in a lawless creating and destroying, a great jester for ever doing and undoing himself.

Islam, had Nietzsche known it, must surely have incurred the same condemnation as Christianity. Beyond their many divergencies, the two faiths are one in their conviction of man as under ethical authority, as a citizen of a cosmic order, ruled by a Divine rectitude, by a God of justice who wills the law of the good and the true within which life belongs and to which its mortality returns.

There is, indeed, no more complete ethical theism than Islam. Its genius, we often find it said, is law rather than theology. The point is well made. But it would be truer to say that its strength lies in theology as law. It understands the world and man as set under God, constituted by creation, guided by revelation and summoned to submission. Awareness of God is, therefore, primarily awareness of obligation and accountability. Just as the law from Sinai set Jewry under the claims of the Divine Lordship within what they understood as sacred history, so the Divine law in Islam makes all life and activity the realm of God's authority and man's obedience. The knowledge Islam enjoys in the revelation has to do directly with the demands of God and only indirectly with His nature. Law, we may say, is religion and religion is law.

The *Sharī'ah*

The general term embracing both law and religion is *Sharī'ah,* or "way," or right path of action, both ritual and ethical. This is the Torah of Islam, received through the Prophet and elaborated in the first three centuries of Islam through the gathering experience of Muslims in its custody. Law is often denoted by a term earlier than *Sharī'ah,* namely *Fiqh,* or "understanding." The *fuqahā',* or "legists," were the men of discernment who drew out, for actual jurisprudence, or life-direction and due order, the implications of the Divine will. The word *Fiqh* combines the twin ideas of directive and response, of God in command and man in surrender.

Total and inclusive as it is, this *islām,* or law-abidingness, of man within the structure of Divine direction is not properly seen as passive or servile. It belongs with the dignity of man as entrusted with the dominion *(khilāfah)* of the world,

44

and as undertaking the *amānah,* or trust, of suzerainty under God. (See Surahs 2:30 and 33:72). The earth is the Lord's and not man's. But the "empire" over it is given into man's hands and presupposes capacities of intelligence and freedom, as well as of loyalty. In that responsibility to God with and for the world, lies the issue of man's being.

The intelligent nature of man's *Fiqh,* or conformity to the Divine will, does not mean that the *Sharī'ah* is derived from rationality. On the contrary, it is given by God and has no other ground. Even where its contents take their definition from sources other than the Qur'ān and tradition, they possess, nevertheless, the same revelatory and mandatory quality. The *Sharī'ah* is what God commands and what men obey. The very legalism it may engender is, arguably, a lesser evil than the reduction of its imperative force. Submission is tested, exemplified, made concrete, even in exacting rituals and matters that reason may find pointless. One can more wholly register Divine demand by discerning no other point, of utility or arguability, in what it enjoins. The spirit that complains against the letter may soon have no more context in which either to complain or to attain. That debate, of course, continues—and not only in Islam.

In this way Muslims seé in the *Sharī'ah* an all-embracing sacred law, the source of which is God's will and the motive obedience to Him. Its content is understood, classically, as governing and determining all areas of life—personal, communal, social, civil, political, and cultic. The strictly ritual and devotional provisions are the sacramental *foci* of what is throughout religious, in the sense that is God-aware, God-responsive and God-ordained. One does not rightly speak of religion *and* morality, of morality *and* law: they are identical—though the problems implicit in seeing them so are serious and lively. There is a sense in which one can only equate law and life, religion and existence by neglecting either the ideals of the one or the realities of the other. But the hope of their identity is magnificent, provided we are alert to its perpetual frustration. There lies the whole inner tension of Islamic law and ethics.

The Godward relation of men, in this exceptionless quality, was, from the earliest centuries, understood as threefold. Things to be believed are given in *Īmān,* or faith: it is the obligation of man to receive and confess them. Things to be done in rite and ordinance are given in *Dīn,* or religion: it is the duty of man to perform and do them. Things commanded as good and vetoed as evil are also given, in what Arabic calls *Al-Amr bi-l-Ma'rūf* and *Al-Nahī 'an al-Munkar:* it is the obligation of man to fulfill the one and abjure the other. In the whole *Sharī'ah* are the gathered prescriptions and regulations legislating for the whole complex range of human affairs and relationships.[2] By all these the innate calling, freedom, and stature of man, in body and soul, in family and society, in order and well-being, are to find their realization. Within the whole there are wide stretches of moral option or neutrality, where the *Sharī'ah* does not tediously enjoin, but yet hallows and conditions the choices and works of Muslim mankind.

The articles of faith, or *Īmān,* are God and His unity, the books, the prophets and messengers of God, angels as bearers of God's commands and revelation, the last day and judgment, and the Divine decree of good and evil, that is, the Divine criteria or determination, of reality and of destiny. There have been endless debates on these themes, not least the last, and a diversity of emphases and interpretation. But broadly they constitute the dogmatic structure of Islam, set the doctrinal texture of Muslim thought and give the house of Islam its character-istic temper of soul. It was the intention of our first three chapters to indicate their main significance and their historical genesis in seventh century Arabia.

The faith acceptance of the right Muslim, however, is summed up and articulated in the briefer *Shahādah,* or confession, prefaced by the singular: "*I* bear witness . . ."

To confess: "There is no god but God and Muhammad is the *Rasūl* of God" is the first of the five articles, or "pillars," of *Dīn* and joins both faith and practice. Its personal, vocal avowal is the doctrinal criterion of being Muslim, though from time to time inconsistency of conduct led purists to insist that it had to be corroborated by fidelity of life. Neglect of the rest of the *Sharī'ah* disqualified *Shahādah* also. At the crux of this issue was the worth of the "intention," or *Niyyah* with which a valid confession had to be made. Three other pillars of religion, namely *Ṣalāt, Ṣaum,* and *Ḥajj,* prayer, fast and pilgrimage, respectively, will be discussed in the next chapter. They belong under Law but may be more conveniently studied in the context of Liturgy.

Zakāt

The remaining pillar is *Zakāt,* or almsgiving—an institution which under-girds a whole philosophy of social responsibility in Islam. From a very early point, allegiance involved obligation to fellow Muslims who were poor or victimized. The help of the Medinan converts to the Meccan emigrés became an abiding theme of tradition and example. The needs of the original and growing commu-nity were for solidarity, mutuality, interdependence, and resources for propaga-tion, as well as the sealing of accessions. All these, as the phrase went, were "in the way of God." *Zakāt* was thus the cement of Islam, always joined with prayer in the double Quranic phrase: "Perform the *Ṣalāt* and bring the *Zakāt,*" and willful withholding of it a sign of rebellion. The *jizyah,* or tax on non-Muslim minorities surviving under Islam, was always carefully distinguished from *Zak-āt,* thus further enforcing its communal character. Both the paying and the disbursing signalized participation in the household of the faith.

"Lend to God a good loan" says Surah 73:20. *Zakāt* is understood as a means to repentance and atonement, as a way of practical reconciliation, and as a parable of brotherliness. It also symbolizes those voluntary acts of generosity that season common life. As a tradition says: "A camel lent out for milk is alms, good works are alms, your smile to your neighbor is alms." These deeds, some-times called *Ṣadaqāt,* to distinguish them from legal alms (though the term is not consistently held to that sense), should not, however, excuse the doer from *Zak-āt* proper. The obligatory cannot rightly be displaced by the voluntary. Nor, in the eyes of literalists, can *Zakāt* be equated with state taxation for social welfare purposes, since then the element of obligatoriness is not of the *Sharī'ah,* but of the fiscal authority of the state. For some modern thinkers, nevertheless, the ideology arguable from this pillar of religion, namely an active social conscience, may be seen as inspiring, under the different conditions of the modern world, the patterns of state action. The organization of the mosque and of the religious leadership cannot feasibly cope with the task of collecting and disbursing even a modest poor relief in the teeming, complex world of this century. It is surely not an un-Islamic doctrine that what is enjoined by religion can be organized and implemented by the political power.

At all events the intelligent enunciation of *Zakāt* today makes the case for socialist economy. The root meaning of the term is "to purify." Surah 9:103 say: "Take of their wealth an offering [*ṣadaqah*] to purify them and cleanse [*tuzakkihim*] them thereby." The doctrine is that property is validated as a private right and enjoyment, provided a portion of it is devoted to the common need, in token of the corporate awareness that should characterize all personal possession. This paid portion "purifies," that is, legitimizes, what is retained. Without this active conscience, retention and ownership would be impure and disqualified. The community has not only a stake in, but also a claim on, the individual's *amwāl* or substance. It is easy to see a direct line of argument from this central thesis of the faith to the Marxist doctrine of the labor theory of value, of the community as the source and context of all worth, and of a communal ownership of what is vital to common life. The last theme, however, must be subject to the implicit approval of ownership, once socially conscious, which is involved in the whole ordinance of *Zakāt*. The abolition of private ownership would terminate the feasibility of the pillar of *Dīn;* and that, argue the orthodox theorists, could never be the intention of God.

Clearly, there is room for wide divergence of view here about the mutual bearings of Islamic alms and ideologies of wealth and of communism. There were, likewise, through the centuries, many varieties of interpretation on the practical aspects of *Zakāt,* the proportions of income payable and their variation according to the kind of income involved. Intricate as these are, they have little bearing on the religious dimension. Agricultural *Zakāt,* wrote Al-Fīrūzābādī,

> . . . is only obligatory on cereals eaten for food and cultivated by men, such as wheat, barley, millet, sorghum, rice and the like: then it applies to vegetables such as lentils, chickpeas, vetches, beans, and peas. Fruits are not subject, except for dates and grapes, to which Al-Shāfi'ī used to add olives, turmeric, and safron . . . The taxable minimum, when the grain has been threshed and the fruit dried is five camel burdens, for sixteen hundred Baghdad *ruṭls,* but for rice . . . the minimum is ten camel burdens.[3]

We leave the threshing-floor and the weighing-shed, the tax-gatherers and the peasants, to return to them and their whole society, in another guise. The specific pillars of *Dīn* uphold the house of Muslim conduct and character as the

Sharī'ah enjoins them. The Qur'ān, as we saw in the quotation in Chapter 3 from
Surah 25, mingles general ethics with particular commands and prohibitions. Our
exposition had better seek to study first the right moral "manner" of the true
Muslim, and then the explicit legal provisions. The whole, however, needs to be
prefaced by some reference to the sources of Islamic law and ethical ideal.

The Sources of Law

Given the Qur'ān and the tradition, the notion of a need for reference to the
sources of Islamic law may seem, at first sight, perplexing. Is not the sacred
Scripture a sufficient source in itself, as amplified by the *Sunnah,* or example of
Muḥammad, already reviewed? The answer, plainly, is no. The Qur'ān is complete as a criterion, as the test of repugnancy. But it antedated many themes and
issues encountered by Islam in its expansion. It relates to a setting which, limited
and circumscribed in time and place, could not afford the precedents and directives demanded by an unlimited future. Even within its own scene, there were
matters on which it was silent. There had, then, to be a superstructure of law,
built upon it. The large growth of tradition to supplement it is evidence enough
of this necessity and of its legitimacy. As a second source of guidance, tradition,
or *Ḥadīth,* draws its authority from the general exemplariness and inspiration of
Muḥammad as distinct from his Quranic role proper. The status of the revelatory
instrument sanctions an enlargement of the law. The dead yet speaketh.

Yet together, these two still do not suffice. Sunnī Islam relies upon two
further sources. One is *Qiyās,* or analogy. By this, the legists argued from the
intention of some specific rule of Qur'ān or *Sunnah,* to cover some matter,
arguable from, though not stated in, the original. The compulsory recording of
commercial transactions to prevent fraud might be said to cover, by analogy, the
registration of marriages, where in fact a far more serious transaction of trust is
involved. Such extension might well be resisted on other grounds and the debate
over legitimate analogical extension of the *Sharī'ah* was often profuse and divi-
sive. But the principle, and that of *ra'y,* or opinion, with which it was linked, was
a useful means of law affirming.

There were, however, pressures of necessity which could in no way be
satisfied in these terms. Recourse was had, therefore, to a fourth and much ampler
source of law, namely *Ijmā',* or consensus. Founded on the conviction that the
community as such would not long, or finally, "converge on an error," *Ijmā'* in
effect entrusted the enlargement of law to the collective fidelity. Innovation—a
concept always close to heresy in Islam—would be saved from excess, from
pretension, from distortion, if it commended itself, in the long run, to the whole
household of the faith. Here seemed to be a sure principle of development which
would be secure against the vagaries of individualists and the deviations of the
sectaries. Was there not safeguard in numbers? Had the Prophet not agreed that
after the Qur'ān and his example the community would be the proper referee?

Where else in fact could faith custody turn, if not to the faith custodians, the believers incorporate? Is not this principle, in some measure, universal through all religions, at least those which do not retreat into the mystical and the exotic?

Thus matters of new, or newly interpreted, law were to be authenticated by the agreement of the common mind, always, of course, consistently with the other primary sources. Yet *Sharī'ah* so derived had no less sacred and binding a character.

But consensus does not just emerge. It needs pioneers. It requires opinion initiators, before its mind can be formed. This means the kindred institution of *Ijtihād,* or endeavor, initiative, from which potential *Ijmā'* can arise and by which it may be stimulated. *Ijtihād,* however, needed to be hedged with provisos and prerequisites. It was not open to any and every "lay" Muslim to pretend to it, but demanded expert knowledge of the Qur'ān, skills of grammar, and subtleties of legal acumen, beyond the range of the average believer. Every system begets its pundits—in the case of Islam the Shaikhs, the *fuqahā'* and the *'ulamā',* qualified to venture, with proper circumspection, the initiatives which might, in turn, merit general acceptance.

To these themes belongs the deep cleavage between Sunnis and Shī'ahs which we postpone to our study of the *Ummah* below. Meanwhile, it suffices to note that Shī'ahs disavowed *Ijmā',* relying on their Imāms to "guarantee" Islamic truth. In a different sense from Sunnis, they exalted *Ijtihād* but located it even more stringently in their "spiritual guides," understood as speaking in the name and by the light of the Hidden Imām. Their authority, exempt from the need for *Ijmā',* was the more assertive.

Among Sunnis there was no clear or final dictum as to the area or period within which consensus could be said to be assured, nor as to the precise means of ascertaining it. But the basic idea of *Ijmā'* set the elaboration of *Sharī'ah* squarely within the community, and this was both its strength and its wisdom. Four Sunnī schools of law developed between the eighth and ninth centuries and differed widely in the details of their teaching, namely the Ḥanafī, the Mālikī, the Shāfi'ī, and the Ḥanbalī. The last was the most strict and uncompromising. Every Sunnī Muslim belongs to one or other school, and they are distributed unevenly throughout the whole Islamic world.

Between the schools there were debates about the limits and safeguards of *Ijmā'* and of *ra'y,* and over the powers and credentials of the masters of *Ijtihād.* The most crucial of these controversies concerned the question whether at any time enlargement of law by *Ijmā'* could be said to be complete so that the "door" of *Ijtihād* must be said to be closed. This issue became the main ground of contention between those wanting a static, secure situation, immune from change, and those who sensed the necessity of growth and flexibility. The problem, of course, has been overtaken in modern times by the sheer pressures of irresistible change, requiring not merely an open door but levelled walls. But by the same token the bewilderments of loyalty are the more intense. Yet, even now, the concept of consensus remains both a stay and a solace. For, in the last analysis, it entrusts the continuity of *Sharī'ah* to a living trusteeship, by dint of which it may hope to ensure a living perpetuation.

There were different ways, in medieval times, of assessing the how and where, the whence and whither, of a communal mind. Three ideas, in particular, emerged by the third Muslim century, namely *Istiḥsān,* or what impressed with an intrinsic rightness as "good"; *Istiṣlāḥ,* or what seemed in the public interest as beneficial; and *Istiṣḥāb,* or what had good commendation or associations. These the *fuqahā'* sought either to enlarge or to restrain, according to their instinct for enterprise or conservation. They could be used either to instigate or to curb development, as mood or need dictated. The whole concept of consensus had only the scantiest of direct Quranic ground as far as specific reference is concerned. But it certainly coincided with a deep conviction of solidarity resulting from faith and conformity, a solidarity which could, therefore, in turn attest and discriminate what faith and conformity should entail. It stands, then, as a most characteristic institution of Islam and serves to illustrate a vital principle of religion everywhere—the interreliance of belonging and behaving. It formalizes and regulates what we may perhaps loosely call the compatibility of change.

Even before *Ijmā'* and *Ijtihād* were juridically defined and established, the physical enlargement of Islam had brought about a widening and broadening of its scope of law and practice, simply by the rapid and diversified recruitment of new peoples and cultures. This occurred, in large measure, through contribution of customary law, or *'urf,* as found within the conquered lands, to the *corpus* of the *Sharī'ah.* Conditional on compatibility with the Qur'ān and the *Sunnah,* large areas of local law and custom came, with their peoples, into the fold of Muslim *fiqh.* This generous tolerance of the familiar worlds of new Muslims may be seen, in part, as an application of the clue within *Ijmā',* though much of it happened willy-nilly and without formal auspices. In the first centuries, the fertility of tradition, as studied in Chapter 2, enabled incoming habits and values and practice to find validity and allowance under the authority of Muḥammad's actual or supposed example. This sanction for customary law through the tradition of the Prophet became less feasible with the passage of time and greater remoteness from the Ḥijāz. But the pattern of hospitality has remained and goes far to account for the ready adoption of Islam, not least in Africa. Yet, whatever the compromises thus incurred, they were effectively subdued to the basic identity of the *Sharī'ah*-people, and there was a resilience in the *Sharī'ah* itself against debasement. In the acceptance of *'urf* into *Sharī'ah,* Islam, in the main, was able to allow a gradualism which did not require entire transition in one generation. Meanwhile, the tests of a worthy Islam remained intact, in Qur'ān, *Sunnah,* and community. There were, moreover, plenty of means to their enforcement, for example, in those intriguing officers of Islamic *Sharī'ah,* the *muḥtasib,* or custodian of morals and inspector of trade, and the *muṭawwī',* "the maker-obedient."

Muslim Behavior

To take due stock of the worthy Muslim it is perhaps best to set down here the Quranic passage most resembling a single code and to review, in sequel to it, the major themes of Islamic ethical concern, both of injunction and prohibition, and the more important items of personal law. The passage is in Surah 17, from verses 22 to 39.

Do not set up another god with God, lest you find yourself in shame and desolation. Your Lord has commanded that you serve none save Him. Show kindness to parents, whether one or both of them attains old age with you. Do not be round or impatient with either of them, but speak kindly words to them. Lower to them the wing of humility tenderly and say: My Lord, have mercy on them, as they nurtured me when I was little. Your Lord knows well what is in your hearts, if you be true of soul. He is all forgiving to those who seek Him.

Give to the kinsman his due and to the needy and the wayfarer, and do not squander your substance, for squanderers are brothers to Satan. Satan is ever thankless to his Lord. And if you turn from them, anticipating the wherewithal from your Lord's mercy, then at least speak to the needy kindly.

Do not have your hand chained to your neck; yet do not be open-handed to utter excess, or you will end up with reproach and bankruptcy.

Your Lord gives with bountiful hand and with sparing hand to whom He wills. Truly He knows and observes His servants.

Do not kill your children for fear of poverty. We will provide both for you and for them. To kill them is a most grievous sin.

Come not near to adultery, which is foul and an evil way. Do not kill any man —a deed God forbids, except for rightful cause. If a man is slain unjustly, We have appointed to next of kin the right to satisfaction. But let him not carry his vengeance beyond the due, for there is counter retaliation.

Handle the property of the orphan in all integrity, until he comes of age. Keep your bond, for you are accountable.

Give full measure when you measure, and weigh with just scales. That is better and fairer in the end.

Do not pursue things you have no knowledge of. Hearing, sight and heart—all these faculties of a man will be held responsible.

Do not strut proudly on the earth. You cannot cleave the earth or match the mountains in stature. All such ways are evil with your Lord.

All this is given you by revelation of the wisdom of your Lord, and set not up any other god beside God.

There is, here, a close resemblance to the Decalogue (without the Sabbath provision): anti-idolatry, care and honor of parents, prohibition of infanticide, and of murder outside legitimate vengeance, prohibition of adultery, integrity with property and trade and with rights of orphans. Interspersed with the commands, positive and negative, are directives about attitudes and character, particularly kindliness, integrity and humility.

The traditional ethics of Islam divide conduct, inward and outward, into five categories—things enjoined, things commended, things deplored, things prohibited, and a central area where actions fall into none of the other four categories and may thus be said to be "neutral," though they are not outside the Divine watchfulness or the human responsibility and may readily merge or tend into one of the other categories. There is the severest condemnation for the omission of the obligatory or the committing of the forbidden, and relative censure for the neglect of the desirable or indulgence in the deplored.

The Muslim scheme is readily capable of universality, in that it does not relate contractually to the acquisition of any particular territory, nor is it vested in a private account of history. Its provisions, nevertheless, reflect the time and the economy of its origins. Retaliation is proper, but not beyond due limits. Like the Biblical law of requital, it is concerned with *one* man for a man, not ten. There is throughout a deep, practical note of "what is better in the end," and an underlying sense of common finitude and frailty, of the perennial rightness of "tenderness," and an urgent sense of the final Divine accounting.

The Qur'ān, in several other passages, echoes and enforces these injunctions and qualities, and tradition multiplies their exemplification in the Prophet and the companions. Humanity under Islam is gathered with these prototypes into a sort of corporate responsibility over good and evil. The right and the wrong behavior is not a take-it-or-leave-it individualism. The body communal is there to care for right conduct among all. The very term *Ma'rūf,* noted above, meaning "the good," has the primary sense of "the known," the acknowledged, while evil is *al-munkar,* the (corporately) disowned. Good and evil have their sole definition in the Divine authority, but the care for their recognition lies with the house of Islam. The spiritual resources of this care lie in the conscience and moral health of the whole body of Muslim humanity and in their sense of encounter awaiting in the world to come. Its verdict in debatable issues could take shape in the *fatwas,* or legal opinions, given by the *muftis* within the authority of *Ijmā'* and in exegesis, for the guidance of the faithful.

The character of Islamic law is most readily illustrated in the realm of personal status and matters of marriage, divorce, and inheritance. It was here that the Qur'ān itself was most specific, whereas in other areas of legislation, such as matters of administration and civil jurisprudence it was relatively silent in detail.

Marriage in Islam is a simple contractual relationship or agreement, verbally exchanged between the two parties in the presence of witnesses. It has no sacramental status or quality of "one flesh" in the Christian sense of the "estate" of matrimony. The Muslim bride says simply: "I marry you to myself," and the bridegroom says: "I accept your marriage to me." Sexual relationships outside marriage, except in the case of slavery, are prohibited. The rights of the bride require that due status, contract and provision, be assured, before sexuality can legitimately be taken.

It is important to emphasize this essential dignity of the married state. For while Islam does not give to marriage a status incapable of concurrent duplication, the Qur'ān nevertheless comes very close in certain passages, to a view of the wedded state that sets it among the "signs of God," that ought properly to lead into reverent gratitude and hallowedness. The most notable passage is Surah

30:21: "And of His signs is that He created for you, of yourselves, wives, that you might live in joy with them, and He ordained between you love and mercy."

The benediction of the gift of sex in marriage, however, does not necessarily argue monogamy. Provided each wife has her just rights, the *Sharī'ah* allows up to four wives. The context of this permission needs to be carefully noted in Surah 4:3. For, though it has been taken by the traditional practice for centuries as positive allowance of plurality within the limit of four, the verse makes this hinge on a proviso which, in the view of many today, is unattainable and amounts, therefore, to a virtual prohibition.

In the first place, the whole matter is within the theme of provision for orphans and seems to assume the widowhood ensuing from early warfare. The authority to marry "two, three, or four," if it seems good, is conditioned by the proviso: "If you fear you will not deal equally, then marry only one, or the female slaves." That operative phrase may mean feasible equalities—economic support and rotation of sexual intercourse (a matter that traditions strongly enjoin so that no wife is left forlorn), or it may arguably mean a quite impracticable equality of emotional affection and delight. If the latter interpretation is followed (which a few other passages about the impossibility of "equality" seem to hint), then there is, in fact, no provision at all for plurality. The condition being unattainable, the permission lapses.

From a sacramental perspective about marriage we are still left with the question whether a "virtual" prohibition is appropriate. Will not the notion of duplicate marriage *ipso facto* constitute an unwarrantable injustice to an existing wife, since the self cannot be wholly given save wholly? But Islamic *Sharī'ah* holds that there is no inherent wrong in plurality, and it may be noted that the "fear" referred to in Surah 4:3 can only be proven after the plural marriages exist. The man who feels a confidence can, within this authority, go ahead and his failure to be equal, if it occurs, will be subsequent to the fact.

In current practice this deterring exegesis is more and more widely relied on to sustain single marriage, and in most Muslim societies today even dual, not to speak of threefold or fourfold, marriages are increasingly disallowed. By the same token the abiding Quranic sense of the contractual dignity of sex is reinforced and comes close to the logic that monogamy is its most valid expression. Economic and social factors tend in the same direction. Nevertheless, despite the specific changes in the *Sharī'ah* law of many countries, there are voices sustaining the old exegesis and the former pluralism as more appropriate to the physiological nature of men, more compassionate towards women and more loyal to our liberties under God. Throughout these assessments, however, it is well to keep always in view the *Sharī'ah*'s reprobation of adultery and extramarital intercourse, since this belongs powerfully with its positive and vigilant concept of marriage. There is in traditional Muslim mores an alert jealousy about the sanctity of women's honor and of the duties that belong with men's rights in women.

It is in this context that the provisions about divorce should be set. Traditionally, divorce is possible at the man's will simply by his declaration of it. Inasmuch as it may be followed by reconciliation, up to a third repetition, it has tended to be a safety valve for hasty enmities. Only after a third divorce does a wife cease to be available for remarriage to her husband, though even then she may again become so after an interim marriage to another party. When divorce occurs, according to the *Sharīʿah,* the wife must be freely let go, after the stipulated period to avoid confusion about paternity, and not distrained or exploited. There were several particulars in which Islam brought improvement into the lot of Arab women, and in Khadījah, Muḥammad's first wife, Fāṭimah his daughter and wife of ʿAlī, and other women, it has ensured a strong female element in its heritage of example. There are large grounds for seeing Islam as constituting, in sundry particulars, "a man's world." But its understanding of "the stronger sex" (Surah 4:34) is tempered by the deep sense of mutuality and the tribute of contractuality, tragically as the contract of marriage was desecrated in the fashion of the ḥarīm and the patterns of *The Arabian Nights.*

The Prophet's own marriages, eleven in all, were exceptional in their dynastic concern, in the heirlessness that dogged him, and in the diplomatic and political necessities of his recovery of Mecca. The pattern of his single marriage to Khadījah while she lived is cited as no less relevant than the later situation, where, in fact, almost all Muḥammad's added wives were widows, or divorced.

In matters of inheritance, women normally receive one half of the male share for equivalent relationship, in blood kinship or marital connection. This differential is sometimes justified on the grounds that a Muslim woman is always likely to be within some male relative's provision, whether father, husband, brother, or uncle.

In the brevity of our discussion of personal status there has been a merging of past and present views. The question is, therefore, implicit about the actual status of the *Sharīʿah* when revision occurs. The specific situation in personal status law in the several Muslim states is too complex and diverse for the barest exposition here. In many, plural marriage is precluded and divorced sharply curtailed. In some, notably Egypt and Tunisia, the *Sharʿī* Courts that formerly administered the religious law have been abolished. In Turkey since the nineteen-twenties there has been an avowedly secular pattern of social legislation based on western models and deliberately repudiating both the source and sanction of the old order. But though abandoned or eroded, the *Sharīʿah* concept may still be retrieved in reinterpretation. There is the argument that in its essential dynamism Islam is conserved, not depleted, by such changes. They may be claimed as within the evolving intention of the sacred and in some cases, as in that of single marriage, the gist can be credibly read from, or into, the revealed Scripture. It is possible to digest a wide measure of modern reform, even to the apparent disqualification of centuries of supposedly authentic usage, and still derive it, through a broad appeal to *Ijmāʿ,* from the orthodox heritage.

Such advocacy, however, by the same token, merits and incurs the strictures and rebuttals that an anxious conservatism inspires. Though seldom outwardly successful, these voices have to be respected. For they represent a form of fidelity for which modernity is a menace. The very fact that they hold for an Islam against the odds is a measure of their integrity in it. But the more clearly they see what they *should* be, the more remote they are from being it effectively. There is an easier task for those who align their Islam with the world, than for those who would conform their world to Islam.

Yet, in either case, and through all the varieties between, it is feasible to claim that the end and essence is the Divine authority over loyal people. What then of that final question, returning whence we started? God-aware, God-responsive, God-ordained—is this a viable pattern of law and how is it sustained in the postures of worship? The latter is a theme which takes us into Chapter 5. The former will always be involved in the alternative of human autonomy. But is it really an alternative except as idolatrous? Islam believes men receive the substance of such autonomy only in turning back from its pretension. It sees the values and meanings we experience within ourselves as truly grounded in a Lordship at once absolute and compassionate.

It is the idols that are the conspiracy of transcendence against man. They are disarmed and disowned, not by a secular competition with them, but by a true submission. The "counterdoctrine" which exposes their tyranny and breaks their power is, simply, "God is greater." Islam sees law under God as the true education of man. If religion may be said to be "reading the text of the universe in the original," Islam finds it written in the imperative. And so its worship is erect and prostrate, and then again erect.

5.
Liturgy and the Sufi Path

All religious ritual, according to Immanuel Kant, is "pious playing"—*Frommes Spielwerk* he called it, adding that the only valid way to worship God was by moral states of mind. To imagine one could do so by words and ceremony is an idle fancy, a piece of superstitious play-acting.

The great philosopher did not know Muslims at prayer, since there were no mosques in Konigsberg, where his days were spent. Had he known them even his rational disapproval might have wavered, or paused to reconsider. For nowhere is there a simpler worship or a more direct ritual. Nowhere is there a religious devotion less calculated than that of Islam to deceive itself about its own significance.

Certainly there is nothing "playful" about the piety of the mosque. "God," says the Qur'ān, "did not create the world in jest." (Surahs 21:16 and 44:38). On that conviction the prayers of Islam rest. There could hardly be a more formal simplicity. There is no priesthood, no bewildering incantation, no solemn music, no curtained mysteries, no garments for sacred wear contrasted with those of the street and of the marketplace. All proceeds within a congregational unison in which the *imām,* or leader, does no more than occupy the space before the niche and set the time for the sequence of movements in which all participate. The essential sacrament, for such it is, is within each person's own privacy, requiring as it does the use of his own limbs and lips. Since all move in rhythm of posture and with identical words, the experience incorporates each individual into a communal whole. No one is spectator of "official" acts. No one is obliged to delegate his own intention to another's action, or liable to annul his physical presence, through inaction, into an absence of mind. The mechanical or the repetitive, which are anyhow unavoidable in all recurrent worship, are such as still to engage each with all and all with each, without distinction of value, function or act, while reducing none to passivity.

Before taking this further we had better first justify the word "Liturgy" in the title of this chapter. It might, at first glance, seem ill-chosen. It is not a normal usage in this context and could stand for features of ritual quite uncongenial to Islam. The root idea, however, is deeply apposite. "Liturgy" in origin means acts of public spirit on the part of private people, gifts in prizes for athletic games, or underwriting the music and arts of the community: the *leitourgia* of the Greeks. It passed thence into Christian currency to describe the acts of personal surrender in the setting of the celebration of the passion of Christ in holy communion or participation, and thence into religious usage as denoting those exchanges of discipleship with Lordship that sacraments embody, always in a social context.

Islam, as we know, has no paradigmatic events for celebration, no Passover because no Exodus, no Lord's Supper because no Cross. Qur'ān-recitation is the nearest equivalent to being "baptized into Moses," or sharing "in the night in which Jesus was betrayed." For it puts into faithful mouths the very utterance that speaks from Heaven. This is clearly a personal activity which needs no formal figuration, no ordered ceremonial, but only a private learning and reciting. But there is the same dutifulness, the same corporate context, the same social implication, and these make "liturgy" the right term to borrow. There are the same threefold elements of Godward duty, personal obligation, and collective response. The Arabic word *Dīn*—things *done* in Islam as distinct from *Īmān,* or things *believed,* and usually translated "religion" or "religious acts"—is very near to this broad nature of liturgy.

For prayer, *Ṣalāt,* is definitely a deed. "Perform—establish—the prayer" is the formula. So it is with all the five pillars of *Dīn* on which *Dār al-Islām* is built, namely Witness, Prayer, Alms, Fasting, and Pilgrimage. Their form and content must be studied as the intensive religious dimension, the duties of Islamic identity *per se.* "Intensive" is an important word, inasmuch as being Muslim is properly to be diffused through all the areas of life and not located in specifically ritual acts. The "extensive" character of Islam, its insistent refusal to isolate religion from the rest of existence, must control the interpretation of the things that are, nonetheless, specifically "religious." The implied paradox here is, of course, inescapable. One cannot enjoin, or even identify, what is only diffused: its very vagueness would be its undoing. Islam is in no mind to exhort to godfearingness and give the exhortation no ritual focus or particular duties. Muslims must stand, and bow, and prostrate, observe a daily fast between the seasons of one moon, pay dues to God, and go on pilgrimage. But these necessary expressions of loyalty are to be taken as the tokens of an inclusive and active sense of God which is more than they.

Worship

So, then, to the washing, known as *wuḍū',* which prefaces the prayer. Is this conceivably a kind of self-baptism? From one angle, certainly, no. For it is self-administered, as baptism can never be. Moreover, it is recurrent and has no twice-born, or transcendent, implication. In a different sense, however, yes. For it is the only formal cleansing in Islam and makes ready the way to the Lord. Mosques and water belong together, where water can be had. Prayer is readiest beside a spring, or well, or pool, and requires for its preparation the simplest of bodily routines. The ritual purity that washing serves is within a private competence. The self does what the self needs and is aware of itself in the doing, and the action moves with the movement of life. There is broadly in Islam no inclusive crisis about sin, only a habitual transaction about sins. The washing of the body serves a sort of hygiene of the self. We approach God through a symbol of purification that demands neither subtlety nor passion. It neither beats its breast nor rends its garments. It prosaically washes hands and arms and face and ankles, and proceeds into the act of *Ṣalāt.*

The daily rites of prayer (*Ṣalāt*) are five in number and consist of between two and five sequences of movement and liturgical recitation. The varying number depends upon the time of day, but each sequence contains the same pattern beginning and ending in the erect posture and including bowing and prostrating. The final sequence of each time of prayer concludes with a salutation to right and left upon all the people of Islam. It is a liturgy of adoration and submission, affirming the unity, sovereignty, and greatness of God.

The surest way into its nature is through the *Fātiḥah,* which it embodies. This is the opening chapter of the Qur'ān, which runs:

> In the Name of God, the merciful Lord of mercy.
> Praise be to God, the Lord of all being,
> The merciful Lord of mercy,
> Master of the Day of Judgement.
> Thee alone we serve and to Thee alone we come for aid.
> Guide us in the straight path,
> The path of those whom Thou hast blessed,
> Not of those against whom there is displeasure,
> Nor of those who go astray.

These words are the heart of Muslim devotion, the only terms in which *Ṣalāt* is ever petitionary. "Guide us in the straight path," the way of the *Sunnah* in the *Ummah,* the doing of the works of *Dīn* and the keeping of the truths of *Īmān,* in contrast with the ways of the devious and willful under the Divine displeasure. This note of distinctiveness in Islam is inseparable from its nature. It is the final faith and its people the community of a "universal election" of favor, by dint of the saving sign of right guidance. No mention of "the fathers" here: the operative pronoun *al-ladhīna,* "those . . . ," incorporates the dead, the living, and the unborn, yet not by any ethnic test, nor in some certainty of blood relationship, but only in the mercy of God, whose counsels are its own and upon which neither race nor esteem may presume. It is the company of "the doers of the will" of God, but it is not within the will of the doers to ensure a claim. Hence the force of the petition: "guide us *in* the straight path." The fact of the Qur'ān already brings us *to* the path. The *Fātiḥah* is a prayer for conformity and acceptability within it. All this stands on the emphatic protestation: "Thee it is we worship; Thee it is we seek unto for aid." Prayer is only true where it explicitly disowns all other recourse, or resource. For our singular dependence is the effective meaning of the unity of God. No *Shirk* here: no "practice" of any other presence, no deviation to an idol for comfort or for succor. To harbor a superstitious soul is not truly to pray. The sanctuary is where the theist may be least consistent. Hence the insistent cry: "*Thee* it is we worship."

The plural there is instinctive. While the confession: "I bear witness that there is no god but God; Muḥammad is the apostle of God," is in the singular, the *Fātiḥah* throughout has plural human pronouns. Yet the *Ṣalāt* need not be congregational save at noon on Friday. Where mosques are accessible they are to be preferred, and especially so in Ramaḍān. But a mosque in the last resort is not a building: it is a place of prostration and any patch of ground in ritual purity suffices where a human frame may stretch itself—a fact about Islam which accounts in large measure for the naturalness of its occasions and the contagion in its expansion. A faith that does not need to house its worshippers has no walls to hide its creed.

The mosque sermon is mainly and by tradition an exercise in exhortation, rather than an exposition of belief. Set between the call to prayer and the full *Ṣalāt,* it is more an expression of the solidarity, than the justification, of faith, and has often been an instrument of social and political direction. The *minbar,* or pulpit, from which it is delivered, developed from the platform, or raised dais, where the Prophet gave his decisions and directives. Some issues around the contemporary preacher will be reached in Chapter 7. It is when the sermon ends that the mosque comes fully alive in the corporateness of the prayer.

Its architecture reinforces the same lessons as the postures of the body. It is bare of distracting intrusions of artistry and exists primarily neither as an auditorium for listeners, nor as a setting for liturgy as drama. It is essentially an essay in religious space: by definition it is a place for prostration. Hence the carpets and the unencumbered expanses of area, whether domed or pillared. The niche, or *miḥrāb,* is not a sanctuary. It is merely a mark of direction, a sign of the radius of the circle of which Mecca is the center. Calligraphy, or script, and color, are the only decoration. Only that sacred text has power to solemnize the context and is immune from the menace of distraction and the distortion of unity that beset representational art. The mosque, it might be said, is the architectural service and counterpart of a devotion consistent with Islam.

But it is not finally to these things that the ultimate achievement of the liturgy is owed. It lies in the corporate piety of the generations and the sharp sacrament of the body in which it takes shape. The individual is one with the centuries in that he renews with his own immediacy of day and hour the routine of all the Prophet's people from that one beginning. This is the historical unity of a single form of words in a single liturgical language. He does so in geographical unity with the whole territory of Islam, by the conscious symbol of the *Qiblah,* the Meccan focus of the prayer, which gathers him in a great circuit, concentrically dispersed, signified as one by the sign of the *miḥrāb* inward and the token of the salutation around to right and left. It is also a local unity, whether in the ranks of the Friday concourse, or in the identity of the pattern among scattered groups of single persons in the presence-to-each-other which the sense of the mosque provides. It is, finally, a private unity of the individual, in the actions of the physical, and the intentions of the mental, part of him. These together are the answer if we ask to know the strength of Muslim piety. To bring the brow to the ground is the better to walk the earth. In prostration the Muslim learns to be erect.

The essence of *Ṣalāt*, then, is the sense of God, the reiterated practice of a religious awareness. This "remembrance" of God is known in Islam as *Dhikr*— a term which in mysticism becomes technical but which properly is inclusive of Islam as a whole. It is closely linked with ritual prayer. Thus Surah 7:206: "Remember your Lord in your soul with humility and reverence and without ostentation. Do so at morn and at eventide, and do not be negligent." It is in fact only by Quranic implication that prayer is fivefold daily. Morning and evening and a "midmost prayer" are mentioned. The recollection of God is the crucial thing, the saying of the invocation: "In the Name of God, the merciful Lord of mercy," known as the *Bismillāh*. Surah 33:42 enjoins: "O ye who have believed, mention your Lord much and praise him early and late." This act of *dhikr* is responsive to the will and mercy of God in the revelation. The Qur'ān is in several places described by the same term. It is God's self-mention, His "reminder" to men that they may be mindful of His ways, and claims. *Ṣalāt* practices this recollection with a will to the sort of awareness of God the Qur'ān teaches and evokes. "Remember Me," reads Surah 2:153, "and I will remember you: be thankful toward Me and do not belie Me."

There is a remarkable emphasis here and one that is easily missed by students of the Qur'ān, namely the antithesis between gratitude and "atheism," between *shukr* and *kufr*. The latter is a very familiar term having to do with the denial of God. But it is not only, or even mainly, contrasted with belief. Instead, here and elsewhere, it is opposed to thankfulness. The clue is that the essential atheism is not to deny God—that may be despair or honest doubt—but to ignore Him as if He were dead or gone. Or, conversely, the core of religion is not proposition but recognition. The meaning of faith in God is, in the end, not a thesis to defend but a gratitude to confess, a profound thankfulness for existence which knows that its proper dimensions are all-compelling. When the Qur'ān ponders human attitudes to God it remarks with an eloquent simplicity: "Most of them never give thanks." *Dhikr*, the gist of *Ṣalāt*, disowns and reverses this "gracelessness of man."

As such, it spells a quality of security and peace. "The Name of the Lord is a strong tower" in the sense that the invocation of God banishes false reliances, annuls the purview of the gods of superstition, asserts an emotional dependence on God alone which liberates from other fears and cares. It hallows times and places and sets them under the single, and sufficient, rule of God against all other powers.

The theological problem of the Names of God we have already considered in Chapter 1. The religious feasibility there sustained is what *Ṣalāt* and the *Bismillāh* presuppose. It is still more widely applied in various extended forms of nonritual prayer, or *du 'ā'*. But in either context, it is important to understand why so much of Muslim devotion—to the puzzlement of some Christian observers—seems to ask for so little. This forbearing to make petition can, by other criteria than the Islamic, be mistaken for lack of confidence, formalism, or even insincerity. What avails it, we may query, to say: *Yā Allāh,* or *Yā Rabb,* "O God! O Lord!" and *Yā Laṭīf,* "O kindly One," and then fail to make petition? The Islamic answer is that invocation *is* petition—all the petition that is needful. One is simply asking God to be Himself. If one calls upon God as "provider" or "compassionate," one does not need to specify what His being such will mean or require, in detail, responsively to my so calling on Him. His wisdom being infinite, no discretion of mine can elaborate the cry itself. For this seeks quite adequately, in the Name alone, the answer of what God is. So "remember God" says the *Qur'ān,* steadily, habitually, modestly, insistently, and reverently. For "in the mention of God the hearts (of men) come to tranquillity" (Surah 13:28). "God suffices as guardian" is the sentiment of many passages. The word there yields the idea of *tawakkul,* or confident trust, an inner reliance of heart that has come to rest in the entire dependability of the One within all the Names.

That characteristic temper of *Ṣalāt* and other prayer, as a quality of those who "remember God," is told in another way if we note that many of the Names by which He is recollected have essentially to do with the crises, the cycles, of mortal existence. They are, in that sense, existential rather than metaphysical symbols. God brings to life and brings to death, nurtures and "mortalizes," provides and sustains, gives and takes, opens and closes, grants and withholds, begins and ends. Responsively to this, there are frequent Muslim prayers, often of the terse and ejaculatory kind, for the major events of life, for childbirth and circumcision, for marriage, sickness and death, for journeys, arrivals and farewells, and also for the more habitual and prosaic occasions—rising and sleeping, eating and cohabiting. Some have a devout formula for the functions of the body and the blessings of a good digestion. Setting out to travel one may say:

> O God, we ask of Thee during this our journey, righteousness and faithfulness to duty and the doing of deeds to Thee well pleasing. Thou art the companion of the road and the guardian of the family.

Or when riding and driving, in terms which might well fit any "technologizing" of daily life:

> "Glory be to Him Who made this subservient to us ... surely to our Lord is our returning."[1]

The preoccupation with death and the beyond figures impressively in the devotion of Muslims. This mirrors, no doubt, the sharp and insistent concern of the Qur'ān with the theme of personal judgment and Heaven and Hell. It also reflects the indeterminate nature of destiny and of mercy. "Let me die a Muslim" captures this temper of knowing what is needful but not presuming to have it, and does so with a haunting kind of directness and simplicity.

In the same context one may well note the recurrent cry for refuge that belongs with all Muslim religion. This *Ta'wīdh,* or "refuge seeking" as it is known, is best pondered in the two closing chapters of the Qur'ān. It is refuge, always, *in* God, by virtue of one or other of His attributes, and it is refuge *from* evils of every kind, inward and outward, temporal and eternal, human and demonic.

Dhikr, like the meaning of *Ṣalāt* and all other devotion in Islam, is not complete without reference to one vital term, namely "intention." The daily prayers, together with all the pillars of religion, are properly prefaced by the phrase, on the lips of the individual: "I have intended the prayer of the dawn," or: "I have intended (this day) the fast of Ramaḍān." Without this confessed intention the form, though otherwise perfect and complete, would not be valid. Merely to rehearse the words of the *Shahādah* without intending to confess them would not amount to a ritual confession. To travel to Mecca in the right month is, of itself, no pilgrimage. This doctrine of the *Niyyah,* this self-alertedness we might almost call it, serves to obviate what is negligent or perfunctory, even if, in the frailties of human nature, one sometimes has to take care to intend the intention. Heedlessness, anywhere, has a way of overtaking even its own preventives.

The Ramaḍān fast and the *Ḥajj* to Mecca complete the elements of *Dīn.* They, equally with *Ṣalāt,* are institutions of man's responsive awareness of God. As enjoined, their performance fulfills the obligation God has set for men. That alone makes them an obedient cognizance of Him. Fasting incorporates—in an almost literal sense of the word—the same principle as the bodily movements in *Ṣalāt,* namely the physical sacrament.

Fasting

Ramaḍān means complete abstinence from dawn to sunset. To transfer food taking and drinking from the day to the night hours, it may be argued, has no logic to uphold it, but is quite arbitrary and highly inconvenient, though less so perhaps, in the Hijāz of the seventh century, than now. But this is to be merely rational. The *imsāk,* as the term goes, the "withholding" of the body from its natural satisfactions from dawn till dusk reminds it, compellingly, of a Divine claim and imposes a pattern of discipline that educates and habituates it for other tasks and realms. The communal atmosphere that Ramaḍān provides powerfully reinforces the collective sense of Muslims, sets them a sort of sacramental sign of oneness, and affords, as experience confirms, an effectual way of becoming Muslim simply by making occasion for participant adherence. There are many whose Islam begins in the month of Ramaḍān, finds its genesis in a day abstinence and a night meal, and is thereby recruited into Muslim standing, however untaught it may remain. This is the real logic of the fast.

That distinguishing mark was certainly the initial character of the fast at its institution. That Quranic directive came in the following terms shortly after the emigration from Mecca:

O believers, prescribed for you is the Fast, for days numbered . . . the month of Ramaḍān wherein the Qur'ān was sent down for a guidance to the people. . . . Eat and drink until the white streaks show clearly to you from the black streaks in the dawn, then continue the Fast until the night . . . while you keep to the mosques (Surah 2:183–187).

It is often seen by historians as the most notable of several developments within the Islamic community, marking a conscious independence of other religions' norms. Ramaḍān differed from both Jewish and Christian fasting, in its twenty-eight day period and its daylight incidence, and in its disconnection from other elements such as redemption or atonement. The Muslim fast is understood, classically, as an absolute prohibition of all bodily sustenance by whatever means and an abstinence from sexual activity. It is a time of intensified devotion and mutual forgiveness. The hardships it imposes, particularly when the cycle of the lunar calendar brings it round into the heat of summer, are to be taken in the stride of loyalty.

That sheer physical strenuousness, however, is less problematic than the issues raised by the letter of the fast in the context of modern industrial and mechanized society. Just as the din of traffic and the rush of cities tend to drown the call to prayer and the preoccupations of work, of shift systems, and the rest, disrupt the fivefold prayers, so the demands of transport, trade, and technology impede the fasting capabilities of many sections of the modern community. Whereas loud-speakers and electronic devices on the minarets can help surmount the competition of the streets, there is no external solution to the dilemma of Ramaḍān-keeping where efficiency competes with it. There have been moves, notably in Tunisia under President Bourguiba, to reinterpret the fast as an inner discipline to be observed, not by a literal loyalty, but by a creative acceptance of its meaning. Ramaḍān is then a confession of the duty of the flesh to serve, and never to engross, the spirit. Islam, says this view, cannot be held to a literalism, feasible only for an economy that has gone into the limbo of the past and thus inappropriate to a dynamic and enduring faith. Even in Surah 2, exigencies of sickness or travel allow a making good of the fast at another time. May not sterner exigencies admit its fulfillment in another idiom?

Others, by contrast, though taking the point of the dilemma, protest that the fast is in fact more viable, even today, than these radical ideas argue. But, more important, they see every spiritual interpretation as needing the anchor of the ordinance, the sacrament of the literal demand. A fast of the mind is no substitute for the reality of the foodless days, the regimen of their full sequence, the hard, experienced fact in its full rigor. Without these, people never know the release, the spontaneous joy, of the nightly comradeship, the sense of achievement and belonging, and the benign satisfaction of the *ʿId al-Fitr,* or "feast of the breaking," with which the fast ends.

Statistics are elusive and impressions precarious. But there is no reason to doubt that in the wide stretches of *Dār al-Islām,* and through all its diverse peoples, the observance of Ramaḍān is deeply felt. Since childhood is exempt, the first keeping of it often marks a memorable sort of initiation into Islam for boys and girls on the threshold of their teens, or earlier. It has an impact all can understand and, though listlessness may be part of the price as the long day wears on, the solidarity and the exactingness that arise from Ramaḍān at least ensure that religion is not negligible. In sensitive quarters, whether radical or conservative, the Islamic mind is aware of the snares of formalism, and meritoriousness, which accompany all religious obligations, and the most rigorous of them most of all.

Pilgrimage

The final pillar of religion, the *Ḥajj*, gives a yearly fulfillment, in travel, to the symbol of the *Qiblah* in *Ṣalāt*. From the local mosque the lines radiate inwards to their focal point in Mecca: in the pilgrimage the faithful make their way down them to the central shrine. The *miḥrāb* is no pointer on an untravelled road. By this annual "congregation" Islam is bound together in a visible sacrament of unity, geographically realized from the ends of the earth. In history the pilgrimage has profoundly served the solidarity of Islam and helped to a strong cosmopolitanism in architecture, tradition, and society, through the contacts it afforded. Each recurring year it mediates through the body of the faithful a vicarious experience of the symbol of Mecca, in that pilgrims share with their neighbors the thrill and emotion of their venture both in retrospect and prospect. In the actuality of the ceremonies themselves in and about Mecca there resides a powerful realization of the incorporate community of Islam, in time and place.

The Quranic directive is in Surah 2:196–97, which says, simply, "Fulfill the pilgrimage and the visitation unto God." The phrase: "But if you are prevented . . ." has occasioned long, exegetical discussion as to legitimate inability. But there is no doubt that a resolute will to pilgrimage is the Muslim's bounden duty. "He who can find a way thither"—to quote 3:97—must do so. To find a corporate and perpetual way there had been the crucial theme of all Muḥammad's policy after the *Hijrah*. That he did so was his most signal victory and the *Ḥajj* is simply its perpetuation into the texture of Islamic emotion in annual renewal. The continuity within Islam of Mecca's role as a city sanctuary terminated all ambiguity about the effect of his mission against idols on the status of their central shrines. It also cleansed and rehabilitated the familiarly sacred territory itself, islamized, as it were, the very symbol of the struggle, making the triumph complete. The individual pilgrim, surmounting his own circumstantial obstacles, is treading the same road.

He is also presenting himself before God in the spirit of Abraham, who, with Ishmael, is believed to have been the founder and builder of Mecca. By this criterion as Muḥammad saw it, the polytheists of the city were usurpers. The cleansing of the *Ka'bah*—the central sanctuary in the great house of pilgrimage at Mecca—had been its repossession, by Muḥammad's arms, in the name of truth.

The Muslim's pilgrimage opens with the *Niyyah,* or "intention," as he draws near to the city, which he greets with the cry: *Labbaika:* "Here am I, Lord, here am I." By these words, the servant presents himself before God at the rendezvous of revelation and of community. There follows the *Tawāf,* or rite of circumambulation around the *Ka'bah* which stands, cube-shaped, in the center of the mosque court. Pilgrims crowd to stretch arms and breast against the "black stone" and kiss it. Set in the *Ka'bah* wall, the stone is an object of very ancient veneration. The *Tawāf* is only undertaken in the state of *Ihrām,* or "solemn hallowing," as the ritual condition of the entire pilgrimage. Its symbol is the pilgrim garb and it sets apart for the special purpose of the rites both the period and the person, requiring abstinence from sexuality and from trade. The circuits of the *Ka'bah* are followed by *sa'y,* or running seven times, to and fro, through one of the principal thoroughfares of Mecca towards Marwa, a distance in all of almost two miles, recalling the desperate search of Hagar for water for her son, Ishmael.

The climax comes between the eighth and the tenth day of pilgrimage, with the journey, through Mina, five miles eastward of Mecca, to the plain of 'Arafāt, nine miles beyond it. After a night en route the whole pilgrim concourse "stands" from noon to near sunset at 'Arafāt, recalling, with the aid of sermons, or *khutbahs,* the *wuqūf,* or "standing" of Abraham, the great iconoclast, staunch against idolatry. Then, at sunset, the passage to Muzdalīfah, halfway towards Mecca, for the night, and on the next day the "stoning" at Mina, which recalls Abraham's rejection of the evil Satan. The pilgrims cast seven stones at a low pillar in the main square of Mina, in repudiation of the archrejector of the Divine will.[2]

The pilgrimage proper ends with the sacrifice at Mina of animals in ritual slaughter. These ceremonies, known as the *'Id al-Adhā,* or *Al-'Id al-Kabīr,* or *Bairām,* have their counterpart in every devout Muslim household. The simultaneous, universal character of the rite with which pilgrimage is complete makes for a powerful, vicarious sense of its significance. The consecrated animal, provided either by each pilgrim for himself, or in groups, is slaughtered with its head towards Mecca. Part of the flesh is eaten by the worshippers, part distributed and part left at the place of slaughter. This climax of the *manāsik,* or pilgrim obligations, is followed by a shaving of the head and a partial desacrilization. The state of *Ihrām* finally ends after the last circuit of the *Ka'bah.*

There is a lesser pilgrimage or *'Umrah,* distinct from the *Hajj* proper, which may be performed at any time and which does not include the journey to 'Arafāt. Throughout the ceremonies there are ejaculatory prayers as in *Salāt,* and four official *khutbahs,* or sermons, are delivered. Pilgrims may also include Medina in their travels and do honor to the Prophet's grave. But these devotions are outside the pilgrimage itself as also are the various salutations at the tombs in the Meccan vicinity. Home-bound pilgrims traditionally take with them water from the well of Zamzam, the holy spring in Mecca where Hagar saved her life and Ishmael's in their distress.

They also take the memory of a deep religious transaction, an encounter with history and with the world-community of which they are part. Modern conditions have gone far to alleviate the old risks and rigors of the *Ḥajj.* The trials and fears of earlier generations of Mecca-seekers have passed into history. But there remains, unique to Islam and only for the Muslim, the pull of its single magnetism, reaching to the corners of the earth. It is the terrestrial sign of the *Ummah,* or community, which is the theme of Chapter 6.

The Islam of the Mystics

Our review of the liturgy of Islam in prayer, fasting, and pilgrimage, with the earlier exposition, under Law, of witness and alms, is now complete in respect of the orthodox terms of *Dīn.* But its significance requires to be set also within the concepts of Islamic mysticism. Liturgy is certainly the right place for a treatment of this most creative, if also—from an orthodox perspective—wayward, manifestation of Muslim religious life. Aspects of Sufism, as Islamic mysticism is termed, belong squarely with social history and the *Ummah.* Indeed its influence permeates everything Islamic—philosophy, commentary, economic life and popular institutions. But it is in devotion that it most deeply lives. It gave its own special meaning to the idea of *dhikr,* or recollection, which we saw to be central to *Ṣalāt,* bringing the practice of Divine remembrance to a highly deliberate, even technical, art. It did so by cultic forms of spiritual concentration and by passionate loyalty to masters or saints of such practice, around whose persons or legends the Sufi fraternities gathered.

The first factor in the story of Sufism was the arguable example of Muḥammad himself, whom the Qur'ān, in Surahs 73 and 74, describes as "enmantled," or "enwrapped." As early as the eighth century there were those who sought to practice absorption in the Divine, in line with, if not in imitation of, the Prophet's story. Did his encircling cloak or mantle not serve as a means to, and a symbol of, his being "hidden" with the word or spirit from God? The journey by rapture, spoken of in Surah 17:1, might be understood in the same sense. Where ordinary tradition desired to conform to Muḥammad's patterns in general moral behavior, the Sufis aspired to participate in the way of his spirituality.

There was, of course, no suggestion of further Qur'ān. The Scriptural finality was total. The hope, simply, was to conform to the direction of will and posture of soul, to which, in Muḥammad's case alone, the Scripture had been granted. The mystics were eager to follow a careful pattern of existential devotion to the Prophet's example.

A further factor in the emergence of the Sufis was revulsion at the moral laxities and luxuries of the Umayyad Caliphate in its metropolis at Damascus— compromises which anti-Umayyad historians probably exaggerated, but which were dismaying enough to provoke political unrest and theological questioning,[3] as well as the characteristically mystical reaction which determined to find a countering personal austerity. This repudiation of the pervasive worldliness of "establishment" Islam in the eighth century is the probable explanation of the term *Ṣūfī,* which is derived from *ṣūf* (wool). For wool rebuked, in its plain simplicity, the silks and satins of the Damascus court, the affluence and indulgence which had forsaken the primitive discipline of the first disciples and companions of Muḥammad. Sufism, in this sense, meant "other-worldliness" against "this-worldliness." It gave warm and intimate expression to Muslim religion both in ardent personal form and, by later development, in local brotherhoods of discipline.

It was also stimulated by a sense of latent discontent with the aridity of dogma by the tenth and eleventh centuries A.D. Some factors in the negative theology we have already noted. On several of the major themes—God and unity, man and will, the status of the Qur'ān, the nature of faith, and the role of reason —a habit of scholasticism developed with a love of abstraction and evasive subtlety. Sufism through the centuries provided a welcome haven from these embittering contentions and attracted those wistful or sceptical souls who find the ambitions of reason dubious or overweening even when they are soundly exercised.

The tension always implicit between doctrine and devotion came to be reflected in the leadership of the Sufis, which tended to pass out of the sphere of recognized religious teachers, into the hands of lower economic classes less versed in the disciplines of law and theology. Some historians relate that development to the influence of other traditions surviving beyond conversion to Islam. Social factors also helped to explain the undoubted fervor in preaching and recruitment that marked the Sufi story. When orthodox repression threatened, they fed on the danger, nourished by their assurance that inner *ma'rifah,* or experienced truth, was superior to the rational *'ilm* of the schools of theology and the *kalām* of the dogmatists.

Among the greatest of the early Sufis was Al-Muḥāsibī, (d. 837 A.D.) whose name means "he who scrutinizes his conscience." He was well versed in scholastic lore but turned from it to ascetic meditation and composed, in his *Ri'āyah li Ḥuqūq-Illāh* (Caring for the Rights of God), a manual of devotion whose influence has been compared to that of the *Imitatio Christi* of Thomas á Kempis. Another notable figure in the same century was Al-Junaid (d. 910 A.D.) thirty times a pilgrim to Mecca, on foot, and by the fame of his ecstacies a magnet for ardent disciples.

The story of the famous woman saint, Rābi'ah, (d. 801 A.D.) has features which approximate closely to the pieties of monasticism outside the Muslim world. Celibate and a recluse, she drew to her seclusion a procession of devotees and petitioners, seeking her prayers, her counsel and her charisma. Her life might be cited as representing the meaning, as the Sufis saw it, of *al-nafs al-muṭma'innah,* referred to in Surah 89:27: "the soul possessed in tranquillity." This was the goal eagerly cherished and pursued by the Sufi mind. To Rābi'ah is attributed the much rehearsed prayer:

"O Lord, if I worship Thee from fear of hell, burn me therein. And if I worship Thee in hope of paradise exclude me from it. But if I worship Thee for Thine own sake, then withhold not from me Thy eternal beauty."

What was this Sufi spirituality and God-possessed love?

"I have made Thee the companion of my heart.
But my body is present for those who seek its company,
And my body is friendly towards its guests.
But the Beloved of my heart is the guest of my soul."[4]

The answer can best be found in the life and thought of Al-Ghazālī (d. 1111 A.D.). Like Al-Junaid, a citizen of Baghdad in his mature years, he was the most noted architect of Sufi thought and its most erudite exponent. His monumental work, with the title (literally rendered): "The Revival of the Sciences of Religion," was quoted in Chapter 1. It was in fact a thoroughgoing study of what might be called "The Art of Being Islamic," and an extraordinary compendium of profound spiritual and psychological insight. He himself had come to a quality of theology involving a deep personal revolt against scholastic rationalism, and yet clothing the Sufi ardor in patient, disciplined thought. The story of Al-Ghazālī's renunciation of Baghdad and intellectual careerism and his long pilgrimage of spiritual search remains a supreme classic of Islamic religion. His eminence gave powerful reinforcement, as well as good repute, to the Sufi movement. It was in default of such leadership that its history tells a more chequered story as it comes closer to the modern period.

Yet no one had more clearly diagnosed the temptations of the would-be Sufi or charted his path of disciplined vocation than Al-Ghazālī. That path, already known as the *Ṭarīquah,* lay in a life of devotion, usually shared by a cult group or brotherhood committed to its practice, though there were also solitaries. The word means "a way," "a path of going," and signifies a soul-progress from the temporal to the eternal, from the self-preoccupied to the true being, from sin to God. The goal was differently interpreted, whether as periodic realization of the Divine glory from which the soul should return to mundane existence in the illumination of the experience, or as a passing away of self-centric being in the unbroken unity of God.

It was this thought of *fanā',* or escape from the empirical self into the unitive state in God, that lay behind the tragic fate of the Sufi martyr, Al-Ḥallāj (d. 922 A.D.) Claiming just such an absorption into God, he was able to say, with entire mystical integrity, *Anā-l-Ḥaqq,* "I am the Real," "I am the truth." But his hearers mistook him for a blasphemer, presuming to an individual identity as God, as if he had displaced the Lord of the worlds, and so committed the most flagrant *shirk,* or self-deification. Such a charge utterly misconstrued the mystical meaning. What Al-Ḥallāj meant, beyond the perception or the malice of his foes to apprehend, was that in his awareness of truth he had passed the frontier of a subject/object religion into a mystical *Tauḥīd,* the unity which is not the exterior assertion of a unitary "He" but the beatific confession of the unitive "We."

That goal, however understood, necessitated a prolonged discipleship in the "Way," leading through stages and their corresponding states, towards the destination. There was the seeker, the wayfarer, and the initiate—the three categories, broadly understood, of Sufi experience. Their movement of soul was from acquisitiveness to renunciation, from pride to humility, from anxiety to inner peace, from love of abundance to contentment with adversity. This inner progress was often linked with the idea of *Jihād,* inwardly interpreted as being a struggle "in the way of God," having its beginning in the turning of the heart or *taubah,* meaning a conversion of concern. This inaugurated the sustained search after self-abnegation, patience, fear, solitude, abstinence, and the sense of the Divine *murāqabah* ("Thou, God, seest me"). Prospered by the Spirit and by steadfastness these were rewarded by the knowledge and love of God.

The stages and states differed between varying masters of the way, and precise analysis defeats itself. What mattered was the hunger of the heart and the reality of self-surrender. Al-Ghazālī's autobiography, known as "The Deliverer from Wandering," yields us the most worthy and illuminating narrative.

> I . . . turned with set purpose to the method of mysticism (or Sufism). I knew that the complete mystic 'way' includes both intellectual belief and practical activity; the latter consists in getting rid of the obstacles in the self and its stripping off its base characteristics and vicious morals, so that the heart may attain to freedom from what is not God and to constant recollection of Him.

After full study, he continued:

> It was clear to me that the key to all this was to sever the attachment of the heart to worldly things by leaving the mansion of deception and returning to that of eternity, and to advance towards God most high with all earnestness . . . I realised that I was caught in a veritable thicket of attachments . . . I examined my motive in my work of teaching and realized that it was not a pure desire for the things of God, but that the motive impulse moving me was the desire for an influential position and public recognition. I saw for certain that I was on the brink of a crumbling bank of sand and in imminent danger of hell-fire unless I took my state in hand . . . I sought refuge with God most high as one who is driven to him because he has no other resource . . . He made it easy for me to turn away from position and wealth, from children and friends.[5]

This was Sufi interiority at its noblest.

It was after Al-Ḥallāj and Al-Ghazālī that the Sufi motif within Islam began to develop tendencies responsive to Gnostic and theosophic teaching. This was particularly the case in the Persian and Indian spheres of Islamic dispersion. Whereas the earlier pioneers had exemplified a simple piety allied with moral zeal and rigorous discipline of life, notable figures of later Ṣufism engaged in esoteric speculation and couched their teachings in elaborate poetic imagery. One may contrast, for example, the directness and simplicity of Ḥasan al-Baṣrī (d. 728 A.D.) with the subtleties of Ibn al-ʿArabī (d. 1240 A.D.). The former wrote:

> "God has said: 'When My servant becomes altogether occupied with Me, then I make his happiness consist in the remembrance of Myself, and when I have made his

happiness and his delight consist in that remembrance, he desires Me and I desire him, and when he desires me and I desire Him, I raise the veils between Me and him and I become manifest before his eyes."

But "the veils" in the latter have to do with the contingent so that its contingency is revealed:

". . . but the veils continue to be a concealment, and so it must be. Consider this world in regard to the raising of the veil, for He spoke of consuming, by the glory of His countenance, the creature who apprehends it and sometimes He says of Himself that the creatures can see Him and not be consumed, declaring that the veils are raised in the Vision, and the Vision itself is a veil."[6]

Characteristic of this more eclectic and philosophical type of Sufism were terms like *ishrāq,* (illumination), *qurb,* (proximity), *wajd* (ecstacy), *waṣl* (lit. arrival, or unitive initiation), and *ittiṣāl* (integration into the Divine). Other terms denote the devotee in the various states of his soul progress, as *faqīr,* or *darwīsh* (poor one, dervish), *murīd* (seeker), *mutawakkil* (trusting) and *wālī* (saint).

The structural patterns of later Sufism developed out of its theories of knowledge and its systems of discipline. Whether simple or speculative, ascetic or Gnostic, its forms both produced and required the *quṭb,* or founder prototype, as the spiritual focus of the Sufi path. Disciples gathered round the proven master to learn his wisdom, live in his shadow and see by his light. Thus grew the several mystical Orders which played so central a part in the vitality of Islam from the twelfth century to the twentieth. Many factors, social, economic and cultural, contributed to their growth and influence. They gave communal solidarity to their members and spiritual shape to trade interests and craft guilds. In each case the master developed the ritual *dhikr* by which to achieve the state of absorption and manuals of prayer or litanies of devotion grew from his pen or around his reputation.

The cultic patterns varied. *Taṣawwuf,* or the art of being a Sufi, lent itself to a wide diversity of technique and emotion. Long recitation of the word *Allāh,* or elaborations of the *Takbīr* (i.e., saying: "God is most great") or the use of the *Taṣliyah* and the *Ta'wīdh* in swaying chant and sequence, as well as other means, gave to the Orders in their local "cells" or groups both an intense experience of community and an access, in some sort, to the world of *al-Ghaib,* as their masters knew and told it—the world of unseen reality, the true home of the disciple.

The earliest Order was the Jilāniyyah, founded by 'Abd al-Qādir al-Jilānī (d. 1166 A.D.), sometimes known as the Qādiriyyah. Its ritual was simple and its temper tolerant. It had numerous subbranches, owing, in part, to the many sons of the founder's family. From its origins in Baghdad and its strong roots in the Arab world, it spread very widely in both North Africa and East Asia.

An Order native to North Africa was the Shādhiliyyah, named after Abū-l-Ḥasan al-Shādhilī (d. 1258 A.D.), with a more subtle pattern of *dhikr* than Al-Jilāni's, but with a strong early emphasis on remaining in the world of labor and exchange. Al-Shādhili taught a constant recourse to God and a stoic indifference to external fortunes. Originating, it would appear, in Tunis, his Order attained a broad dispersion throughout the Maghrib and also in Arabia.

Probably the most justly celebrated of all Sufi *quṭbs* was the Persian poet, Jalāl al-Dīn Rūmī (d. 1273 A.D.), from whose striking conversion to faith came both a stream of exquisite poetry and a community of spiritual illumination, named the Maulawiyyah, after the Maulana (master) (or Mevlevi). He had migrated westward from his birthplace, Balkh, to Baghdad, and thence to Konya in central Turkey, where his center was established. Shams-al-Dīn Tabrīzī, a wandering Sufi, was the critical influence in the spiritual crisis which made Jalāl a poet, releasing from hitherto dormant reaches of his personality the hidden force of love and letters which breathes in the long religious poem, the *Mathnawī*. In its six great sections, it is the supreme work of Persian Sufi spirituality, expounding but also enveloping its doctrines in stories, symbols, maxims, and poetic imagery.

The Maulawiyyah Order is familiar for its whirling dervishes with their technique of *dhikr* by rhythmic, all-engrossing movement of the body to induce the trance of recognition. Its shrine is Jalāl's tomb in Konya, a focal point of Turkish Islam, but cherished, too, wherever the Persian tongue is loved.

Unique among Turkish Orders are the Bektashis, whose origins, in the fourteenth century, are shrouded in obscurity. Their most interesting feature was a communal meal of bread and wine and a practice of brotherhood confession, with a considerable discounting, or distrust, of the outward works of *Dīn*. Their story illustrates the syncretistic liabilities of the Sufi mentality, holding loosely to orthodox demands.

But undoubtedly the most adventurous and libertarian forms of Sufism are those we encounter when we pass into the Indian milieu. In its long and chequered tenancy in the subcontinent, Islamic religion has reacted with Hinduism and other elements in a manifold fertility. The Suhrawardiyyah (founder, Shihāb al-Dīn Suhrawardī, d. 1234 A.D.), the Chistiyyah (founder Mu'īn al-Dīn Chisti, d. 1236 A.D.) and the Naqshabandiyyah (founder Muḥammad Naqshabandī, d. 1389 A.D.) and their offshoots, are the most famous in Indian Islam. Their influence extends far into South and East Asia.

Sufism served to enrich Islam with many strains of cultural and social expression and liberated its common folk into a self-transcending intensity of spiritual life they could have reached in no other way. With its manifold energies of soul, its strenuous demands and its vast diffusion through the lands and centuries of Islam, the life of the Sufi Orders might lay claim to being the finest achievement of Islamic religion.

As such, however, it has generated powerful reactions both of admiration and criticism among historians and theologians within and beyond Islam. Mystics anyway, by their pursuit of sanctity, tend to imply a reproach of society. Sufi patterns of discipleship related uneasily to the standards of dogmatists and called into question the egalitarianism of Muslim *Ṣalāt,* by their temptation to become an aristocracy of the spirit. They held loosely to the letter and even to the routine

claims of *Dīn,* if these impeded their private discipleships. They made bold to
spiritualize the pilgrimage and the fast. When degeneracy overtook them they
became a prey to charlatans. But on all counts their long and vital role in Islam
is eloquent both of the needs it measured and the resources it possessed. Despite
all its contemporary stresses, Sufism remains a hopeful factor in the interreligious
relations of Islam. Mystics are always easier neighbors than dogmatists.

We conclude this cursory review of a vast and rich territory of the Islamic
soul with the words of one of its rarest poets, a Cairene, Ibn al-Fāriḍ (1181–1235
A.D.) whose tomb is still a place of veneration in Cairo's Muqaṭṭam Hills. He uses
the familiar image of the veil. "Occultation" is the state of unknowing wrapped
around by merely external senses.

> "Take a single time
> For thy consideration—no great while—
> And thou shalt find all that appears to thee
> And whatsoever thou dost contemplate
> The act of One alone, but in the veils
> Of occultation wrapped: when He removes
> The curtain, thou beholdest none but Him,
> And in the shapes confusion no more reigns."[7]

6.
Ummah

Cohesion and a sense of solidarity are vital factors in the continuity of great religions. In Islam they belong with the fact and concept of the *Ummah*—a term which is difficult to translate into one single, English equivalent. It has elements of "nation," "community," "people," and "religion"—all fused into characteristic Islamic quality and ideal. *Ummah,* we might say, is the collective dimension belonging to Muslims, in the trust of the Qur'ān, the obedience of Muḥammad and the fulfillment of law and liturgy.

"We did not find our ancestors in such ways," said the Prophet's townsmen in Mecca, in rejection of his preaching. (Surahs 2:170; 5:104 and 10:78.) "Our fathers," they went on, were (literally) "upon a community," that is, "of an *Ummah.*" That corporate loyalty the pagans did not intend to abandon at the call of an upstart.

Islamic Community

Already in the earliest encounter was the tradition of the collective, the living and the dead, in religion. Beyond all the commercial instincts lay the anxiety for the persistence of the tribal worship. By the same token, Muḥammad's goal had to be a new *Ummah,* unitary in worship, supratribal and decisive. The clear active enunciation of this policy, its crucial point of departure, was the *Hijrah,* by which Muḥammad and his community left Mecca and established in Medina. It is from that watershed of development, appropriately, that the Islamic calendar begins.[1] Historians saw in it the real hinge of Muslim genesis. It is striking that they did not locate the date of definition either in the birth of Muḥammad or in the initiation of the Qur'ān. When Muslims, who were already his disciples, were faced with a decision to emigrate and throw in their lot with a cause against their own kin from a center outside—then the Islamic era opens. This was, in its critical quality, a bigger decision than a confession of faith or the endurance of the community's hostility while still resident within it. Faith-solidarity was now actively pitted against blood-kinship.

This was the decisive thing. Some modern writers see in it the emergence of a new personalism destined to transform the Arab mentality. If this be too romantic a view, it was certainly a basic revision of tribalism, a new pattern of priority. This was the new *Ummah* implicit in the *Hijrah.* The emigrants were cast upon the aid and comfort of "alien" Medinan partners and involved in separation, material and emotional, from their kindred left in Mecca. That there were some kinship ties within Medina does not diminish what was meant by an espousal of new citizenship.

But the new *Ummah,* founded in unitary religion, was not just another
"tribe." By those religious origins it was committed to all compatible access of
membership. Its first postures were necessarily alert and militant. For the situation was liable to subterfuge. Jeopardy was its "native air." Medina, moreover,
was at first only partially secure and had to be consolidated into identity of
interest with Muḥammad and the non-Muslim Medinans persuaded, cajoled or
maneuvered, into the cause which, if it did not now "make" their city, would
certainly, by failure, unmake it, through Meccan retaliation. The narrative of that
consolidation we need not retell: its political and military opportunism we have
already noted. The build-up of resources, the worsting of Quraishī power and
counsels, the campaign of arms and negotiation leading to its capitulation, are a
classic story of successful leadership.

Throughout, even at its most militant, the open *Ummah* idea is never lost
to sight. Even the *Hijrah* was not allowed to close the doors behind it. Stragglers
who were ready to come late were not precluded on the ground that they had lost
their chance or lacked a timely heroism. For timidity could have a change of
mind, or intimidation be defied with a better courage. All sincere accession is
timely.

In the sixth year of the *Hijrah,* in the armistice of Al-Ḥudaibiyyah, Muḥammad negotiated the first pilgrimage to Mecca of Islam as such, the Quraish
agreeing to evacuate the city for three days, the next year, for this purpose. More
adherence accrued from its consequences than from thirteen years of preaching.
The prestige of negotiating with the Quraish as an equal, the symbolic value of
the pilgrimage to be made, the ten-year freedom of either party to make what
alliances they wished (thus affording cover for acceding tribes)—all these far
outweighted the concession by which he dropped the title of *Rasūl-Allāh* from
his formal style in the document—a concession which angered and dismayed his
less perceptive followers. For the substance of the *Rasūliyyah* was emphatically
set forward.

When, by these military and diplomatic measures, Mecca was finally conquered and incorporated into Islam, there were two historic capitals, the city of
the preaching and the city of the power. The *Ummah* of Islam acquired thereby
an abiding sign of its supralocal, intertribal character. There were soon to be a
score of cities. Mecca was quickly and almost painlessly brought into the fold.
The idols did not die hard. They surrendered, the historian may say, in the human
surrender of their city. Therein is both fact and symbol. It was power which
brought the Quraish to heel: but it was power generated by and for a faith about
God needing no city for refuge and claiming all cities for empire. Islam had
become a state. Their mutual victory was indivisible.

It was soon to seem everywhere repeatable. Some time after Mecca's capitulation and during the steady, if not always unchallenged, Islamization within
Arabia, Muḥammad, it is alleged, sent letters to rulers in the world of that day,
to Byzantium, Egypt, and Ethiopia, requiring their adhesion to Islam. It is
suggested in some quarters that if they had agreed to let their peoples embrace

the Muslim faith and liturgy, their political authorities would have been preserved intact in their hands. We can only imagine how Islam would then have been organized, with politically "independent" national accessions and no *Jihād,* or religious war, ever proclaimed and pursued. Islam, existing thus religiously under a variety of persisting sovereignties, would not have been the great *Dār al-Islām* that history knows. Mecca had set the precedent for religio-political surrender and the external world was to learn the same pattern.

The main interest of the tradition about the letters is the implicit *Cuius regio, eius religio* principle—the summons of rulers to the faith as the key to their peoples' adherence. In rejecting or ignoring Muḥammad's letter, its recipients had no notion of the incredible sequence that history held in store. They could not have known that the new Islamic *Ummah* was poised for massive victories altogether phenomenal in their reach and finality.

The Tide of Expansion

Our concern here with the story of the expansion that brought Islam across North Africa, the Straits of Gibraltar, and the Pyrenees, and far into eastern Asia, within a century of the Prophet's death, is more for its deep consequences in the religious temper of Islam than for its dramatic chronology in detail. At the death of the second Caliph, 'Umar, in 644 A.D., Egypt and Libya to the west had been conquered, and northward and eastward, the Fertile Crescent, Syria, Iraq, and Persia as far as Hamadan and Isfahan. The third Caliph, 'Uthmān (644–656 A.D.), continued the advance westward into Tripolitania, northward through Armenia and on to the Caucasus Mountains and eastward into Khuzistan and the borders of Afghanistan. Under the early Umayyads, the Maghrib (Tunis, Algeria, and Morocco) and Spain, almost to the Pyrenees, were added to the Muslim realm. The tide in Europe was only turned, in the heart of France by Charles Martel in 732, at the Battle of Tours, exactly one century after Muḥammad's death. It continued to flow in the east as far as Sind and the Indus River. The tale, and the enemy toll, of battles, the collapse of great Byzantine and Persian provinces, the military prowess of 'Umar himself, of Khālid and Amrū and other famous generals, the very yielding, as it seemed, of history, to the Muslim will—all these gave to Islam the habit of assurance and the instinct of dominion. History itself had become tributary to Muslim destiny and all its other peoples and beliefs their subjects.

The religious "logic" of the Islamic expansion takes in its stride the underlying factors of historical explanation. The first was the *élan vital*—as the French might say—of the Muslim armies, their unfailing ardor, their inner zest. Muḥammad had touched the deepest springs of valor and sanctified them in the notion of *Jihād,* making the living as invulnerable and the fallen as already immortal in the heavens. "In the way of God" was the phrase from which their temper drew its strength and generated what nothing mercenary could match. Rather it dispirited all that blocked its way—forces which were already undermined by the long contentions of the Byzantine and Persian Empires, by the restiveness of the border provinces, by the heavy grievances of the populations and the enfeebling controversies within eastern Christendom. In places the Muslims' successes owed as much to the welcome of the conquered as to the weight of the conquerors.

There were also in the reckoning powerful economic factors—the attraction of the cultured lands that proved so readily reducible, the pressures of poverty and numbers within the Arabian peninsula. There had been earlier eruptions of the "desert" into the "sown." But the seventh century had the indefinable, unprecedented factor of Islam to fuse all else into irresistibility. The experience, in turn, gave Islam a corroboration of finality and a freehold on power.

It also opened to it a vast influx of new adherence, new peoples and old cultures, with their customs and traditions, to be absorbed into the Islamic whole. But the assurance of that advent and its sanctions of supremacy were such as to bring them effectively into Muslim mold. Islam in turn gained a new sophistication both of mind and doctrine, by contact with dimensions of being unknown in its hearthland. It became heir to Plato and Aristotle and to the metaphysical aspirations of the Greek temper. Its theology responded to influences deriving from the long preoccupations of the Christian faith and developed its own form of the problem of Divine and human will, of faith and works, and of the status of the word of God in the Quranic Scripture.

But its reactions of receptivity in all these myriad ways never yielded the essential definition which the origins of Islam had given. Hospitality there was, together with ambivalence, yet always within a capacity to preserve and impose the inner identity. It was not the sword, in the sharp and naked sense, in ruthlessness and anger, that made its triumph. Any such thesis oversimplifies and distorts the story. The authority of empire is the proper summary of the means of its displacement both of potentates and faiths. Islam did not speak from catacombs, for it told only what it knew in its own emergence, and it assumed that its reception should conform to that same experience. It saw the way of truth as passing always through thrones. There was, therefore, a reciprocal relation between conversion and submission, between conquest and *Ṣalāt*. How, indeed, should it be otherwise? But it reserved its intolerance only for idolatry and all defiance of the God Who had empowered it.

That religio-political authority found its focus in the Caliph and the concept of his office.

The Caliphate

As briefly noted in Chapter 2, the institution of the Caliphate had already been created in the immediate aftermath of Muḥammad's death. Under the second Caliph, 'Umar, it became the most formidable of thrones. For long in practice, and always in theory, it constituted a symbolic headship of the community, believed through the tradition to have Divine sanction. It provided a focus of allegiance and embodied, among other implications, two general truths of the Islamic *Ummah,* namely the subject's duty of total obedience and the ruler's obligation of "representativeness" under God. "Representativeness" is deliberately used, at some risk, in this context. It is not that the Caliphate was ever popularly elective in suffrage sense, but that its holder was to be the first of those who pray and the executant, not the author, of the sacred *Shari'ah.*

The second of these aspects is more easily told. Muḥammad had personally led the prayers in the post-*Hijrah* community. He prostrated at the *miḥrāb* as well as governed from the *minbar.* From the outset his successors followed the same habit. Wherever the Caliph was present he was the congregational leader among the faithful. The pattern became general through the lower echelons of government, provincial and local. Truly any individual, however lowly, could lead the *Ṣalāt.* The custom by which the political authority in its highest, or highest available, personage presided at the liturgy may be seen as the Islamic form of the theory of the state, of the interplay of the Divine and the temporal sovereignty. Not here the sacral kingship or the coronation of emperors, but the ritual centrality—without essential distinction of liturgical action—of the politically supreme figure. This is the Imamate inherent in the Caliphate.

It stands, also, as a token of the theoretical subservience of the Caliph to the *Shari'ah.* He bows with the rest. He is not the Prophet, nor the Prophet's "son." Prophecy was sealed in 632, with the death of Muḥammad. The Caliph administers the law rooted in that finalized revelation, as completed by the other Divinely willed sources. The law is preserved and fulfilled under the wing of the Caliphate but it is not subdued to it. In Sunnī theory, it is the community, not the commander, of the faithful, who is the guardian and guarantor of the *Shari'ah.* His power, however, is the condition of its operation. The Sunnī *'Ulamā',* or learned experts, were able, for the most part, to make good their claim to custody and interpretation of the law as their proper role.

The duty of the subject of the Caliph was one of implicit obedience. The Shī'ah, because of their disaffection over 'Alī and his cause, and certain other minority sects, sought, from time to time in the first two centuries of Islam, to assert a right of nonobedience. But among Sunnis, the authority of the Caliph was a paramount religious principle. From the beginning, in 632 at Muḥammad's death, there were urgent practical necessities for swift and undisputed succession. The rapid expansion of Islam in the following decades intensified this need. The weakness of 'Uthmān, the third Caliph (644–656 A.D.) and the ensuing strife under 'Alī (656–661 A.D.) underlined the same lesson. Mu'āwiya, who displaced 'Alī in 661, to found the Umayyad Caliphate, with Damascus as its center, ruled vigorously and began the practice of designating the son who was to succeed and of ensuring public recognition of him in advance. This application of the hereditary principle, which had not obtained from 632 to 661, was intended to ensure continuity of effective control and to avoid the crises of succession. It also provided for the legal requirement that the Caliph should be descended from the Quraish of Mecca.

The autocratic character of the Caliphate became more marked under the 'Abbāsids, who took power from the Umayyads in 750 A.D. and ruled from Baghdad. Persian traditions of despotism supplanted the Arab ways of the Umayyads. New and more pretentious titles were assumed: "the Caliph of God" (rather than ". . . of the Apostle") and "the Shadow of God upon earth." Though they had profited from temporary alliance with disaffected elements to unseat the Umayyads, the 'Abbāsids were not minded to permit a repetition of the tactic. The tendency to link centralized power with a growing emphasis on "official" orthodoxy increased in the ninth century. It coincided with the growing authority of non-Arab elements in Islamic life—a development which, while attesting its universalism, strained its unity.

The heyday of 'Abbāsid power passed by the tenth century, though it continued in formal line and yielded a theoretical succession to the Ottoman Caliphate in the fifteenth century. The intervening centuries saw the rise and flux of numerous smaller and rival "caliphates" or vassalages. The territories west of Tunis, and the Spanish peninsula never in fact came into the orbit of 'Abbāsid Baghdad. The Umayyads who continued there, and their successor potentates, made good a pattern of separatism that came to be general throughout the east. The vicissitudes of the Ikhshidids, the Tulūnids, the (Shī'ah) Fāṭimids, of Egypt and Tunis; the Buwayhids of Baghdad; the Ghaznawids across Persia from the Caucasus to India; the Almoravids in Spain and the Maghrib; and others of lesser range in time and place, belong to political history rather than the study of religion. But, in their turbulent sequence, and in the tensions of the Crusades in the eleventh and twelfth centuries, the tribulations of Mongol invasion in the thirteenth, the struggles of Seljuq and Ottoman Turks in the fourteenth, lies ample proof of the durability of the Islamic way and of the capacity of its inner forces to take its outward conquerors in hand. In that sense, the persistence of the *Ummah* defies admitted fragmentation and the stresses of military and cultural invasion. The other salient fact in the long story of Islam up to the sixteenth century is the contribution of the Persian and the Turkish languages to the service and adornment of its thought and meaning.

Though never after 750 A.D. a sovereignty physically coextensive with Islamic territories, the Caliphate did not cease to symbolize what it failed to embrace. It stood for the fundamental axiom of Islamic existence, namely that the state is the sign and surety of the faith and the faith is the ground and seal of the state. So it had been in the dispensation of Muḥammad, and the Caliphate was the historical perpetuation of that partnership. That it was unable to preserve effective unity through tumultuous centuries across three continents does not diminish the concept of which it was the organ.

The Significance of the Shī'ah

The first, and the most essential rupture of the unity of the Islamic *Ummah* was the emergence of the Shī'ah. As the body's primary and permanent schism, the Shī'ah are a subject of deep relevance to the student of religion. They are also a topic of much complexity for the historian.

From 632 to 644 the Caliphate was a story of unity and success, in which the first two holders of the office were not challenged—though later Shī'ah theory insists that even in the first instance, in 632, 'Alī, cousin and son-in-law of Muḥammad, was wrongfully passed over. It was, however, under the third Caliph that disaffection, gathering round his claims, became bitter and open. The unrest of 'Uthmān's years (644–656 A.D.) deepened when 'Alī, in compromised circumstances, finally became Caliph in 656 A.D. Opposition to him never accepted his rule. Disaster overtook his reign and, after his murder in 661 A.D. his following, the 'Alids, could make little headway against the shrewd and determined *de facto* authority of the first Umayyad Caliph at Damascus. But on his death, the smoldering 'Alid cause erupted into brief flame, in the ill-starred venture of Ḥusain, younger son of 'Alī, who challenged the next Umayyad Caliph, Yāzīd, and was annihilated with almost his whole retinue in the massacre of Karbalā' in 680 A.D.

It was the horror of this event, coupled with the murder in 669 A.D. of the elder son of Alī, that gave the aura of martyrdom to their ill-fated house. So tragic a destiny befalling the nearest kinsmen and the only grandsons of the Prophet cried out for the spiritual recompense of an immortal devotion, and Shī'ah Islam was born in the response. The continuing political frustrations of the 'Alid party only sharpened its intensity. Even when the Umayyad Caliphate gave way to the 'Abbāsids, their external fortunes, despite their service to the change, remained fitful and forlorn. In his lifetime 'Alī had enjoyed an ardent reputation for his chivalry and saintliness. That memory, hallowed by the pathos of his family and of Fāṭimah, his wife (d. 632 A.D.), took shape in a passionate, ardent allegiance. It was one of those occasions in history where mingling anger and pity, wrought into the cult of suffering, evoked a staunch refusal to forget or, by forgetfulness, to conspire with the injustices of fate and leave the spilled blood silent in the sand. It is this quality which, despite the vagaries and the divisiveness, gives Shī'ah Islam its fascination for the student of religion.

External, political privations, however, were only one factor. Underlying the Shī'ah form of Islam is a divergent concept of the guarantees of living continuity in faith. Whereas Sunnis rely broadly on the *Sharī'ah* in the community to ensure a true standing in Islam through the generations in their sequence, Shī'ahs believe in renewed mediation of Muḥammad's finality through a sequence of Imāms. These are much more than the prayer-leading figures known to Sunnī Islam. They stood in lineal relation to Muḥammad and only through them did the faithful in each generation stand within the authentic truth. The Sunnī scheme took the lengthening ages of Islam back, as it were, horizontally in the plane of history to the fountainhead in the Prophet, and bound them into one by the criterion of the *Sharī'ah*. Shī'ah Islam saw that final source linked afresh to each generation, vertically, through the Imām, without whom the faith and the faithful could not coinhere. In doing so, they did not impugn the finality of the Qur'ān: they believed they possessed it through renewed emanation of the original "light of

Muḥammad." This light was guaranteed by hereditary succession and designation of the previous Imām.

The first Imām after Karbalā' was "the young 'Alī," a survivor of the massacre and son to Ḥusain, who came to be known for his piety as Zain al-'Ābidīn, "the paragon of worshippers." From him derived a succession which, numbering from 'Alī, counted seven Imāms and, for another segment of devotion, twelve Imāms. The schism between the Seveners, (*Al-Sab'iyyah*) and the Twelvers, (*Al-Ithnā'Ashariyyah*) was a central cleavage within the Shī'ah loyalty. The division came after the Imamate of Ja'far (d. 765 A.D.). The Seveners recognized Ismā'īl, Ja'far's son, who had predeceased his father and whose sect is thus known also as the Ismailis. The Twelvers took Mūsā Kāẓim, a surviving son of Ja'far, from whom the line continued until the twelfth Imām, Ḥasan al-'Askarī (d. 874 A.D.). At that point the Twelvers adopted a position comparable to that taken by the Seveners at the earlier date, namely belief in the concealment of the true Imām, to await manifestation in God's time and to guide the faithful meanwhile out of hiddenness. The hidden Imām for the Seveners was the lost son, Ismā'īl. For the Twelvers it was the son of Ḥasan al-'Askarī, who mysteriously disappeared at Samarra, at about the age of seven. He may have been abducted or killed, but piety believed that he had gone into *ghaibah*, or seclusion, from whence he continued to preserve his followers in the true faith.

The intricacies of Shī'ah Islam in both these main segments are too complex to be disentangled here. There was, in its generative principle of immediacy, an instinctive tendency to sectarian division, as devotion or partisanship came to attach, competitively, to different figures in the sequence up to "concealment," and in the situation that followed it. The notion of "the hidden Imām" both necessitated and invited fissiparous tendencies wherever loyalties and emotions were finalized at competing points. The chronic sectarianism of Shī'ah Islam is seen by Sunnis as justifying the firm discipline of the Sunnī alternative, with its rejection of personal cults outside the final Prophet and its relative immunity thereby from the excesses and unpredictabilities of Shī'ah eschatology.

The emotional strength and cultic deviation of the Shī'ahs is most readily indicated by a study of their shrines, which through long periods asserted effective priority over Mecca itself. Pilgrimage as the unitary ritual in Islam became itself an instrument of separation. The concentric gave way to the eccentric. 'Alī's grave at Najaf; Karbalā' itself, both in Iraq; Mashhad in Persia, being the shrine of Imām Riḍā, as well as the burial place of the great Hārūn al-Rashīd; and the Kāẓimain in Baghdad, where Mūsā, seventh Imām and Muḥammad, ninth Imām, were buried, all became Shī'ah centers of devotion and the first three, in particular, powerful rivals of the orthodox *Ḥajj* itself. Political tensions and provincial passions also contributed, from time to time, to curtail or divert the classic pilgrimage. Though Shī'ahs have compelling religious reasons, through the Prophet and 'Alī and certain of the later Imāms, to hold faithfully to Mecca and Medina, the local loyalties as well as Sunnī enmities have often assured to Mashhad and Karbalā' and Najaf a more dominant devotion.

The Shīʿah divergence is equally striking in tradition, piety, and Quranic exegesis. The history of partisanship begat a partisanship about history. The controversies over succession and schism embittered the narratives. How "bad," for example, were the Umayyads? There was sharp contention, too, about the currency and credentials of the traditions, studied in Chapter 2, wherever these involved issues bearing on Sunnī-Shīʿah positions—which were, of course, numerous. Traditionalists were ranged in hostile camps.

The cleavage persisted likewise through the entire cultic life. *Ṣalāt* and its *Dhikr* were of necessity common to both. But the Shīʿah segment had its own patterns of mysticism and, as might be expected, developed by far the most esoteric forms. Aside from the *Ṭarīqahs,* Shīʿah piety showed itself far more receptive than Sunnī Islam to the influences of the environment, giving birth for example in early nineteenth century Persia to the cult of Bābism from which, in turn, Bahāʾism sprang.

Nowhere, however, was its characteristic energy more intense than in the genesis and persistence of the commemoration of the Passion of Ḥusain. The pathos and pain of this reenactment of the tragedy of Karbalāʾ have no parallel in Sunnī Islam. Through the centuries it has remained as a focus of emotion. The faithful mourn the fallen saint and relive the grim details of the tragic day when all but five of "the elect seed" and retinue perished, including the daughter of Ḥusain in her bridal array.

This drama of the tenth of Muḥarram gives moving voice to Shīʿah belief in the self-renouncing virtue of Ḥusain's death. Devotion sees him as the martyr at the hands of evil, who went to his death saying: "I have washed my hands of life; I have girded myself to do the will of God." Shīʿahs do not believe that he could have been so tragically a victim except by Divine foreknowledge. Clearly, then, he was an oblation for the cause of Islam and from his innocent sorrows redemption must flow for the community of faith. Pardon, mediation, virtue are to be found in the vicarious sacrifice which cruelty exacted—a cruelty that in its telling staggered with horror the whole Muslim world and in its recollection represents for all Shīʿahs the epitome of human crime.

Beyond these divergencies over history, authority, tradition, and cult, Shīʿah Muslims differ from Sunnis over the Qurʾān itself. The absence of ʿAlī's name from it, and its silence about explicit Shīʿah claims, inspire the charge that it has been in places corrupted or adjusted by Sunnī hands. There are, it is alleged, at least two Surahs wanting which would have given the Shīʿahs comfort and confirmation. Ingenuity also can help supply what is lacking by slight alterations to vary the sense, in forced and artificial ways which certainly command no support among Sunnis. With their concepts of the Imāms, Shīʿahs tend, further, to insist that all interpretation must be allegorical, requiring the special illumination that only the Imāms, or their spokesmen, the *mujtahids,* could attain. Ismailis, in particular, find every statement of the Qurʾān eluding direct or literal meaning and, therefore, out of the range of normal *tafsīr,* or commentary. More extreme forms of this attitude eliminate exegesis almost entirely, setting the

Qur'ān totally within the secret purview of the hidden Imām. There is also the claim that the official text is relative to the original book which the hidden Imām will finally reveal.

Shī'ahs, in varying ways, read their sectarian interest where the text gives opportunity. Thus, for example, the familiar words in Surah 33:33. "People of the house (*Ahl al-Bait*), God only wills to put away from you all uncleanness and to cleanse you." The phrase "people of the house," usually understood as either Muḥammad's wives, or the denizens of the *Ka'bah* precincts, is taken by Shī'ah thought to refer to 'Alī, Fāṭimah and their family. The verse then becomes the ground for a doctrine of the immaculate Imāms. Passages which seem to indicate prophetic sinfulness are handled in such a way as to exclude that implication.

Despite the many legacies of estrangement, a will to rapprochement between Sunnis and Shī'ahs has been at work in recent years and much progress has been made. The abatement of fanaticism has contributed to this. Insofar as Shī'ah allegiance belongs with national identity, whether Persian, Indian, East African, Yemeni, or the rest, modern conditions of interpenetration have served to allay its sharpness and to disqualify some of its more extreme forms of deviation.

Yet there is truth in the view that the abiding Sunnī-Shī'ah cleavage, deep as it is, relates to a common unity. It is a family quarrel. It concerns fundamental issues of authority and community which could not divide if they did not, in measure, unite. It witnesses to the intensity with which Islam registers ultimate problems of religion. Each segment exemplifies postures of faith and aspects of establishment that recur with comparable divisiveness in other creeds. For all their antipathy, they still express the *Ummah* they disrupt.

Non-Muslims Under Islam

The *Ummah* theme may be assessed from quite a different angle by taking stock of the Islamic attitude to outsiders and its resulting theory of toleration. Paganism, polytheism, and atheism are repugnant to Islam and must be characterized as *Dār al-Ḥarb*—realms to be brought by *Jihād* under the authority of the true faith. From the outset the view was that the Caliphate and idolatry could not coexist. The latter must be eliminated.

But there were tolerated minorities, Jews and Christians, known as *dhimmis,* who were allowed to maintain their faith and worship within their own families. They were subjected to special taxation and suffered several disabilities, varying from time to time and place to place. The greatest was the prohibition of all external recruitment. Only those born Christians could be Christians, and likewise for Jews. It was assumed that the minorities would never receive adhesions from among Muslims. They enjoyed a freedom only to persist, not a freedom to baptize or to receive. It was thus a toleration ensuring freedom to remain but not a freedom to "become," except in one direction, namely into Islam. Since the Muslim was already there, he had no options. It was axiomatic that he should never seek to change. If he did, the law of apostasy forbade the notion and barred the way on pain of death and disinheritance. It was impossible to de-Islamize. Islam was a faith no Muslim was outwardly free to abandon. There is no more eloquent demonstration of the meaning of *Ummah* than this situation. It was a principle of irreversible and irreducible community continuity. Change of faith was equivalent to political treachery.

But the permitted minorities had the option of remaining as they were born, or of becoming Muslim. In the course of the centuries they accepted this account of themselves. Such option was better than open persecution. But it meant existence by the sufferance of an empire and an authority properly and only wielded by the one faith, Islam. Those who embraced Islam were accepting religiously the sovereignty that had already acquired them politically. Those who held to their faith did so despite its complete political displacement. The notable position that individual Jews and Christians came to enjoy in the management of financial, educational or, in Ottoman days, military, aspects of the Caliphate, should not obscure the basic disabilities of their communities, since there were prudential or personal reasons for their functions. In its measure of toleration Islam never abandoned the axiom that it was made to rule.

An abiding legacy of this system was the communal separatism which came to characterize the legal and social order under Islam. Initially there was considerable interplay between Muslim thought and practice, and minority cultures, following the Arabicization achieved within the first century of expansion. That process continued with a steady penetration of original Islam by concepts and vocabulary drawn from Christian and Jewish sources. Even in controversy all talked much the same mental language. Doctrines tended to arouse very similar issues and to generate comparable heresies. Controversies within Islam about freedom and destiny, faith and works, authority and reason, the eternal and the temporal, closely resembled, from different premises, those of early Christendom. The question, for example, of the Qur'ān's being the eternally pre-existent speech of God seems parallel to Christian doctrine as to the pre-existent Christ. And there was the question how men could be, at the same time, morally accountable and essentially unfree.

But with the gathering assurance of Islam and the enervating Christian experience of subjugated status, there came an increasing isolation of the respective theologies. Clues that might have been discovered in the similarities of inward debate became lost in mutually hostile attitudes. The sense of otherness sharpened. Fixed prejudices hardened and where there was mutual cognizance at all it was for purposes of refutation and rejection.

It was this mental isolation that came to be symbolized in the Millet system during the Ottoman centuries. The word Millet derives from the Quranic term *millah,* meaning a community. Thus Islam itself, in Surah 2:135 and other passages, is described as "millat Ibrāhīm," the fellowship of Abraham's faith and loyalty. But in the Ottoman legal system the Millet denoted any religious group of *dhimmī* status, allowed to administer its own law of personal relationship—marriage, divorce, inheritance and the like—and to regulate its own communal

education. In this manner Copts, Greeks, Armenians, Syriac Christians, Maro-
nites and others, enjoyed the necessary means of communal identity under law.
Not being Muslim, they could not be regulated by Islamic personal law. The
Millet system left them in legal possession of their communal selves, in all that
concerned their family and their faith, within the overriding dominance of a
citizenship belonging uniquely to Islam.

This traditional communalism still survives in the Near and Middle East,
only partly modified by the pressures of secularism that tend towards a single
citizenship within a common law. But an even more persistent legacy is the
mentality it expressed—a mentality that has long habituated the religious mind
to noncommunication.

There was, of course, a strong element of paradox in the Islamic requirement
that other religions must be merely sects. Claiming for itself the unilateral possession of the state, and requiring all other religious groups to exist "just as religions"
without benefit of power, Islam decreed for them a pattern that it held to be
intolerable for itself. Islam could not properly be Islam except in political dominance. Other faiths must contrive to be themselves despite the denial of political
opportunity.

There was, however, nothing new in this. All dominant faiths have tended
to assume that the political arm was theirs by right. To ask for an idea of equal
citizenship, within which religious allegiance would be a matter of indifference
to the state, is to ask for the twentieth century and secularism—a form of things
to which Islam's adjustment, as we shall see in Chapter 7, proves more difficult
than almost any other faith's. It was the assurance and finality of Islam, as the
Millet system registered it, which gave the religio-political equation in Islam a
firmer hold and a longer survival than in any other tradition. Such was the vigor
of the Islamic sense of a destiny to dominate, by virtue of being historically final
among religions. History, therefore, belonged with Islam's authority and all else
must subsist in subordination.

So it was that one of the profoundest problems of modern times developed
when history itself, in the form of the Western empire, seemed to belie the Islamic
assumption that sovereignty is inalienably Islamic. This was to become the inner
dilemma of the nineteenth century. It is significant that, when the challenge came,
it came from outside, so well secured was the docility of the *dhimmī* communities
and of the Millet system.

Through the dominant centuries the Islamic assurance about power was
never radically shaken. It is interesting to observe that it successfully persisted
even where the populations that had the understatus of "minorities" were, in fact,
actual, even overwhelming, majorities. The most notable example is Islamic
India, where non-Muslim subjects of the Mughals always outnumbered the Muslims. Here, of course, the *dhimmī* status, confined in the Arab world to nonidolat-
ers, could not apply in the same form. The sheer weight of Hindu masses and the
indestructibility of Hindu culture and mentality were such that, though many

conversions took place, Islamic statehood was always minority-power. *Dār al-Islām* was outnumbered in its own house. The Meccan, Medinan and Middle Eastern pattern of inclusive dominance was not physically repeated. Nevertheless, the sense of destiny, of birthright to rule, remained unimpaired until weakness supervened and a Western Rāj displaced it.

The student of the Islamic theory of non-Islamic elements inside the *Ummah* might usefully pause to reflect on a salient example of what we might call the retaliatory principle, of an effort to reverse the Islamic "right to power." It took the form of an external challenge, namely, the Crusades from the west. Other more successful incursions from the east—Turkish, Mongol, Tartar—unseated Muslim rulers but then themselves submitted to Islam. These were simply history's ethnic and political eruptions, assertions of the sheer will to conquer. The Crusades were a response of emulation. They were a Christian pursuit of the Islamic conviction that power-in-territory is a *religious* mission.

Numerous economic, feudal, social, and political considerations were also in the picture. But the crusading theory that the holy places needed to be possessed, in hard fact, not merely in deep reverence; that rule must corroborate worship; that alien religion should not be left enjoying the sovereignty—these were strongly Islamic convictions. To see this is not to claim that their formulation was a conscious borrowing. The two realms were too far apart in temper for that. But it is to say that the parallel is close. The "infidel," the Crusaders believed, should not be left in charge. Force to dispossess was a legitimate enterprise of "the true faith." The Crusades proceeded upon a sort of *Dār al-Christianity* concept of the Holy Land where, for sacramental reasons, Christendom bitterly resented Muslim occupancy. To say, as we must, that it was a tragically misguided enterprise, which had mistaken the true vocation both of the Church and of the Holy Places, would not be a verdict congenial to the Islamic mind. The Islam of the Fertile Crescent, notably under the great Ayyūbid, Salāḥ al-Dīn (Saladin) (1138–93 A.D.), resisted magnificently. But the historic rivalry itself lay between two closely comparable philosophies of what religion ought to do in the world.

It is noteworthy, in this connection, that the Eastern Churches, which suffered under the Crusaders hardly less than the Muslims, had no stomach for western "liberation." This is, in part, a measure of the degree to which they conformed, by that time, to the Islamic account of their role. The externally planted Kingdom of Jerusalem lasted less than a single century. In the long retrospect of eastern Christendom it appears as no more than an episode in the firm pattern of Christian submission to Islamic conditions of power. But, in western intentions, it was an episode aiming to emulate those very conditions and affirm them against Islam. In defeat and withdrawal, the Crusaders left behind them an eastern Christendom painfully confirmed in its quiescence under Islam. They themselves carried back to Europe seeds of experience they had never thought to receive. The external challenge to Islamic power-possession was not renewed until the recent centuries of the western empire.

The *Ummah* in the Mirror of Its Cities

As we have seen earlier, study of Islamic origins belongs firmly with two cities, Mecca and Medina. The student of Islamic civilizations does well to rely on the same urban clue and explore the nature of the *Ummah* in the symbol of its great city centers. In its unity and diversity Islamic culture is a tale of many cities. Any civilization—as the name implies—has its apex in the city, sustained and shouldered, furnished and feared, by a tributary agriculture. Islam is no exception. Indeed it is a conspicuous exemplar. The map of its culture is a web of cities. Mosque and city have always been mutual partners, making for each other's renown.

Having characterized the *Ummah* in its caliphal office, in its central Sunnī-Shī‘ah duality and in its relation to "the stranger in the gates," we now turn to savor it in its broad sweep of time and place, taking cities for our guides. Some, like Baghdad and Cairo, were the native creation of Islam, but most were capitals of established fame and, therefore, focal points of the *Ummah*'s engagement with the world.

Damascus of the Umayyads

The first focal point was Damascus, seat of the victorious Umayyads from 661 to 750 A.D. Blessed with superb gardens and orchards, fed by the snows of the Anti-Lebanon in streams that make their paradise before losing themselves in desert sands, Damascus presided over the first great cycle of Islamic power. Its sway reached from Biscay to the Indus River. Once Mu‘āwiya, the first Umayyad, had made it the caliphal capital, Medina never regained any political centrality—a strange fate indeed for the seat of Muḥammad's own personal power and the site of his most formative decision.

Mu‘āwiya owed much to the governorship of Damascus which he had enjoyed under the Caliph ‘Uthmān and turned to such good advantage against ‘Alī. But he corroborated its assets with great resources of personal character and ambition. History sees in him an exponent of the characteristic Arab virtue of *murū’ah,* or "manliness." That he continued and consolidated for twenty years was, by later standards of his dynasty, a triumph in itself. "I apply not my sword where my lash suffices," he said, "nor my lash where my tongue is enough . . . When men pull, I loosen, when they loosen, I pull." His competent opportunism laid the foundation for the heydey of Islamic Damascus, despite the vagaries and discords of his successors.

The Umayyad court was a strange amalgam of restless bedouin energy and the new arts and excesses of acquired culture. Poets abounded, their hearts still in the desert but their amours in the palaces. The Great Mosque of Damascus was the work of one of the most profligate of the caliphs, Walīd I (705–715). The fourth holiest edifice in Islam, it occupied the entire area of the great Cathedral Church of St. John which Walīd demolished to make way for his vast design.

Immense sums were spent on its erection. Craftsmen—a veritable army of arti-sans—and shiploads of gold and silver were recruited from far and wide. When accounts of the expenditure were finally brought to the Caliph, it is recorded that eighteen camels were needed for their delivery. The Caliph refused to look at them with the words: "Verily we have spent this for God and will have no accounting of it."

Damascus life is a historian's mirror of many of the continuing tensions of the *Ummah*. There was the struggle, for example, between the pull of worldly indulgence and the austere disciplines of pious Islam, the former symbolized by Walīd II (743–744) with his habit of swimming in a wine-pool from which he drank copiously, the latter by 'Umar 11 (717–720), who came to be known as the "saint" of the Umayyads and the first of the "renewers" whom Islam by tradition expects at the turn of every Hijrī century. He could often be found, with patched clothes, mingling in the mosques with other devotees, hardly recognizable as the ruler of domains as far as the Pillars of Hercules.

Another stress in Damascene society was that between the Arab and the non-Arab elements within Islam. The local population which had Islamized—the *Mawālis* as they were called—often exceeded the immigrant Muslims in their zeal for the faith, a zeal which they visited on the *dhimmīs* they had forsaken but which failed to gain them a status of equality with the Arab Muslims to whom they had acceded. The racial contrast was firmly applied and the Arab "originals" distinguished from their "client" coreligionaries. Umayyad society recruited vast numbers of slaves—black, yellow and white—from its conquered territories.

Under Umayyad auspices Islam developed aspects of culture and expression that set the lines of its intellectual history in the later centuries. Provincial centers like Kufa and Baṣrah often played as great a role as the capital itself. There Arabic philology and grammar were developed, partly in response to the needs and zeal of non-Arab converts. Even Mecca and Medina brought their quota of celebrities in lyric poetry and amorous verse, both the inspirers and the inspired. The great John of Damascus, first of the notable Christian "dialogicians" in Islam, was a product of the Umayyad administration and, before his withdrawal to Mar Saba, in the Judean wilderness, is said to have debated in the Caliph's presence. Mosque preaching grew into a more conscious and deliberate art under the Umayyads, perhaps stimulated by the vast and lavish architectural splendors they achieved to house it.

The most justly celebrated of these, outside Damascus, was 'Abd al-Malik's erection of the Dome of the Rock in Jerusalem (691 A.D.). The third in sanctity of all Islam's Holy Places, celebrating both Abraham and the Prophet Muḥammad in the mother-city of the Jewish and the Christian faiths, the Dome remains the most enduring legacy of the Umayyad time to the ethos and symbol-ism of Islam. It is sad that the dynasty with the imagination to retrieve, and so splendidly to adorn, a focal site in history should have succumbed within three-score years to the decadence that the rising tide of the 'Abbāsids swept away.

Baghdad and the 'Abbāsids

The main architect of the new order, and of its capital Baghdad, was the Caliph al-Manṣūr (754–775 A.D.). The center of the government of the *Ummah* now moved to the banks of the Tigris under a dynasty which was to survive through thirty-seven reigns, until 1258, but had its apogee within its first century. After Al-Manṣūr, its most renowned and effective rulers were Al-Mahdī (775–785), Hārūn al-Rashīd (786–809), and Al-Ma'mūn (813–833). Under these rulers Baghdad became a splendid metropolis, presiding with verve as well as ruthless power over a vast dominion, enjoying a far-flung commerce and housing one of the greatest intercultural centers of intellectual exchange across the continents and the centuries.

Al-Manṣūr built his *Madīnat-al-Salām,* or "city of peace," on the west bank of the Tigris, a city planned in concentric circles with the royal palace at the heart and four gates opening to the four points of the compass. Hence it was called *Al-Mudawwarah,* "the circular." His famous viziers, or ministers, the Barmakids, built their lavish palaces and gardens on the eastern bank where the city spread with three broad bridges spanning the river. The Tigris, with its sister river, the Euphrates, within easy reach westward, had the Persian Gulf downstream as a gateway to the commerce of India and the Far East. Northward and westward the rivers linked the city with Syria, the Fertile Crescent, and beyond to Byzantium, with whom the early 'Abbāsids battled long, and with Charlemagne, the Frankish Emperor, whose delegations they received in elegant diplomacy.

Heir to all the physical advantages of an ancient cradle of civilization, the new metropolis rapidly climbed to a peak of cultural achievement. The Arab qualities of the best Umayyads, fed from desert origins, gave way to a largely Persian and cosmopolitan style of authority. Under the greatest 'Abbāsids Islam developed a sophistication it had not hitherto known. Only the religious definition and the Arabic language endured within the revolution in identity which the eighth, ninth and tenth centuries achieved.

Worlds away from the Qur'ān is that other great classic of the Arabic tongue, *The Thousand and One Nights,* which epitomizes Hārūn al-Rashīd's Baghdad. It is a composite array of character and circumstance drawn from sources as widespread as Persia, India, Egypt, Syria, China and Greece. Yet it represents a powerful local mirror. The travels of Sindbad certainly reflect the far-ranging merchandise of the city's traders. The escapades of caliphs, courtiers, artisans and peasants tell the tale of the society that lived and loved them in their unfailing profusion. Hārūn's boon companion, the poet Abū Nuwās, roamed the streets with his royal master and commanded vast sums for his poetic ventures. The resourcefulness of Shāhrazād in sustaining the nightly recital was no more than the resources of wealth, of intrigue, of magnificence, of curious lore, that lay to hand around the palaces and gardens and *sūqs,* or that belonged with the travellers, the slaves, the eunuchs, the *qāḍīs,* the viziers, the merchants, the knaves, that haunted it.

But Baghdad's incredible urban genius had other, more serious, qualities. Al-Ma'mūn founded his *Bait al-Ḥikmah,* or "House of Wisdom," which housed a library as famous as any in medieval history, and was nursery of many of the celebrated names and works in Islamic scholarship. The most abiding achievement of its scholars was the steady translation of works of Greek and Syriac learning into Arabic. By this means the writings of Aristotle, the medicine of Galen and Hippocrates, the geometry of Euclid and, later, *The Republic* of Plato found their fertilizing way into Muslim culture and ultimately, by this circuitous route, back to the Western, European world, through Latin versions of the Arabic. One famous translator was the 'Ibādī Christian, Ḥunayn ibn-Isḥāq (809–873), whom Al-Ma'mūn appointed director of the translation academy, and who, with the assistance of members of his family, transmitted Greek sciences via Greek/Syriac/Arabic to eastern readers. In this way anatomy, astronomy, medicine, chemistry, philosophy and literature, grammar and logic, penetrated Islamic thinking with rich consequences for its subtlety and depth and alertness. Another notable translator, a Sabian, was Thābit ibn Qurrah (d. 901). The stimulus they gave to learning and enquiry may be gauged from Ibn al-Nadīm's *Al-Fihrist,* or "Index" completed in 988. The "Index" was a remarkable compendium of writings in Arabic, with notes on contributing authors, compiled by one of the numerous booksellers of Baghdad and a mine of erudition, as it were, about erudition, and covering a multifarious culture from perfumes, botany and pharmacy, to history, geology and astronomy. Even the slave girl, Tawaddud, in *The Thousand and One Nights,* could pass muster in an exacting catechism by the learned, extending through twenty-three "nights."[2]

Al-Ma'mūn's *Bait al-Ḥikmah* had its own observatory and teaching facilities and book loan. In the eleventh century an Academy, *Al-Niẓāmiyyah,* was founded in Baghdad to provide residential teaching on what later became the university model. Though by that time a strong theological dogmatism had overtaken the exciting intellectualism of the ninth and tenth centuries, it was this 'Abbāsid culture which lay at the root of the mental competence which even dogmatism by then required. Meanwhile the skills and aspirations Baghdad symbolized had been busily applied to the vexing problems of revelation and reason, dogma and philosophic enquiry, Divine and human will, which we noted briefly in Chapter 1. The *Ummah* in its Baghdad vintage generated one of the most significant theological tensions—Shī'ah issues apart—in its long history, that between the Mu'tazilah and the upholders of what only later we call "orthodoxy." The former, who were much persecuted until they found caliphal favor under Al-Ma'mūn, when they themselves turned persecutors, present a somewhat bewildering picture of what may be loosely called theological subtlety and zealous dogmatism. They were involved—what theology is not?—in the human aspects of revelation. How could the eternal Qur'ān be enmeshed in the very temporal vicissitudes of the Prophet's time and place? To the doctrine that the Holy Book was "uncreated" they opposed the notion of its "createdness." *Tanzīl,* by which it "came down" upon the Prophet, necessarily involved its contents, and its nature, in temporality. It could not, therefore, be described as "uncreated." The opponents of the Mu'tazilah insisted that *Tanzīl*, however paradoxically, mediated the eternal into time without affecting its eternity. The problem really had no solution, in the terms within which the controversy set it. But it was, none the less, a measure both of the temerity thinking had by then acquired and of the sophistication by which "orthodoxy" needed to be equipped. The controversy could not have arisen in the Damascus of the Umayyads.

Cordoba in Iberian Islam

Damascus found its Baghdad in the far west. When the first 'Abbāsid, with vicious brutality, had sought the total liquidation of Umayyad heirs, 'Abd al-Rahmān escaped and fled in disguise through North Africa, eluding 'Abbāsid spies and pursuers. In the best tradition of his Arab ancestry he succeeded in establishing his rule in Cordoba in 756, rallying Umayyad Spain to his side and frustrating the efforts of the 'Abbāsids to undo him, despite their attempts to recruit Charlemagne against him. During his reign the foundations were laid for the splendor that reached its secure zenith in the long reign of another 'Abd al-Rahmān (the third) between 912 and 961. Again the quality of the Islamic *Ummah* embodied itself in the architecture, the letters, the society, of a great capital, in emphatic demonstration of its ubiquitous vitality.

As in Damascus, the capital's crowning glory was the great Mosque, with its forest of pillars, which the first 'Abd al-Rahmān erected to be the focal point of the city. Cordoba came to muster a population of half a million, served by more than three hundred public baths, some seventy libraries and seven hundred other mosques. The householders provided street lighting by a system of lamps hung outside their dwellings. In the ninth century the capital was able to establish close intellectual links with Baghdad, bringing poets, translators and lawyers, and emulating, from 970, the "university" pattern of mosque academy pioneered by *Bait al-Ḥikmah*. Its Cordoban equivalent was the work of Al-Ḥakam (961–76). Among the famous canon lawyers was Ibn Yaḥyā (d. 849) who brought the "school" of Mālik ibn Anas from Baghdad.

Many of the social strains that had characterized Umayyad Damascus were reproduced in its western offspring. The status of the Christian *dhimmīs* was comparable, though the near adjacence of the Christian powers of Castile, Aragon and Leon within the Iberian peninsula, and the ebb and flow of strife with them, sharpened the religious antipathies. The recruits to Islam, known in Spain as the *Muwalladun,* or "the generated," rivalled the Syrian *mawālis* in their zealousness, and incurred much the same inferior status as compared with the genuine Arab Muslims. This situation was further complicated by the racial mixture, including Berbers from North Africa, recruited by Islam in its passage across the Maghrib for its ventures into Spain, and the Goths and other strains. Cordoba records some of history's most puzzling instances of Christian self-immolation and ardent martyrdom by the sword of Islam and of the passions begotten of religious antipathy.

The student has to go beyond the collapse of Umayyad power in Cordoba, in 1031, into the confusion of the eleventh and twelfth centuries, to encounter Cordoba's greatest intellectuals, namely Ibn Ḥazm (994–1064) and Ibn Rushd (1126–98). The former, the grandson of a *muwallad,* was a prolific writer in theology, philosophy and tradition. His most famous work "On Sects, Heresies and Creeds," makes him a pioneer in the careful, detailed study of "varieties of religious experience," at least as these were formulated in historically recognizable expression. Ibn Ḥazm's *The Ring of the Dove,* is a delightful treatise on the art of love and the psychology of manners, as well as a skillful portrayal of Cordoban society. Ibn Rushd, known in the west as Averroes, was *qāḍī,* astronomer, physician, commentator on Aristotle (via the Baghdad Arabic versions), and a seminal figure in the philosophic ancestry of Thomas Aquinas. He countered the anti-intellectualism of Al-Ghazālī with his reassertion of the role of reason. Averroeism, as understood in the west, was thought to involve the concept of two kinds of truth, the one rational and the other revelatory—a notion which Aquinas set himself to transcend in his effort after a *Summa* of unitary truth. Ibn Rushd, both in his antecedents and his legacy, was a frontier figure in Islam and, as such, a powerful personal symbol of his native city.

Cairo, the Fāṭimids and Beyond

When 'Amru, the victorious Muslim general, set up a simple mosque in his camp at Fusṭāṭ, on the Nile, in 642, it was the first Muslim place of prayer in Africa. It was the beginning of the saga of Cairo (*Al-Qāhirah* in Arabic, "the conquering"), first of today's Islamic cities.

It took centuries to bring it into prominence. In Umayyad times and through the 'Abbāsid heydey, it was a provincial center. But when Baghdad began to decline in the tenth century, the Ṭulūnids, followed by the Ikhshīdids, gave Cairo a new destiny which blossomed when Al-'Azīz (975–996) brought the Fāṭimid dynasty from Tunis (where it had been established in 901) and inaugurated a régime that lasted until 1171. Al-'Azīz claimed descent from Fāṭimah, the Prophet's daughter. The Fāṭimids were Shī'ahs and their story illustrates the vagaries to which Shī'ah attitudes are subject. The sixth Caliph, Al-Ḥākim (996–1021), originator of the Druse religion, was mad. Declaring himself an incarnation of deity he broke away from the generally mild attitudes of the Fāṭimids towards their *dhimmī* subjects and inflicted fierce persecution, destroying the Holy Sepulchre in Jerusalem. In part, thereby, the provoker of the Crusades, it is fitting that his dynasty was finally terminated, in 1171, by Salāḥ al-Dīn, the Ayyūbid, the successful antagonist of the Crusaders.

The Shī'ah character of the Fāṭimid Caliphate did not deeply endanger the strong Sunnī temper of Egyptian Islam, which Salāḥ al-Dīn quickly reasserted. It did mean, however, that a Shī'ah impulse generated what was to become the most famous of all Islamic centers of Sunnī theology and law, namely Al-Azhar, the great mosque-university, built in 972–973. Its traditional pattern of Quranic exegesis, scholastic theology, logic, grammar, rhetoric, and *fiqh,* set the classic form of orthodox education, by memorizing, citation of authorities, and utter respect for the faithfully transmitted past, of which Al-Azhar became the supreme exemplar. Its great open court, or *Ṣaḥn,* and the pillared porticos and colonnades *(arwiqah),* have housed generations of Muslim students from the whole dispersion of Islam in an abiding ritual of educational fidelity.

There were other adornments of Fāṭimid Cairo, resembling but hardly equalling the architectural and scholarly exploits of Baghdadis and Cordobans. Among the illustrious names is that of Ibn al-Haytham (known in the west as Al-Hazen) (965–1039), the father of modern optics. Fāṭimid art was strong in wood carving, tiling and glazing; it produced exquisite textiles, and brought a standard of excellence to the craft of bookbinding.

The second era in Cairene history was that of the Mamlūks, the slave dynasties which succeeded the Ayyūbids around 1250 and were finally overthrown by the Ottoman Turks in 1517. The greatest of Islamic writers, and the most prolific in those years, was Jalāl al-Dīn al-Suyūṭī (1445–1505), a Cairo light of encyclopedic range. But out of a confusing, and often sordid, welter of political changes and short-lived rulerships, it is well to focus on Ibn al-Fāriḍ, the finest of Cairenes, a contemporary of Francis of Assisi. It is tempting to speculate that possibly they met when Francis, in 1219, visited the Ayyūbid ruler, Al-Kāmil. Ibn al-Fāriḍ, who was born and died in Cairo, and whom we quoted at the conclusion of Chapter 5, was the greatest of all Sufi poets of Arab birth in Islam. His breadth of religious sympathy, though hardly representative of Mamlūk Cairo, deserves to be allowed to represent it. He wrote in his *Dīwān:*

> "And if the mosque's *miḥrāb* be lighted up
> By the Qur'ān, no church's massive pile
> Is wasted with the Gospel open there;
> No synagogue, wherein the Torah's scrolls
> Moses delivered to the chosen folk
> Are nightly read by rabbis at their prayers.
> And if, in idol-house, the devotee
> Bows down to stones, rush not in zealous rage
> Beyond the disavowal faith requires.
> Many a one, unspotted by the shame
> Of polytheist idol-mongering,
> In spirit worships Mammon . . ."[3]

The greatest of the adopted sons of Cairo was Ibn Khaldūn, whose synoptic view of the *Ummah* and of history will conclude this chapter.

Istanbul and the Ottomans

From 1517, until its termination by the Turks themselves in 1924, the Ottoman Caliphate dominated western Islam. Broad areas of Eastern Europe, as well as Turkey proper, the Arab East, Iraq, the eastern and western littorals of Arabia, the Yemen, Egypt, and North Africa as far as the west of Algeria, belonged within its authority. Even in weakness and decay it retained a legend of forceful power. When it was abolished, it was sharply mourned by the Khilāfatist movement in India where it had never ruled. Its greatest personalities were classic exponents of Sunnī Islam.

Istanbul was their symbol and shrine—a city which, both in dramatic seizure at the hands of Islam in 1453, and calculated rejection by Atatürk in 1925 as the relict of a repudiated concept, has epitomized the fortunes of Islam for half a millenium.

When Constantinople fell to Muḥammad II it was the long delayed achievement of a lasting Muslim dream. As early as 669, Umayyad forces had reached its very walls. Hārūn al-Rashīd had won his spurs more than a century later in battle for the Bosphorus. But the Citadel of Byzantium contrived to hold out against both Caliphates and to survive the Crusaders. The tides of struggle oscillated across Asia Minor between the dynasts of the two religions. The tiny princedom, which was at length to gain the day, had been set up at Brusa close to Constantinople in 1326: Its petty rulers, the Osmanli Turks, had originated, like so many other makers of destiny in Islam, from the racial melting pot of Central Asia or Chinese Turkestan. From their base on the southern shore of the Sea of Marmora they consolidated and, in the fateful year 1453, attained the long coveted prize.

The event was as climatic for Islam as it was cataclysmic for Eastern Christendom. Islamic power now stood firmly across the bridge of Asia and Europe, and within a century the Ottomans were established from Muscat to the Danube. Their story, in some measure, resembles the initial expansion of original Islam and there were several of the same factors—nomadism seeking new lands, a love of arms for their own sake, a will to conquest, a readiness to absorb older culture on condition of total surrender. Only the central Asian origins made the different quality. The Ottomans shared the Umayyads' instinct to adopt where they had physically supplanted, with the same ruthless self-consciousness of power, and the same urge to dominate in stone and splendor. Islamic institutions drew new strength from Turkish vitality, while the Turkish will and spirit found superb occasions in Islam. This periodic mutual kindling of peoples and religion is what makes the *Ummah* so fascinating for historians.

If we liken the Ottomans, in these ways, to the Umayyads then their Muʿāwiya was Sulaymān the Magnificent (1520–1566), whose reign might be claimed as the most glorious in all the annals of Islam. Unlike Muʿāwiya, he built on others' foundations. Warrior, statesman, legist, builder, and potentate, he supremely expressed the vital forces of his race and creed. Also known as *Al-Qānūnī*, "the lawgiver," he achieved a massive codification of law and set the pattern for the characteristic centralization and bureaucratic organization which, in feebler unscrupulous hands, was to become the undoing of the Empire.

The great Saint Sophia Cathedral of Constantinople, home of Justinian and John Chrysostom, became the Mosque of Islam in Istanbul, its eastern sanctuary giving way to the dais of the Muslim *minbar* and *miḥrāb*. The angles of orientation, of course, did not tally, and the abiding symbol of a religious astigmatism is there to this day, when the Saint Sophia has become a museum. Was it, conceivably, for that reason that Sulaymān determined to build newly and outdo the inherited edifice with his vast Sulaymāniyyah Mosque, its dome even larger still? Sinān, his architect, ardently concurred and Istanbul became a city of endless minarets and domes, its architectural glories outdoing in number, size and grandeur every other capital in Islamic history.

Sulaymān's court also vied effectively with those that have become legendary in Islam. The arts, poetry, music, and crafts flourished. Ottoman literature, written in Turkish in Arabic characters and with endless word borrowings from Arabic and Persian, boasted many famous historians, poets and mystics. The greatest of the poets was Bāqī (1526–1600), ornament of the court of Sulaymān. His most famous piece was an elegy mourning the Caliph's death . . .

> "That master-rider of the realm of bliss
> For whose careering steed the field of the world was narrow.
> The infidels of Hungary bowed their heads to the temper of his blade,
> The Frank admired the grain of his sword.
> He laid his face to the ground, graciously, like a fresh rose petal,
> The treasurer of time put him in the coffer, like a jewel."[4]

Caliphal passing meant tragedy for the brothers of the successor. It was the barbarous Ottoman custom to put to death all brothers and their pregnant wives or slave-women, in a ruthless procedure to preclude intrigues against the succession. Fratricide was performed by strangling with a silken bowstring, as a mark of royal dignity. Though this system, first promulgated by the conqueror of the city, helped, as he said, to "preserve the order of the world," it also contributed deeply to Ottoman decay. When the law of primogeniture took effect around 1618 and the Ottomans ceased to liquidate their close relatives, they immured their princes within the Seraglio, to live with their mothers and their women. Either way, they squandered their vitality and in the long run drained themselves into degeneracy.

Yet, even when the splendor had departed, the imposing edifice persisted. In the long reign of Sulṭān ʿAbd al-Ḥamīd II (1876–1908), Istanbul became a symbol of brutal tyranny to rising movements of Arab nationalism within its Arab provinces, movements which the Young Turks, and their predecessors before 1875, had paralleled within Turkish society. But the ideals of liberal government were not to prevail in those terms. The Ottoman regime finally went down in the debacle of the First World War and out of the ruins a secular, laïc, Turkish nationalism, with Muṣṭafā Kemal Atatürk (1881–1938) as its supreme architect, warrior and token, emerged. It affirmed its new temper by opting for a new capital, Ankara, around the ancient Ancyra, and turned its back on the legend and the reality of Istanbul.

Modern bulldozers have since played havoc with the old domiciles and *sūqs*. Despite its downgrading, Istanbul proves irrepressible. Its majestic shrines and commanding natural endowments sustain it against all adversity. Even the dervish Orders are alive again, after their three decades of secular proscription under Atatürk. *Islambol,* "full of Islam," a version of Istanbul which sometimes appeared on Ottoman coinage and decrees, is a neat sufficient word but *not* an epitaph.

Bukhara, Samarqand, Tashkand

Between the Oxus and the Jaxartes Rivers, south and east of the Aral Sea, Umayyad Islam established a distant frontier with Chinese Turkestan and with Buddhism. "What is beyond the River"—as the region was known in Damascus —namely Transoxiana, resembled the Umayyad capital in its joy of waters and its delectable gardens and orchards. Travelers likened the Ṣughd valley to a paradise, joining the two cities of Bukhara and Samarqand in a single fertility, one hundred miles apart. Some two hundred miles further east was the Uzbek center of Tashkand. The area was subdued by the Umayyads in the first two decades of the eighth century, though Tashkand itself was not occupied until 751.

The region attained its finest flower in the period of the Sāmānids, who ruled from 874 until the end of the tenth century. They were nominally tributary to the ʿAbbāsids but contrived to enjoy a virtual independence. Their capital, Bukhara, was celebrated for the most eminent of Muslim physicians, Al-Rāzī who, under the Latinized name Razes, was to be a germinal figure in the history of medicine in the West. The great traditionalist, Al-Bukhārī (810–870), took his name from the city and gained a reputation for sanctity as great as that of any other person in Sunnī Islam, after the Prophet. His corpus of edited traditions is among the most widely cherished sources of Muslim piety. An inveterate traveler, as all traditionalists needed to be, his fame exemplifies another feature of "the golden road to Samarqand,"—the highway along which a cosmopolitan variety of traffic passed.

One of the region's most important commodities was paper, which first became available to the Islamic world, via the three cities, in the ninth century. Each became a busy center of its manufacture or sale, especially Samarqand, where book merchants operated from distant parts. There were numerous *madrasahs* for the study of theology. The youthful prodigy, Ibn Sīnā, was the most famous student of the Bukhara academy. Its relations were very close with Baghdad.

But, if fertile and cultured, the territory of the three cities lay athwart the path of successive invaders from Central Asia, including Jenghiz Khān, the ruthless despoiler of the Middle East, and Tīmūr (Tamerlane), whose devastations at the turn of the fourteenth century in Baghdad (sacked 1393) and Damascus (1401) and beyond, fearfully battered the whole fabric of Islam. Tīmūr made his capital at Samarqand, where he died in 1404. The region had a modest recovery of local pride and prosperity under the Shaybānids, whose authority exactly spanned the sixteenth century. One Shaybānid ruler sent to the Punjab to inquire into the dubious religious innovations of the mighty Akbar.

For all the strength of Sunnī *'ulamā'* from the renowned academies of this region, its most vigorous form of Islam was its itinerant Sufism, especially of the Naqshabandiyyah and Chishtiyyah Orders. The wandering dervishes brought a vivid, if compromised, Islam to nomadic peoples northward and eastward from these cities. With their *zāwiyas,* or devotional meeting points, and cultic chants and prayers, they could be readily absorbed by tribal patterns and may often have been received as the ancestral *shamans* had been.

Cities and nomads, the region was Islamic frontier territory. It is interesting to recall that Bukhara, time-honored *Quṭb al-Islām,* "pole of Islam," and Tashkand, were important centers of Muslim encounter with the Communist revolution. Russia occupied the area in the 1860s. The fortunes of the cities and their peoples before and after the coming of the Soviets, though little known generally in the West, illustrate several facets of Islam. Even before the turn of the twentieth century, but especially after Russia's defeat by Japan in 1905, there were stirrings of socialist ideals. These were directed both against the tyranny of the Tsars and against the conservative Muslim *'ulamā'.* Known as *Jadīds,* or renewers, these reformers drew some of their vigor from the dynamism of Jamāl al-Dīn al-Afghānī (1839–1897), a leader of pan-Islamic revival, who traveled at least to neighboring Afghanistan, if not to Bukhara itself, and whose stimulus touched many Arab and Turkish "renewers" also, including Muḥammad 'Abduh, in Damascus, Cairo and Istanbul.

Muslim socialists of the Bukhara region drew their inspiration from orthodox sources in Islam, interpreting the original mission of the Prophet—as many others have done in this century—as a movement of social protest against established privilege and exploitation. At the same time, Islam helped to toughen their ethnic revolt against Russian pressures. After the Soviet Revolution, the same ethnic loyalties meant a deep ambivalence. Russian dominance persisted and ethnic-Muslim thinking had either to accept it and join in militant irreligion, or inwardly reject it and close ranks within a persecuted faith. In the years between 1917 and World War II, Muslims in the Bukhara Tashkand region underwent fierce anti-Islamic suppression. Though methods since 1950 have been less militant, the essential, ideological hostility to Islam remains. In that ideology the picture of original Islam is radically transformed from that of the *Jadīds.* Official Communist pressure sees Muḥammad's mission as "providing religious pretext for plundering expeditions organized by the Arab aristocracy." The Prophet himself it sees as "a member of the feudal ruling classes"—a far cry from the *Jadīds'* heroic resister, on behalf of the poor, against the capitalist merchant-bankers, the Quraish.

What Al-Bukhārī, the traditionalist, would make of this contrasted interpretation of his central figure, eleven centuries after the completion of his great corpus of tradition, is hard to guess. While ideologies, as the name implies, are always ready to find in classic history the ideas they seek, the objective critic would certainly have to conclude that the *Jadīds* and those like them were much nearer to the reality in Muḥammad's Mecca.[5]

Delhi and the Mughals

Umayyad expansion had brought Islam knocking on the northwestern gates of India. But after reaching Sind in 712 it proceeded no further, aside from traders on the Kerala coast of Malabar, for another three hundred years. Expansion was not resumed until the arrival of the Ghaznavids in the eleventh century under Maḥmūd, who conquered most of the Punjab. He and his successors originated from Central Asia, one of the several Turco-Afshar peoples that erupted both west and south from those traditional breeding grounds of military conquest. It was Muḥammad of Ghor who, in 1191, established what history knows as the Turkish Sultanate of Delhi and, with him, that city began its distinctive role in the story of Islam. The architectural symbol is the famous Quṭb Minār which Muḥammad erected around the year 1200 to celebrate his victories. A circular tower, five storeys high, in red sandstone and marble, with Arabic inscriptions and fine tracery, it served to mark Delhi on the map of the imagination.

The Sultanate of Delhi which, a century later, had spread its authority southward into the Deccan and which endured until 1398, was primarily a military occupation, depending upon the cities and martial control. Unlike the later Mughals, the Sultanate made little effort to accommodate to Hinduism, preferring a rough Muslim idol breaking, and inflicting the indignities of *dhimmī* status and the *jizyah* taxes upon the conquered. Its greatest positive service was that it guarded the northern approaches and preserved India from the ravages that Jenghiz Khān might otherwise have inflicted.

It was unable, however, to halt the invasion of Tīmūr, who sacked Delhi in 1398. It was out of a century of subsequent confusion and obscurity that a descendant of Tīmūr himself, and the first of the Mughals, Bābur by name, began the dynasty that brought forth one of the most enigmatic and personally powerful figures in all history, Akbar the Great. Bābur, who was himself illiterate, fostered the arts and encouraged a coterie of scholars, poets, architects—a Charlemagne, it could be said, of Islam. Essentially a soldier, he built a strong regime and a vigorous administration by dint of dynamic energy and a magnetic quality of leadership. It was his son and successor, Hūmāyūn, who made Delhi his capital in 1526. Mughal power extended steadily southward and, although Muslims were probably never more than a quarter of the population, contrived to dominate and govern vast areas of the subcontinent and to preside over an astonishing fertility of culture and ideas.

Akbar, born in 1542, came to power at the age of thirteen in 1556. He was Islam's closest approximation to Plato's philosopher-king, but only by deliberating abandoning Islam in the second half of his reign. His early boyhood years were quickly left behind in a resolute pursuit and exercise of power. His ideas developed with a fascinating logic of their own. He began in "the straight path."

But he married a Hindu princess, in a calculated move to relate both his faith and his power to the Hinduism that dominated his domains. Not for him the crude iconoclasm of Muḥammad of Ghor or the policy of mere martial and fiscal suppression of the multitudes. But what he gained in Hindu approval, he forfeited in Muslim disquiet, at least among the pundits. This led, both for state and personal reasons, to increasing claims on his part to a dominant role in the interpretation of Islam itself. He felt his way towards something not unlike the concept of the royal supremacy so central to the English Tudors and Queen Elizabeth (almost to a year his exact contemporary). This is one of the most uncanny, and unconscious, parallels in religious history.

Akbar required the *'ulamā'* to look to him for Quranic interpretation and claimed for himself a direct role in the very orientation of the Muslim believer. There may have been Persian elements in this tendency such as those which, within Shī'ah Islam, had issued into the mediatorial Imāms, and the *mujtahids,* with their esoteric sources of Divine wisdom. In parallel progression, Akbar also drew closer to Hinduism. He abolished the *jizyah* tax in 1579. He welcomed Hindu thinkers to his court, where Jesuit emissaries from the West also debated with him. He was fascinated by the comparison of religions.

Finally in the second half of his reign he forsook Islam decisively and set up in its place a sort of royal theosophy, the *Dīn-i-Ilāhī,* an eclectic monotheism, with prostration symbolically to himself, vegetarianism strongly enjoined, and a rite of initiation drawn from baptism. Devotees pledged property, life, honor, and faith to Akbar and committed themselves to wisdom, chastity, courage and justice as the final virtues, abjuring the Trinity and the Prophet alike.

Thanks to the force of his personality and the vigor of his power, Akbar's intriguing experiment in religious invention held together while he lived. But it did not long survive his death. It earned him the enmity of orthodox Islam and demonstrated the enormous problems of the religious innovator even when in possession of total political authority. But, in the abstract, and in intellectual range, it was a rare phenomenon in Islamic life, an attempt to come to terms with the irreducible presence of Hinduism, and to tackle the problems of religious pluralism within a single statehood.

It was under Akbar's successors, Jahāngīr and Shāh Jahān, that Delhi came by its most elegant monuments. Akbar's own capital had been either Agra or Lahore, and Ajmer was the center of the pilgrimage of his new religion, an Indian substitute for Mecca. It was Shāh Jahān who built the majestic Tāj Mahāl at Agra, and the Great Mosque and Red Fort of Delhi, where the most splendid glories of the dynasty are found. In the long reign of the last of the dominant Mughals, Aurangzeb (1657–1707), the house returned sharply to Islamic orthodoxy, after a sanguinary start in which close members of Aurangzeb's own family were brutally eliminated, in a *takht yā takhtah* ("throne or coffin") struggle of succession. Steady decline began to set in before Aurangzeb's death and accelerated after it. Delhi's centuries of Mughal authority descended into the confusion and fragmentation that preceded the emergence of British India, with quite different versions of the perennial problems for which Akbar had offered his at once ambitious and naïve solution. The ultimate partition that followed the demise of the British in India was only further, bitter evidence of how intractable were the problems of Hindu/Muslim society, to which Akbar had turned his strange and lively genius. The Muslim renegade is one of Islam's most towering figures.

Iṣfahān—Glory of "The Great Sophy"

Persian influences played their part in Akbar's India and, grafted on to Hindi, produced Urdu, "the language of the camp." The amalgam, in many other spheres, of things Persian with things Islamic is an absorbing theme for historians of Islam. The Persian genius, it is fair to say, has always been related ambivalently to Islam. It accepted the fact of conquest and its finality, from the early days of the Umayyads. But it has always insisted on its own stamp upon Islam, while Islam, too, thus culturally removed from its Arab origins, has accepted adaptation. The Shī'ah divergence, which we have already studied, is emphatically part of this Persianizing of the first faith, and indicates this cultural resilience of Islam. Persian Muslims became, and have remained, overwhelmingly Shī'ah in allegiance. But Persia has strongly domesticated Islam to itself in numerous other ways, not least in the realm of mystical religion, in art and poetry. It is arbitrary to confine these Persian-Islamic equations to a single symbol of them, or even to Persia itself. But if one has to be chosen, Iṣfahān must qualify. It was the resplendent capital of Shāh 'Abbās, most famous of the Safavids, who flourished from the beginning of the sixteenth century until 1736. "When Isfahan was Isfahan," its wits used to boast, "Cairo was one of its suburbs." The rhyme *Iṣfahān-nīsf-i-jahān* claims that "Isfahan is half of the world."

"The great Sophy," as Shāh 'Abbās was known in the West, reigned from 1586 to 1628. He created a truly celebrated capital along the Zandah Rūd, the only sizeable river on the plateau of mid-Persia, forming a sort of elongated oasis contrived into gardens and courts and reflecting the color and symmetry of tiled domes and minarets. The great Maidān, a vast rectangular area, had the bazaars to the north and the superb Masjid-i-Shāh, or Royal Mosque, to the south, with the smaller Luṭfallāh Mosque on the east, opposite to the 'Ālī Qāpū, or royal "dais" three storeys high from which all could be surveyed. West of this area was the Chahār Bāgh, or four gardens, making a central highway, and housing the most beautiful of *Madrasahs,* with which the city abounded. Southward the river itself was crossed by three unique bridges. These led to the suburb of Julfa, where Shāh 'Abbās concentrated a settlement of Armenians, to whom he gave special immunities in return for the stimulus he expected and received from their ability as traders and artisans. Brought by forced migration from Azarbayjan, they found compensations in their exile, and the Armenian community at Julfā, with its cathedral and library, provides an intriguing chapter in the history of Islam's minorities. In grimmer terms, the Shāh made extensive use of Kurd settlements for defensive purposes on his northern borders beyond Tabriz.

The Shāh was not all sweetness and light. There was, as the cynic might say, "the other half of Isfahan." He had two of his sons put to death and two blinded, in callous, suspicious defense of his throne. Though in theory the slave of the hidden Imām of the Ja'farī or Twelver branch of Shī'ah Islam, he practiced a pattern of autocracy built on notions of Divine right, in which some historians have seen a legacy of Sassānian culture, with its Zoroastrian mystique of power. Certainly the fact that Shī'ah Islam was officially established contributed to the power and repute of the Safavids. It brought large numbers of Shī'ah scholars, exegetes and theologians, and Isfahan, with other cities of Safavid concern, notably Qumm and Mashhad, became lively centers of Shī'ah erudition and exchange.

It was Shāh 'Abbās's policy to localize Islamic pilgrimage for purposes both of trade and prestige. Mashhad, with the tomb of the Imām Rezā, became a serious rival to Mecca itself. Its eminence, under and after the Safavids, is another token of the vital role played by pilgrimage in general in the status and conflicts of Islamic states. Shāh 'Abbās himself set his seal on Mashhad by going there from Isfahan on foot—a journey of some eight hundred miles. The poet celebrated his diligent humility tending the candles at the shrine.

> "The angels from high heaven wing like moths
> Around the candles lighting this paradise and tomb.
> O tender of the wick, use scissors carefully,
> Lest you should clip the wings of Gabriel."

Travelers moved by piety were also regaled with arts. Isfahan's supreme craft was weaving and textiles, but metal ware and the painting of miniatures were highly developed skills.

The last Safavid fell in 1736, to be replaced by Nādir Shāh, founder of the Afshar dynasty, sometimes known as "the Napoleon of the East." He campaigned as far as Bukhara and Afghanistan, lustful for an empire far wider than the Safavids had ever sought. He could not make it good. The splendor had departed. Contemporary Iran is roughly the same territorial expression Safavid Persia had been and the Safavids remain its finest Islamic symbol.

Achen to Gresik: Southeast Asian Islam

With the break up of Pakistan into two separate states, Indonesia has become, numerically, the largest Islamic nation, stretching across a vast archipelago around the main islands of Sumatra, Java and Borneo. It is in Sumatra and Java that Islam has its greatest strength. Some areas, like the country of the Bataks and the island of Bali, have been steadily resistant to Islam. But these are rare exceptions in a region which, with Malaysia, forms a great southern flank of world Islam, always well represented in the Meccan pilgrimage.

The most significant single feature of its history is the degree to which the diffusion of Islam coincided with the assertion of local, ethnic identity against the inroads of Portuguese, Spanish, and later, Dutch, penetration from the West. There is no region of the world where the strength of Islam owed so much, for so long, to the local trading interests facing western competition and the instinctive ability of the religion to move with them.

But the beginnings go further back into the tenth century. Muslim merchants and missionaries, probably from the Malabar coast of South India, and possibly from beyond, planted small communities of adherents around the north tip of Sumatra, notably at Samudra. Early in the thirteenth century Malacca emerged into prominence as an important center of trade and navigation, sited as it was so advantageously on the Malay peninsula by the strait that bears its name. The rise of Malacca brought still more commerce and stimulated Muslim growth on the Sumatran shore in the Partak region, where by the end of the fourteenth century the Sultanate of Acheh was consolidated. From there Islam spread along the coastal areas eastward as far as Gresik on the eastern tip of Java. It is convenient, therefore, to take these two points as representing the dispersion of Indonesian Islam. It is probably wise to assume that this mercantile pattern of Muslim expansion was confined to the centers of trade and only slowly penetrated interior tribal areas. Marco Polo, who visited Sumatra in 1292, writes that the island was very pagan but that the ports were "so much frequented by the Saracen merchants that they have converted the natives to the law of Mahomet."

Indian emissaries from the Delhi region are heard of in the fourteenth century and one, Shaikh Ismā'īl from Mecca, brought the Shāfi'ī school of law which has always predominated in Indonesian Islam. His efforts were furthered by the zealous *Jihād* of Mālik al-Zāhir, a great general in northern Sumatra, whose wars against the tribes inland reproduced the traditional pattern of original Islam. Meanwhile, in the far east of Java, Malik Ibrāhīm was vigorously propagating the faith. His tomb at Gresik (d. 1419) became a place of great veneration in the region. In the same period Megat Iskander Shāh (d. 1424), ruler in Malacca, strengthened the hold of Islam in the peninsula. Hindu and Indian influences are very evident and there were close links with the Sultanate of Delhi.

In 1511 Malacca fell to the Portuguese. The date is an important milestone. In the antecedent struggle for the Straits and in the sequel, through centuries of western presence down to the midtwentieth century, the spread of Islam takes on the character of a race with the West. The confrontation was, in its essence, commercial. But the implications for religion were far reaching. Local rulers—the Achenese are a conspicuous example—were also chief merchants. Their power rested on trade and their income of dues, harbor rights, customs, and markets. The office of *shahbandar,* or port controller, was a crucial factor. Muslim traders came to a virtual monopoly of this function, by their knowledge of the commerce and their ability to harness and to serve local feeling against the European intruders. Religious antipathy coincided with commercial causes and Islam was greatly helped among pagan communities, or among Muslim rulers with pagan hinterlands. Christianity, by the same token, was sadly disserved by the company in which it came. Islam, in the person of *shahbandars,* and their vital role, came to be seen as the natural ally of the locale, and its adoption as the effective means to defense.

As the leading Sumatran Sultanate, Acheh is a useful symbol of this process. It is important also to have always in mind the effect of pilgrimage to Mecca in ensuring cosmopolitan contact and enthusing local forms. Acheh developed a vigorous scholarship with traveling *'ulamā'* and holy men. A Javanese hagiology, *Badad Tanah Jawi,* relating popular sainthood, has been likened by one historian to the Venerable Bede's *The Ecclesiastical History of the English Nation.* The parallel is a suggestive one, that of an identity cherished and renewed by the mediation of the past. After Iskandar Mūdā, its greatest ruler, who reigned from 1608 to 1637, the power of Acheh fell into eclipse.

Throughout, Islam in the archipelago has shown strong Indic and animist influences. The latter tended to develop when, after the coming of the Dutch in the seventeenth century, long distance trade passed out of the hands of the harbor towns, and local commerce turned more into the interior in a web of local marketing. Despite the steady influence of pilgrimage to Mecca in relating the faith to classic standards, and despite the vigor of puritan movements in the nineteenth century of Wahhābī style, Sumatran and Javanese Islam has remained strongly syncretistic, inclined to theosophic, illuminationist mysticism and to popular amalgam with animist cults. By and large, it was also what has been called "an oppositional Islam," supplying the emotional counter to European colonialism, and fortifying itself in the process.

Timbuktu, Saharan and African Islam

The name of Timbuktu has long fascinated western minds, perhaps for its remoteness, and for the sound of its syllables. Its status as a legend is, of course, no final warrant for choosing it here. But how better, if we have to do so, could we symbolize Islam by a single African city? If we link it with its neighbors, Jenne and Gao, on the long crescent of the Niger basin running through the Songhai, it may fittingly stand for the whole Sahara, for the trans-Saharan trade in salt and gold, which was so large an element in the diffusion of Islam, for the great medieval empires of Ghana and Mali, and for the vast sweep of the geographical *Sūdān,* country of the black peoples. This no doubt excludes the seaborne and military penetrations of Islam into Somalia and the east African coastal areas down to Zanzibar. But, otherwise, Islam in Africa may concede to western imagination the poetry of this famous name.

Islamic penetration into Africa came mainly via three routes—the Nile valley and diffusion into the eastern Sudan; the Red Sea and Arabia into the Horn of Africa and southward down the *sawāḥil* (hence Swahili as a language name) or littoral of Kenya and inwards into Tanzania and Uganda and Mozambique; and across the Sahara from the Maghrib and the Berbers of North Africa, and likewise round the great bulge of the western shore of Africa and into the valleys of rivers like Gambia and Senegal. These three main routes of geography in varying degrees complemented one another. The western Sudan came powerfully under the influence of Islam of Maghribi sources.

Along the first route, Islamic expansion did not in the initial seventh century proceed beyond approximately the present southern frontier of Egypt with the Sudan. In Nubia, two powerful Christian kingdoms, Muqarra and 'Alwa, survived into the fourteenth century. By Arabicization and strong Sufi propagation after the fall of those two states, Islam steadily extinguished Sudanese Christianity and came to dominate the entire region.

In the Horn of Africa, the coastal tribes and islands Islamized very early in the Umayyad period but the highlands of Ethiopia formed a bastion of Christian culture which struggled with varying fortunes against the tide of Islamic influence from the coast. The holy city of Harar provides a symbol of Islam's authority in this region, which at times, notably in the sixteenth century, surged with temporary success into the heart of the highlands. The strength of such Muslim conquerors as the Gallas was consolidated, in much steadier and vital terms, by the vigorous activities of Muslim mystics, with their popular following of disciples and itinerant traders.

Trade and small coastal entrepôts, like Mombasa, Malindi and Kilwa, appear to have been the main factors in the story of Islam along the East African shore. Penetration into the interior does not seem to have been seriously attempted until the nineteenth century. The orientation of the *sawāḥil* was towards Arabia and the Ḥaḍramaut. No Bantu communities embraced Islam until the time of Sulṭān ibn Sulṭān (d. 1856) of Muscat, who ruled from Zanzibar and helped to bring about a fusion of Islamic and Bantu cultures into the present Swahili amalgam. Trade then penetrated deeply into Tanzania and Mozambique, where the Yao peoples form the most solidly Muslim element today. Conversion followed trade and seems to have been greatly promoted by the direct or indirect consequences of colonial empire. It is in the latter context, also, that Indian Islam came to play an appreciable part in the fortunes of East Africa, where the Ismà'īlī sect of the Shī'ah is strongly represented, and where indentured laborers came from the subcontinent for railway building and similar development, planting large communities of Muslims in Kenya, Uganda and Tanzania, and indeed as far south as Durban in Natal.

The story of Islam in West Africa is closely bound up with trans-Saharan trade, whether by the westerly route through Marrakesh, or Sijilmasa, to Awdaghost and the ancient empire of Ghana; or through Taghaza, Timbuktu and Gao; or through the central Sahara from Tunis, Tuat, Hoggar and Kano, or easterly from Tripoli to Kanem, with an eastward route from Kanem through Darfur and the Sudan to the Nile. North African sources had brought Islam into the Senegal region by the eleventh century. Salt from the north, so vital to sub-Saharan economies, was traded for gold and slaves from the south. The Almoravids of Morocco *(Al-Murābiṭūn)* (1056–1147) conquered the Ghana capital in 1076 and hastened the disintegration of its power. Islam became the religion at least of chiefs and traders, while the tribal nomads remained largely pagan. Out of the disintegration that followed the superficial authority of the Almoravids, the great empire of Mali developed in the thirteenth century. It produced one of the most colorful and splendid of Muslim potentates, Mansa (king) Musa (d. 1332), who ruled from Senegal to the Hausalands east of the Niger. It was then that Timbuktu, founded around 1100 as a Tuareg trading post, came into its own as a major center of Islamic culture. Mansa Musa made a spectacular impression in Cairo and in Mecca during the pilgrimage he undertook in 1324–1325. He had no less than eight thousand retinue with him across the Sahara and gold enough to cause a glut of it on the Cairo market as he passed through. His fame was known in western Europe and contemporary travelers bore enthusiastic witness to the good order of his empire and the prosperity of his people.

Timbuktu and Mali power fell into decline a century and a half after Musa, to be replaced by a kingdom, based at the Songhai region along the great loop of the Niger River. Under its greatest leader, Askia Muḥammad (1494–1528), Timbuktu, with his capital Gao, resumed a lively authority. The Askia made his own pilgrimage in 1495–1497, with the same éclat, bringing to Mecca the eloquent tribute of a religious rulership extending almost as widely as the Mali power before it. Askia Muḥammad's regime established itself by a definite policy of Islamic comprehension of the tribes, in contrast to the combative, and animist, character of Sonni 'Alī's power whom he superseded.

After Askia Muḥammad's death the regime was plagued by problems and finally succumbed to Moroccan invasion at the end of the sixteenth century. Paganism regained ground strongly. By the eighteenth century the effective hope of the Islamic future lay with the Qādiriyyah and the Tijāniyyah Orders who, in the eighteenth and nineteenth centuries, brought a strong revival, the former by pacific and the latter often by compulsive means. Various Hausa kingdoms had by that time embraced Islam, and in 1775 a noted Fulani leader, 'Uthmān Dan Fodio, preached a Wahhābī style puritanism which developed into a veritable *Jihād* in the first decade of the nineteenth century. Dan Fodio's son, Muḥammad Bello, established the new Fulani empire at Sokoto. Father, son, and a brother 'Abdullāhi, were all scholarly men, and their leadership inaugurated a powerful new chapter in West African Islam, within which whole areas of paganism were absorbed and a more sophisticated, meticulous form of Islam, with considerable Arabicization, developed, the impetus of which was maintained until the colonial period.

In a geographical dimension so vast, no summary can do justice to the endless diversities and vicissitudes of religious life in African realms.[6] The African and the Islamic fused in a bewildering variety of forms. The single worship of God inherited, but did not always subdue, the plural associates of the pagan high god. Ramaḍān often became the first element in Islamization, with pagan rites, divination practices and ancestor veneration persisting, before Ṣalāt or Zakāt were truly understood. Throughout, the pilgrimage was the great leaven, serving to bring the diffused compromises within the correctives and the spell of the Meccan focus.

Old cults die hard. Religious change is liable to be accompanied by attitudes of adaptation and the divided mind, in which the believer retains emotionally what he has renounced formally. But, though the African ethos, in all its incredible fertility, sets its own unmistakable imprint upon the Islam it absorbs, it is fair to say that Islam, however diluted or tentative, has, over the generations, a tenacious and durable quality. The African Muslim may not belong well, but he knows that he belongs.

The *Ummah* in a Travelogue: 1325–1354 A.D.

If the student asks how this vast dispersion might come imaginatively alive at some chosen moment in its long sequence, Islam has the answer in the person of Ibn Baṭṭūṭa, the most tireless of its many wanderers. Born in Tangier in 1304, he began his long saga when he was twenty-one. In all he covered no less than seventy-five thousand miles, driven by an insatiable curiosity, a restless energy and an enjoyment of human esteem. He was an emissary for potentates as, for example, in his mission to the Mongol Emperor of China on behalf of the Sultan of Delhi. But it was the pilgrimage impulse, several times renewed, which first set him on the road. In some cities he made protracted sojourn, serving as a *qādi.* With the possible exception of Gresik, every one of the cities we have just reviewed fell within his tireless itinerary.

His generation did not coincide with the high peaks of Islamic splendor. But the broad plateau, as it was in the second quarter of the fourteenth century, lay open to his observant eye and his ubiquitous inspection. The mere catalogue of his journeys staggers the prosaic mind, though it is eloquent of the cosmopolitan openness and cultural interpenetration of Muslim communities: Tangier, Egypt, Syria, Mecca, Syria, Iraq, Khuzistan, Mecca again for three years, East Africa, Mecca again, Constantinople, Khurasan, Delhi, the Maldive Islands, Ceylon, China, Assam, Sumatra, Malabar, Syria, Mecca again, Egypt, Libya, Tunis, Algeria, Morocco, the Niger, Mali, Andalusia, and finally again to his birthplace, Tangier.

It appears that he kept a book of notes. But many of his reminiscences were written down by a scribe, Ibn Jubayy, at the great man's dictation years later. Some critics have questioned his veracity. Often, like T. E. Lawrence generations later, his situations were such that no independent evidence avails. But where it does, there are grounds for believing that Ibn Baṭṭūṭa does not willfully deceive. And finally, accuracy must be seen as a relative issue, given the interpretative interests of the man, the feel he can communicate of what he chose to note and what he recollected. Much of what has passed into the telling of historians derives from his observation. It is to him, for example, we owe the details about Mansa Musa of the Mali state. After referring to the high degree of public security under Musa's rule, Ibn Baṭṭūṭa continues:

> "They are careful to observe the hours of prayer, and assiduous in attending them in congregations, and in bringing up their children to them. On Fridays, if a man does not go early to the mosque, he cannot find a corner to pray in, on account of the

crowd. It is a custom of theirs to send each man his boy with his prayermat: the boy
spreads it out for his master in a place befitting him (and remains on it) until he comes
to the mosque. Their prayer-mats are made of the leaves of a tree resembling a date
palm, but without fruit."

At Timbuktu, he encountered hippopotami by the Niger (which he mistook for
the Nile) and "marvelled at their enormous bodies, taking them to be elephants,"
and registered his amazement when they took to the water.

Animals, mines, customs, cooking, furniture, manners, buildings, coinage,
complexions—everything is grist for the traveler's mill. He came upon Bukhara
at a sad ebb in its fortunes.

"We travelled for a whole day through a continuous series of orchards, streams, trees,
and buildings and reached the city of Bukhara. This city was formerly the capital
of the lands beyond the Oxus. It was destroyed by the accursed Tinkiz (Jenghiz
Khan), the Tatar . . . and all but a few of its mosques, academies and bazars are now
lying in ruins . . . There is not one of its inhabitants today who possess any theological
learning or makes any attempt to acquire it. We lodged at a hospice in the suburb
of Bukhara called Fath Abad. The shaykh entertained me at his house and invited
the principal men of the town. We spent a most delightful night there: the Qur'ān
readers recited in pleasing voices, and the preacher delivered an address, and then
they sang melodiously in Turkish and Persian."

Revisiting Damascus after twenty years absence, he wrote:

"I had left a wife of mine there pregnant, and I learned while I was in India that she
had borne a male child, whereupon I sent to the boy's maternal grandfather, who
belonged to Miknasa in Morocco, forty gold dinars in Indian money. When I arrived
in Damascus on this occasion, I had no thought but to enquire after my son. I went
to the mosque where, by good fortune, I found Nūr al-Dīn al Sakhāwī, the īmām
and principal shaikh of the Mālikites. I greeted him but he did not recognise me, so
I made myself known to him and asked him about the boy. He replied: 'He is dead
these twelve years.' "

From a Tangier scholar in the same city he learned of the death of his father
fifteen years earlier. A year later, after another Meccan pilgrimage, he decided
in Cairo to return home,

". . . moved by the longing called forth within me by memories of my home, by
yearning for my family and friends, and by love of my country which surpasses in
my eyes all other lands."[7]

But even this, in 1349, was not the end. Spain and Mali and Bornu still lay ahead.
He survived fifteen years after his final return, enjoying his native Morocco. There
is no more intriguing human measure of the Islamic *Ummah* than this indefatiga-
ble traveler.

Ibn Khaldun—Theorist of Islamic Society

Our survey of the *Ummah* in its city symbols, cursory as it is, has at least
indicated the range of Islamic dispersion and diversity. It could not be better

concluded than by a brief reckoning with the great Ibn Khaldūn. For he was, more than any other figure in Islamic writing, a philosopher of civilization, ambitious to relate the finality of everything Islamic, in which he profoundly believed, to the entirety of human history. In the breadth of his interests, he not only anticipated modern sociology, but also broached in his own context the urgent modern theme of the relation of religion to humanity as a whole. For that reason he can serve here as a fitting prelude to the contents of our final Chapter 7.

Born in Tunis in 1332, Ibn Khaldūn died in Cairo in 1406. He lived through acute, if sometimes petty, crises in North African and Spanish Muslim politics. In successive stages of his diplomatic and political career we find him in Fez, Tlemcen, and Bougie, towns of the Maghrib, and in Granada, Damascus, and Alexandria. In the thirteen-eighties, he spent five years on pilgrimage to Mecca, and later lost both goods and family in shipwreck. When he forsook diplomacy for teaching and judgeships, he was still dogged by adversity. There was, therefore, an existential quality about his interrogation of history.

But it was not so much a philosophy of history in the speculative sense which he sought. It was rather a study of the flux of historical movement, an analysis of the life-cycle of states and the rise and fall of empires. He was interested in the bearing of climate, landscape and race on the patterns of culture. He assessed the survival power of human institutions and attempted to describe a geography of politics. All this was contained in his *Al-Muqaddimah,* an introduction to his *History of the Berber Peoples,* which was the fruit of more than fifty years of reflection and scholarship. As a sociology of history it still fascinates twentieth century historians.[8]

The range of his vision had a truly noble quality. It was combined with a sympathetic realism about human foibles. What strikes the modern reader is the fusion of a lively perception of man and an entire faith in revealed dogma. He sought a rational understanding of the panorama of history. But he refused to grant to reason any role in the sphere of religious truth. Revelation meant for him a disallowance of rationality, except in the confirmation of dogmas accepted in their incontrovertible right. "We must believe and know," he wrote, "what we have been commanded to believe and know." "We must not seek to prove its correctness rationally, even if rational intelligence contradicts it." All that must be left to God through the Prophet, as the supreme Lawgiver.

In the same manner, his readiness for the external relations of Islam, for inquiries outside the Islamic civilization, did not admit of any relativity in things Quranic. His universal interests were dogmatically conditioned. He conceded that external philosophy and culture had influenced Islam and that scholastic controversy with non-Muslims without, and heretics within, had tempted the true faith into speculation. But the implicit reliance on intellect that this involved, Ibn Khaldūn deplored wherever Islam was concerned. Even Plato, he noted, had ended in uncertainties about the Divine. "If, after all the trouble and toil, we find only conjectures, the conjectures we had at the beginning may as well suffice us."

Thus his wide-ranging sociology proceeded within the premises of a dog-matic theology which he took wholly on trust and trusted wholly. He responded to Islam's faith about God as "Lord of the worlds" with an eager, even encyclope-dic, interest in the worlds of human time and place, but always under that Lordship dogmatically confessed. He looked for patterns in historical flux, but still received Islam as somehow outside it. The study of history, for him, was expected to illustrate God's dealings, confirm His moral order, attest the Qur'ān, and edify the faithful. His belief in creation, providence, and the seal of prophet-hood in Muḥammad both inspired and circumscribed his motive concepts. He achieved a noble expression of inclusive sympathies, but did so from an entire Islamic self-sufficiency. Perhaps the deepest personal significance of his scholarly labors is that they gave solace to the tribulations of his own biography, all of which makes him an appealing, as well as a monumental, figure.

Is it not the quality of the questions of modern time that they demand the range of mind that Ibn Khaldūn exemplified, although they no longer stay within the borders of the dogmas where he dwelt? He was potentially modern in a medieval time, when Islam was outwardly in command of its world. How should we draw the equation between the *Ummah* and the world now?

7.
Questions of Modern Time

There is, in Surah 56:60, a statement that God is not overtaken by events. "It is not We," says the verse, "who are among the outpaced" or the forestalled. The phrase suggests a man who comes to market and finds that others, there before him, have cornered the goods, or a runner whom other competitors leave behind. The immediate reference in the verse is to the certainty of death, which nothing is going to forestall. But the idea affirms that other aspects of time and history are never such that God is not there before them. So Islam devoutly believes.

But the changes and stresses in the modern world have in them that which makes it look the contrary to wistful, puzzled Muslims and, indeed, others too. It seems as if a time may have arrived in which religion and dogma, if not the God they speak of, have been "overtaken" by developments and left behind by a relentlessly moving history.

The purpose of this final chapter in the religious life of Islam is to face this basic question, to review the Muslim experience that poses it and to explore the various moods and attitudes that respond to it. So doing, we shall be close to a universal religious experience running comparably through all dogmatic systems in the contemporary world.

Our glimpses of general history in the previous chapter sufficed to make us aware of the great resilience and the wide diversity of Muslim culture and institutions. But the twentieth century has become acutely exacting. Issues only latent before have now a sharper urgency and demand a more conscious reckoning than the past has given them. The instinctive Islamic view that history moves forward in the trust of a past finality and an original perfection is strongly challenged by the scientific view that fuller truth is on ahead, or the despairing view that reality is no longer, or nowhere, to be found with certainty.

What, in summary terms, should we say are the prevailing elements in Islamic experience in modern times? The answer broadly is: a nineteenth century forfeiture to foreign empire of a truly Islamic existence; a twentieth century recovery of authentic existence in *Dār al-Islām* once again itself; a discovery that with that restoration were also deep and baffling changes in the world; and contrasted attempts to deal with them. Our business will be to develop in sequence these four themes.

The *Ummah* and the Inroads of the West

All our studies in the previous chapter of cities and their states and caliphates had to do with Islam master in its own house, or houses. The rulers everywhere were Muslim. *Dār al-Islām* existed both by the political test of "Who is the ruler?" and by the religious test of "Are the mosques open and the duties of religion fulfilled?" It was essential that both questions could be answered in the affirmative.

In the nineteenth century (even earlier in India and Indonesia) Western empire came, dislodging and subduing Muslim sovereignty and taking it into non-Muslim hands. It is important to see how this experience represented something, in Muslim eyes, almost as drastic as exile was to Jews in Babylon. True, the Muslim multitudes stayed, for the most part, in their ancestral lands. But those lands ceased to be, politically, *Dār al-Islām*. True, by the merely devotional test of whether the faith could be practiced, Islam was altogether intact. Western viceroys and administrators did not impede Muslim piety. But, for Islamic instincts, such "freedoms" were totally incomplete. Without the right to rule itself Islam was clearly "in exile" from its true being. History, which from the beginning had delivered power into its hands, had bewilderingly gone awry and left Islam to subjugation.

It is true that the Ottoman Empire remained its formal self until World War I. But in fact only Turkey, Afghanistan, Iran and Arabia escaped political tutelage to non-Muslim Europe, and not always these in its indirect forms. Every other part of the Islamic world passed directly into western custody. The British Raj in India and the Dutch Empire in the East Indies were the largest and longest of these alien dominions over Islam. The story in the Arab East is briefer but more bitter. Algeria was finally conquered by France in 1848, Tunis was annexed in 1883, and Morocco was occupied from 1912. Britain set up its protectorate in Egypt in 1882, and shared with France the mandates over the Arab provinces of the Ottoman Empire after 1921. Russia seized control of various Muslim Khanates in Central Asia between the seventeenth and the nineteenth centuries. In Africa, too, Europe took Muslim power from Muslim rulers, in varying ways, until within the last two decades. The *Ummah* of Islam, we may say, was apoliticized. Muslims were governed instead of governing.

The dilemma was very painful for Islamic peoples. Its measure can most easily be taken by reference to Muslim India. The Indian Mutiny of 1857, (or the Indian War of Independence depending on where you read your history), against the British Raj had, in part, to do with this issue. Abortive as it was, it led to a still firmer entrenchment of British power. The Muslims had played a major part in the Mutiny/War and fell back into greater frustration. The regime, it is true, was neither corrupt nor persecuting. Ramaḍān was kept, pilgrimage made, mosques open. But the Ruler was Queen Victoria, not Aurangzīeb, British not Mughal, "Christian" not Muslim. Islam was reduced to being just a religion, and this condition had never been its understanding of itself and contradicted everything that Muḥammad had ever been and thought. And in post-1857 India, British power seemed set in perpetuity. Had God been forestalled?

While the majority of Muslims languished in sullen apathy and dismay, a few, like Sayyid Aḥmad Khān, (1817–1898) ventured to think that perhaps political powerlessness was not a hopeless tragedy, that the situation might even be read as *Dār al-Islām* after all. Indian Muslims, argued Aḥmad Khān, must emulate Western competence and embrace education and progress, welcoming the outlook of their overlords. So ran a pioneer argument of "modernism" within India. Its author was no mere stooge. On the contrary he believed that Islam must carry its credentials to the West, affirm as well as receive, and interpret the one to the other. This he set himself to do by travels to the West and by the establishment of Aligarh College to foster modern education and train a Muslim leadership for new initiatives. For it was pointless to repine and wait abjectly for the days of Mughal splendor to return.

Aḥmad Khān's vision served a purpose and there were some fainter echoes of his philosophy elsewhere in the East. But the future lay with a more assertive style of nationalism. Independence, in the familiar twentieth century sense, undoubtedly represented the real practical and psychological prerequisite for true identity and for self-responsibility. To that extent the view that said, "The British presence makes us virtually *Dār al-Ḥarb,*" was right. The irrepressible Islamic instinct was not to reconcile to external sovereignty, but to require history to come again into a true Islamic pattern of Islamic power.

Islam Politically Restored to Itself

Manifestly, Islam has been politically restored, though in diverse ways, right across the Muslim world in the last half century. Statehood has been recovered everywhere and the Western empire, politically speaking, hardly survives except in a few island outposts of negligible meaning. The British Rāj has gone from India and Pakistan, the Dutch from Indonesia, the French from North Africa, mandating power from the Arab Middle East, French and/or British rule from Saharan and sub-Saharan Africa, and the British from Malaysia and Singapore. The only salient exception is the Palestinian, where the statehood of Israel poses a bitter and tragic dilemma. True, within the form of "freedom" for Indian Islam goes the fact that some fifty million Muslims live in perpetuity without benefit of Islamic government (to this significant phenomenon we will return). But that situation was the price, through partition, some had to undertake for the sake of the statehood of others.

We can best appreciate the nature of this Islamic recovery of the political power by focusing on the genesis of Pakistan, while remembering that the instincts there at work were vigorously present in every other part of the Muslim world, in local variation.

During the 1940s it became increasingly clear that the British days in India were numbered. The two major religious communities on the subcontinent had broadly combined in their will to independence and had often visualized a united India in independent terms. But, steadily, Muslim opinion—though not without strong exception—swung in the areas of Muslim majority towards the notion of separate independence. For these minds the concept of religious "communalism" (arguing a unitary independence) had to give way to religious "nationalism." The demand of the Muslim League, under the opportunist leadership of Muḥammad 'Alī Jinnah (1876–1948), was for the right of Muslim majority areas to separate statehood in the form of Pakistan. The League claimed that no other policy had the right to call itself Islamic. Extending, in a grim sort of way, the old "hostage system," majority Muslims wanted a state of their own where they would have some Hindus under their aegis, as a counter on behalf of Muslim minorities elsewhere under Hindu aegis. They preferred this to a unitary subcontinent in which they, the Muslims, would always be the minority and possibly, also, hostages to Hindu mercy, without political security except the worth of Hindu promises.

But, deeper than this more calculating stance was the instinctive Muslim conviction that independence must be Islamic. If this necessarily involved partition, it could not avoid condemning other Muslims within Hindu India to non-Islamic statehood. But that paradox could not stand against the logic of historic instinct. When independence from Britain became a near reality, the soul of Islam, in what was to become Pakistan, took a long look at Hinduism and opted for separate statehood. In so doing, it was loyal to the deepest assumption of Muḥammad himself, namely that Islam could not fully be itself except in power.

That insistent philosophy is the more evident for having been also so cruelly selective and so costly in the implementing. It is a most important index to the twentieth century recovery of Islam. Circumstances were not so dramatic or so paradoxical elsewhere. But everywhere the achievement and the conviction about statehood were similar. Like a receding tide the Western imperialism withdrew, leaving Muslim peoples broadly belonging to themselves. The long aberration in which history itself had gone awry was at an end. This is *the* salient fact of Islam in this generation.

Islam Politically Restored in a Changed World

Restoration to itself, however, has proved a deeply ironical satisfaction, inasmuch as the world that independent Islam has to face is so new and intractable. For one thing the very nationalism that has everywhere motivated the attainment of independence is itself dubiously Islamic, for it breaks up the unity of the faithful and creates the different denominator of "citizen" in place of "believer." All these new Islamic nationalisms have to operate in a world where the Caliphate has been more than half a century defunct and has no chance of being resuscitated. Yet the *Ummah* in its historic form was never an ethnic concept, suited to be fragmented into different "nations." Some thinkers, like Muḥammad Iqbāl, liked to persuade themselves that nationalism was only a negative force, necessary to speed the departure of the West, and capable of being "rested" when its work was done. But history gives the lie to that illusion.

Nationalism, moreover, for a variety of reasons internal to modern statehood, tends towards a secularization of law, and the breaking up of caliphal unity statewise develops into the breaking up of the over-all identity faithwise. A loose Pan-Islamism, based on political considerations, is no substitute for what earlier generations would have recognized as *Dār al-Islām.*

There are other radical changes within the new autonomy of Islam that are of external origin. We have no need to rehearse all the accumulating and accelerating consequences of Western technology—oil, speed, mechanization, urbanization and the rest—compounding and confounding, and the revolutions in mentality, and between generations, that go with them. Since Napoleon's invasion of Egypt in 1798, the East has been reacting to external pressures, kindling innate resources of culture, and thus transforming the physical and mental scene. And the end is not yet. Has God been overtaken? is a question which cannot be dogmatically quieted if it is to be adequately answered.

The return to autonomy naturally aroused a deep confidence and an eager enthusiasm. It was not simply that the aberration was at an end: the opportunity was at hand. Islam, which had been ideologically neutralized, as it were, by Western usurpation, could now demonstrate that it had what the modern world takes. Both the key and the lock were in its own hand. Independence, for example, in Pakistan witnessed a spate of pamphleteering on almost every theme, setting out the *Islamic* solution to all the problems, of peace and war, society and justice, freedom and equality. This was a natural and legitimate accompaniment of self-responsibility. Its ready exuberance does not qualify its sincerity.

But retrospect has brought a more sober, chastened mood. Pakistan has not, sadly, held together. Its geographical duality and racial and economic tensions have proved too strong for the Islamic cement to hold. The bitter breakaway of Bangladesh in 1971, facilitated by Indian scheming but harshly wrought out of festering Muslim recrimination against Muslim, has finally shattered the sanguine confidence of 1947 that Islamic identity alone could contrive to weld a single expression, across a thousand miles of intervening territory, out of the diversities of Punjabis, Bengalis, Biharis, Pathans, Baluchis, Sindhis and the rest. That it lasted twenty-four years may be seen as a melancholy tribute of disproof. But, like Pakistan, if not so tragically, every eager independence has had to think second thoughts. Early optimism, which as in Pakistan, tends to defer serious discussion of what Islamic statehood ought to mean in modern terms, evaporates. Then the postponed issues come home to roost and disparate elements fall apart. All this is deeply human, and the Western world has had scant imagination and sympathy with which to serve it. But the mood of disillusion, or at least of greater realism, is unmistakable.

These pressures from without and disenchantments from within are simply the measure of how changed the world is, both from the simplicities of original

Islam and the naïvetés of modern confidence. Autonomy, on one level the legitimate renewal of Islam, is on another a yet more total burden.

In the Mirror of Autobiography

The student's duty here is to measure the burden in the experience of individuals. There are numerous autobiographies which describe, in personal terms, the tension between the old and the new, whether experienced within one locale as an intrusion, or in the other as an exile. Authors like the Moroccan Driss Chraïbe with his *Le Passé Simple,*[1] the Egyptians Aḥmad Amīn and Tāhā Ḥusain, in *Ḥayātī* and *Al-Ayyām,*[2] and Algerians like Muḥammad Dīb, and Albert Mammeri, have vividly communicated the problems of inhabiting two worlds. Most convenient to cite here will be Hamidou Kane's *L'Aventure Ambiguë,*[3] a Senegalese novel which draws in sharp outline the tensions experienced by a traditional believer in encounter with secular men and ·with the modern humanist rejection of the Divine.

Published in 1962, when the writer was thirty-three, the novel's hero (disguising its author), one Samba Diallo, spends his early years in a Quranic school and a strictly Muslim home. Thierno, called "the Master" in the story, is his mentor in the Qur'ān from whom Samba imbibes a total piety. His aunt, sister to the chief of the Diallobé people, recommends that Samba be sent to France to become familiar with the new ways, in order the better to defend his native culture from their subtleties. Her logic miscarries. Far from acquiring a robust defensiveness, based on knowledgeable rejection of secular ways and thoughts, Samba succumbs to the confusion in Paris and slowly loses his Islamic faith. Hamidou Kane traces the gradual, but somehow inevitable, sequence and links it with the sharp contrasts between the deep, Saharan mysteries of nature and the busy boulevards, the logical intellects, the cold precision of Parisian University society. "The Master's" venerable spirituality, rooted in the sense of "the signs of God" in nature among the Diallobé people, somehow pales in the dim grey light of the French skies.

Samba's letters home convey the steady erosion of his beliefs, despite his wistful sense of how precious they are. For he suspects and fears the pervasive materialism of his French friends, for all their rational brilliance, and is under no illusions about the spiritual poverty of his African emigré friends, with their hybrid culture. He is critical of both worlds and torn by the sense of alienation from each. Nor does the author allow him any relief in the sort of blind activism that sometimes eases the tension of inner decision. There is a deliberate concentration in the story on the spiritual and intellectual issues, to the exclusion of politics and emotional indulgence in escapism. This only makes the climax more compelling. Samba cannot be both Diallobé and Parisian, both Muslim and secular. But he cannot escape from either into the other.

He is summoned home by his father who is disquieted by the drift of his letters. "The Master" dies and his place is taken by a traditionalist of the most obstinate kind, who finally kills Samba because the youth is unable to pray at "the Master's" grave. A world is lost but no world is regained. Samba carries in his own person the whole brunt of the conflict. But, as the author implies, the ambiguous adventure goes on. Indeed it has always been so in the past. But never has the inconclusiveness seemed so sharp and bitter as today.

Hamidou Kane's story has been related at length because it captures with great sensitivity what questions of modern time mean in the personal encounter. It is a picture that has to be translated back into the workings of the corporate mind, into the defense mechanism of historic institutions, into the diverse counsels of culture in flux. What, then, are the main lines of Islamic response to the contemporary ambiguity of change and continuity, of flux and identity? How do movements, or moods, within the life of Islam react to the sense of threat and danger, experienced from without and working from within? How do Muslims face the challenge of modern developments in the struggle to be themselves with recognizable fidelity? How does, how should, Islam persist in the context of contemporary pressures?

It is customary to answer these questions, in broad terms, by falling back on the words "conservative" and "modernist," distinguishing between those who will to defend and those who will to revise. The distinction is fair enough, in a rough and ready way, if we keep in mind a variety of types and attitudes within the spectrum between two extremes. The issue within all of them is: what is the true Islam? For all seek and claim to know and show it, and are, therefore, involved in criticizing, and even disqualifying, the "Islam" of their competing or contrasting versions. Arnold Toynbee used the broad distinction between "Zealot" and "Herodian,"[4] between those who resist and those who "compromise." For the former compromise is treachery; for the latter it is creative loyalty. For the former all accommodation to modernity is menace; for the latter it is the right condition of survival.

Wahhābism and Rigorous Conservation

The most convenient example of the temper that resists and entrenches itself in the past is that of the Wahhābī movement. In origin it antedates the modern pressures and has sources that spring from within Islam itself and aspects of decadence which (as Wahhābis saw them) defiled and distorted the true Islam and which Wahhābism set itself to eradicate. Nonetheless, it serves as a telling example of the instinct to defy change, whether it comes from interior temptations or external attack. And it happens that Saudi Arabia, the heartland of Wahhābism, has in the oil beneath its desert sands a most concentrated occasion of twentieth century technology and wealth.

When Wahhābism began, all that was in the womb of the undreamed-of future. Muḥammad ibn 'Abd al-Wahhāb (1704–1792), the founder of the movement, was a native of Najd in Central Arabia. He belonged to the Hanbalī school, the strictest of the four canonical schools of law. He was a rigorist after the example of the famous Ibn Taimiyyah (d. 1328), who disallowed all innovation, pilgrimage to shrines, saint worship, the cult of intercession, and other accretions which had come into popular Islam through the influence of Sufism. 'Abd al-Wahhāb, called simply "the shaikh" by his devoted followers, had a powerful personality. Inspired by early movements of similar temper in India, which he had encountered through pilgrimage to Mecca, he demanded a return to an unadulterated Islam of primitive simplicity—the Islam of the Prophet and the Qur'ān. He considered that popular Islam in his own time was no less *Jāhiliyyah,* or "ignorance," than the pre-Islamic scene. His was a crusade for *Tauḥīd,* for a sternly unitarian faith. *Ijmā',* for him, was limited to the first three centuries: *Ijtihād* was firmly excluded, having all been achieved already. He laid an absolute stress on the Divine unity and held that the Divine will was totally unobligated to any principle or law of being. Those within Islam who contravened his puritan severities he classed as polytheists. He forbade many traditional ceremonies, the use of the rosary and *maulids* in honor of Muḥammad's birth.

It was characteristic of Wahhābism from the beginning to invoke political power and to rely heavily on the state. Thus emerged that close collaboration between the house of Sa'ūd in Arabia and the Wahhābī sect, which, beginning in the mideighteenth century, has endured until today. The Saudis gave political occasion and military success to the dogmatists and enjoyed, in turn, the advantage of the fiery ardor of their allies and their will to fight. The first dramatic successes came early in the nineteenth century, when the twin sanctuaries of Mecca and Medina were occupied. Wahhābī dominion then stretched across most of Arabia and up to the gates of Damascus. Mecca was purged of practices repugnant to its new masters, until the Ottoman power, roused by these indignities, regained control in 1818 through Muḥammad 'Alī of Egypt. Wahhābī fortunes ebbed and flowed and ebbed again, through the nineteenth century, until in 1902 the movement began a steady return to total ascendancy, through the prowess of Ibn Sa'ūd (d. 1953), the great architect of the present Sa'ūdī Kingdom.

Both in success and failure, Wahhābism thus renewed several of the qualities that had characterized original Islam. It came near to being what its ideal demanded, namely the seventh century come alive again. It had the same criteria of early Islam—energy, nomadism, and faith. It was an Arabism in full religious tide, in politico-dogmatic unity and militancy in the name of the one God.

This Sa'ūdī/Wahhābī partnership might well have renewed the wider expansion of initial Islam. But in the discovery of oil lay a far more subtle and ambiguous force than the seventh century had ever face, conspiring with the desert against the ancient simplicity of the faith. Discovered in Arabia in 1938 and massively exploited from 1945, oil ended all possible immunity from the outside world and from alien disruptions of tradition. There were, of course, other factors in change. The first newspaper had appeared in 1924 in Mecca and Arabic radio broadcasts began soon after. But oil proved the decisive quantity, the supreme corrosive of tradition, the bewildering multiplier of a wealth which flooded in a way no dikes could bar.

Wahhābī Islam has, in measure, acquiesced in oil's silent and continuing revolution of society. It has departed from the literal *Sharī'ah* in the legal abolition, in 1962, of slavery. The end of nomadism and many resultant factors have contributed to a weakening of the Wahhābī *élan vital.* Even geology itself thus conspires against a return to the seventh century. Indeed, in its gift of power, it appears to have given to Arab, Iranian and Nigerian Islam, but to the Saudis most of all, a new economic dominance over what remains of the twentieth. The events of 1973, in oil politics and oil pricing, are a portentous development, too recent yet to be fully measured, in what may with double intention be called the fortunes of faith. How odd that Wahhābī terrain should be its major testing ground.

Wahhābī unitarianism, in the main, has set the example for the zealot instinct elsewhere in contemporary Islam. The Sanūsiyyah in Libya, until their overthrow in 1970, represented a similar alliance between rule and religion. We cannot rightly see this zealotism as a consciously deliberative reaction to modern strains. It originated before such strains were present, and grew out of a domestic puritan zeal. Yet its will to defy newness and purify loyalty provides a banner for more sophisticated and conscious reactions to modernity. The Wahhābī assertion of Arabism against Ottoman authority, though differently conceived, did provide a powerful precedent for later Arab nationalism in the Middle East. For here were puritans who had no scruples in directing their militancy, not only against fellow Muslims, but against the Caliph himself. The lesson was not lost upon those who lacked the puritan incentive. The deeply sustained thesis within Wahhābism, of some Muslims disqualifying other Muslims, is one we find recurring through all contemporary Muslim life.

It found echo also in various parallel movements in Indian Islam. Wahhābism repaid its debt to India by deeply affecting Indians in turn. Shāh Walī Ullāh (1703–1765), a very important progenitor of ideas in his day, had a profound respect for Arabia as the true homeland of Islam, and appealed to Arab ways, and to Arabic, in his desire to counter Persian and Indian elements which he believed to be responsible for Islamic compromises. He is not to be regarded as a disciple of 'Abd al-Wahhāb. Shāh Walī Ullāh was a man of independent mind and mystical piety, whose writings were a seed-plot of thinking far wider than Wahhābism. But of the physical links through pilgrimage there is no doubt.

The main legatees of Wahhābī-style conservatism outside Arabia are, broadly speaking, the Muslim Brotherhood in Egypt and the Jamā'at-i-Islāmī in Pakistan. The former, founded in the 1930s by Ḥasan al-Bannā' (1906–1949) aims to rid Islam of moral and doctrinal compromise and to renew its pristine zeal. It differs from Wahhābism in, among other things, its firm subordination of the national element to its view of the *Ummah* of Islam as a single community. It has never been successful in marrying its cause to political power. In study and apologetics it takes stock of the modern world and sees the Qur'ān as affording effective direction for all the economic and social problems of today. It has a demanding sense of urgency and organizes its members in disciplined devotion.

A critical observer would conclude that it oversimplified the meaning of *islām* and the current task of religious apologetic. Its vigor and dedication are, however, a notable current expression of Muslim sincerity, as are the ideals of the Jamā'at-i-Islāmī in Urdu-speaking Islam.

Apart from the intellectual problems they foreshorten, all conserving reactions to current problems tend towards their own frustration because of what we may call the intractable quality of the world and of mankind. Here is a perennial problem of the religious life of man. Zealots stand for a view of Islam (or of any religion) as properly determining what the world shall be. But history and the world seem, obstinately, to have different ideas. In their scheme of discipline the Wahhābīs had the *muṭawwi'*—"the obedience-maker," whose business it was to enforce an undeviating conformity. But, sadly for him, the modern world does not recognize his office. Religions may be "obedience-planners," or "obedience-wishers," or "obedience-exhorters," but no more. Human nature is an ancient evader. And, short of political coercion, or of subversion and conspiracy under a wrong regime, the zealot has no option on the basis of power. He has to move to a more modest and a more persuasive means of actualizing a right *islām* in the world as it is.

Renewing the Understanding of Islam

There is no counterpart to Wahhābism on the side of creative change and adaptation, no movement of comparable strength and durability. What we may loosely call the "liberal" response to modernity is more eclectic and tentative, less sustained, and often indecisive. We cannot really speak of movements, as such, but only of trends and initiatives. It is usual to cite two leading figures, Muḥammad 'Abduh (1849–1905) and Muḥammad Iqbāl (1876–1938), outstanding in Arab and Indian Islam respectively. The former was certainly a pioneer in the liberation of Muslim thinking from *taqlīd,* or sheer traditionalism, the citation of old authorities, and the hidebound frame of mind. In his day, 'Abduh, who became Grand Mufti of Egypt and a notable leader in Al-Azhar, did effectuate a change in mental attitudes and stir a readiness to think. But his own rationale of Islam, in *Risālat al-Tauḥīd,* or "The Theology of Unity,"[5] was a very modest venture, bold though it was in its day.

His resolution of the problems of reason and revelation was to claim that when the former was right and the latter rightly interpreted, they entirely tallied and the problems disappeared. All that science dependably discovered was consistent with the Qur'ān. 'Abduh did not venture any radical view of the relation of Divine Scripture to human intelligence, whether in respect of how prophetic inspiration is to be understood, or of the temper in which to approach exegesis. His work of arousing people out of lethargy was well performed; his direction for their subsequent alertness only partial.

One difficulty was that he had so few adequate successors. His main disciple and biographer, Rashīd Riḍā (1865–1935), turned back to a timid conservatism.

Because of Islam's intensely authoritarian view of the Qur'ān—"a book in which there is nothing dubious"—enterprise of thought has tended to turn away into less exacting spheres of historical scholarship or *ad hoc* reforms of law, leaving fundamental theological issues in abeyance. While secularization of law has been widespread in many countries, intellectual reinterpretation of Islam has been circumscribed, at least in the Arab world.

One interesting figure is Muḥammad Kāmil Ḥusain (born 1902), of Cairo, who sees religious truth as essentially a means to human good, to tranquillity of spirit and inner peace. These goals are not to be confused with abstract dogmatic questions. These do not matter. So long as belief is effectual it is "true." The real miracle of the Qur'ān is that belief in it has achieved this inner soul-peace. We believe in the day of judgment, for example, by the way in which we let it cleanse our souls. Faith is a psychological function necessary to well-being and doctrine should not interfere, still less compete, since there are no criteria, other than effectiveness, for evaluating it.[6]

But these theories are exceptional. It would be fair to say that a practical secularity is very far advanced in many Muslim circles, without being adequately corroborated by the intellectual renewal of the dogmatic structure and the spiritual heritage. Law, anyway, has always had a more fundamental place in Islam than philosophical theology. So it is no surprise to find that Islamic "modernism" is more operative and articulate in the social sphere than in the intellectual.

Muḥammad Iqbāl, it is true, was a vigorous and inventive thinker who sought a subtle harmonizing of Quranic thought with contemporary philosophy, in his case Bergsonian creative evolution. But Iqbāl was a poet and poets can be distinctly elusive even at their boldest. His *Lectures on the Reconstruction of Religious Thought in Islam*[7] were erudite and adventurous and, in that sense, stimulating. Their popular impact was minimal. Iqbāl belongs with Muslim twentieth century history much more as the patron-poet of the idea of Pakistan.

What should, however, be remembered in assessing what scholars and thinkers have tried, or failed, to do in the reinterpretation of Islam, is that a significant *de facto ijmā'* and *ijtihād* are taking place. With the spread of education and technology, more and more members of the faith are finding their *modus vivendi* with modern conditions and this constitutes a living, ongoing reapplication, if not explicit reinterpretation, of Islam. The position of the traditional *'ulamā',* with their ancient skills of erudition, more and more gives way, in the actual world, to the authority and prestige of technicians and politicians. *'Ulamā'* are sometimes left with no option but to follow with more or less grace, less or more protest. While the dogmatic mind has always resisted *ijtihād* other than its own, its erstwhile monopoly of that institution has now broken down.

An interesting element in this picture of an Islam whose definition is coming to be more within the purview of its general practitioners than of its religious experts, is the concept of repugnancy to the Qur'ān. The negative term is at once illuminating. What is *not* inconsistent with the Scripture can be a looser criterion to apply than what the pundits say the Qur'ān enjoins. The will not to be repugnant to the Qur'ān played a large part in the long debate about the Constitution in post-independence Pakistan. That often inconclusive debate was all part of this taking of Islam into more popular, and, therefore, more volatile, less static, custody than that of the religious elite.

We can well link this consideration with our earlier point, in this chapter, about a more modest notion of how much Islam can actually be achieved in society—a notion which a Wahhābī would rule out as blasphemous, but which more workaday folk may find both necessary and honest. So it is that many individuals, and many governments, settle for such approximations to a full Islam as realism will allow and modernity sustain. President Habīb ibn 'Alī Bourguiba of Tunisia might well be cited as a notable advocate of this attitude. In spite of the purist and the doctrinaire, it is likely to be more and more the pattern of the future. Not all the Sambas of "the ambiguous adventure" succumb. Many are already fathers themselves. The Senegal and the Paris of Hamidou Kane's contrasting story are in fact cheek by jowl in every modern society. The issue is not simply between a static society on the one hand and an *alien* education on the other. As a great religion, Islam has its own survival power, on condition that it responds to the movement of history. And the movement and the response are always interacting, and cannot be dictated either by purists or progressives, by pundits or philosophers. At the end of the day, Islam is, and will be, what Muslims say it is.

A fascinating instance of this dictum is the story of Islam in Turkey since secularization under the great Atatürk (1881–1938). After the demise of the Ottomans, Turkey underwent a radical modernization of law and a "laicization" of life, in the most sustained attack on Islamic establishment ever to be made within a Muslim society. The Sufi Orders were proscribed, religious endowments abolished, and all religious education repudiated. Yet Turkish Islam has survived and, in the years since 1950, has recovered much of its lost authority, without reversing the secular revolution. The Turkish nation, it would seem, is ready, perhaps wistful, for the values of religion, having been ruthlessly delivered from its tyrannies.

The Present Significance of Indian Islam

Nowhere is custody of the faith by the faithful more interesting than in India today. The reasons why this is so are not difficult to see. Indian Islam numbers perhaps fifty-five million and Hinduism is always a fascinating and stimulating neighbor. There is also the fact of permanent minority status. As we have seen, Pakistan could only be created by denying to those elsewhere in the subcontinent precisely those conditions that Pakistan said were indispensable to survival. Thus, by Pakistani criteria, Indian Islam has no secure future. It is bound to wither away. Without statehood how can Islam behave, when statehood, or Islamic power, has been assumed from the beginning to be of the very essence of Islam?

And this condition of being without its own state is not a correctable aberration, as it was under British imperialism. It is a permanent condition of existence. There are not going to be future Pakistans for the rescue (if the term is right) of Indian Muslims. Meanwhile the continuing existence of Pakistan *across the border* keeps the impossible alternative continually alive, as an image, while denying it as a prospect. So it is that Islam in post 1947 India is compelled to exist just as a religion—a posture altogether uncongenial to the Islamic genius. Outside the Soviet Union, there is no such Muslim minority of comparable size or centrality to Muslim history.

But if the dilemma is new, could it perhaps be that this very condition could produce a novel and creative response from Indian Islam, not only to disprove the prophets of doom, but to pioneer a wholly fresh dimension of Islamic existence? It is true that the odds against this are very great. There is the ever present danger of some assimilation to Hinduism. Historians remember how Akbar, the great architect of the Mughal dynasty, became syncretistic and ended by substituting for Islam his own *Dīn-i-Ilāhī*. If such perversion could occur on the throne of autocracy, what may minority inferiority produce? Will the innumerable pressures of minority status, within a secular state, attentuate the Muslim will to preserve Islam?

Indian Muslim thought, like any other, has its conservationists, its isolationists, its zealots. But even before partition, there have been lively, creative interpreters of Islam. Among the most notable was Abū-l-Kalām Āzād (1888–1958), one of the leading advocates of a united India, statesman, exegete and thinker, who abjured the whole idea of separatism and played a distinguished part in the establishment of the secular state. He wrote on the Qur'ān with a spiritual insight strangely absent from the speeches and temperament of Jinnah, protagonist of Pakistan, who left no Quranic commentary and no "diary of the heart." Āzād believed the real essence of original Islam to be that *fiṭrah,* or spiritual mind, spoken of in the Qur'ān—the individual's integrity toward God and man. It was this, beyond, and if need be, against, the institutional forms of religion and creed, that was the vital thing. Other writers, such as Hūmāyūn Kabīr and A.A.A. Fyzee have given constructive thought to Hindu relationships and the obligations of Muslim citizenship in a non-Muslim context. Indian Islam, despite Pakistani forebodings, is not likely to wither away. What it is sure to do is to develop new definitions of itself, in practice if not also in theology. So doing, it will be close to issues common to *all* contemporary religion.

Belonging with Humanity

So we pass, in our general review, to the theme of Islam and universal mankind. As we have seen, Islam was never essentially people-centered, or ethnic, as Judaism was. Its Arab Prophet and its Arabic revelation were seen as "a mercy to the worlds." Historically, Islam has made good its capacity to belong with wide diversities of humankind. But always, traditionally, this universality was on the

basis of surrender. *Dār al-Islām* had no territorial limits, but its territory went
where its political power prevailed. What are we to say today of its capacity for
relationship with other faiths, which do not submit to its dogmatic claims, but
nonetheless inhabit the same world and, often, the same country?

To put the matter in different words, is there, as the title of this series of
studies suggests, a religious life of man, in which response to religious diversity
is a new moment in the experience of every tradition? Man is now in a position
to see the human community in a comprehensive way, to "take on," as Franz
Fanon phrased it, "the universality inherent in the human condition." What then
of Islam today in the conscious dialogue of multiform religion?

That question involves the issue of race. For race has always been a sharp
provoker and abettor of religious antipathy. It can be said at once that Islam has
achieved a remarkable degree of interracial coexistence. There have been gross
inequalities, slaveries, racial tensions, distinctions between Arab Muslim and
non-Arab neophytes joining Islam. But from the Prophet's time that evil has
never passed unrebuked. The major tensions have been political rather than
essentially racial, even where, as with the tragic sufferings of Armenians at the
hands of Turks, it seemed to be otherwise.

Those who invoke Islam in behalf of racial hatred are grossly distorting its
real meaning. This is certainly true of so-called Black Muslims in the United
States. Their invocation of Islam as a rallying cry against the white world perverts
its meaning. Black Islam in America appeals to some blacks because its tight
discipline and militancy deter lazy listlessness, give rescue from aimlessness and
offer the solace of deviancy from the normal. The theory of "the lost-found
Nation of Islam in the wilderness of America" is fantasy. It affirms that the black
man, unaware of his own past history and of his future role, has been illuminated
by Elijah Muhammad. White supremacy is a temporary chastisement decreed by
Allah so that, by suffering, the black man could gain a true awareness of his
superior worth. The day of white doom is near. Islam, according to Elijah
Muhammad, has come to announce this fact and to warn against all the false
prophets of integration. For integration is the white man's plot to forestall his own
doom. The nation of Islam must banish the concept of compatibility, deliver the
black from debilitating habits spread by whites for his demoralization, and bring
in the promised liberation.[8]

This powerful myth may be effective in its narrow sphere. But myth it
remains and it has nothing to do with classic, or recognizable, Islam, which has
no such theory of essential human incompatibility. So Malcolm X discovered in
1964 when he made the pilgrimage to Mecca and realized the confidence trick
that Elijah Muhammed had played. Before that experience of Islamic transracial
equality, Malcolm X had seen Islam as an instrument of Black Power against the
white world. His testimony is a moving tribute to the capacity of Islam, and of
the pilgrimage within it, to make actual a genuine transcendence of racial enmities
and passion.[9] Muslim writers like to remind their readers that the first muezzin
calling to prayer was Bilāl, an Ethiopian, who used to pray for the conversion

of the Quraish ("white" persecutors of "black(ed)" believers). His country, African and Christian, was the first to give sanctuary to Muḥammad's persecuted followers when fugitives from Mecca.

In the context of this discussion of race and Islam, it needs to be remembered that Islam has never been related to the rest of mankind with the same sort of cultural and material preponderance that the Western empire wielded. There has been no equal in all history to the exploitative opportunity of the West over the rest of the world in the nineteenth century. Islamic penetration of Africa, by Arab, Fulani, Yao, and the like, was devastating and brutal, to be sure. But Islam did not have the material superiority, the disruptive technology and the instinctive aloofness of Western empires.

We return to our question about Islam's place in the quest for a global unity of mankind, under conditions created by contemporary science. Islam certainly holds within itself deep clues to the religious future. There is its sense of the sacramental quality of all natural experience, as a handling of "the signs of God." Technological man has no profounder need than the hallowing of nature, against all crudely exploitative and acquisitive attitudes. There is the deep truth implicit in the words *Allāhu akbar:* "God is greater"—greater than all that people are liable, falsely, to absolutize. This is the only effective counter to contemporary idolatries in which men make absolute what is only safe when it is relative— science, sex, power, race, nation, production. One has to say of each of these: "Science was made for man, not man for science," and assert the priority of the rightly human against all that degrades it. Such assertion of the human is one side of the meaning of the confession of God. For it is the idolatries against God which prove to be, in experience, the denial of the human. Here lies the final meaning of the Islamic repudiation of *Shirk,* the inclusively damnable thing, namely "not letting God be God." In these senses, at least, Islam may be substantiated in its claim that its heart convictions are indeed the essence of the religious interpretation of life.

We may be a long way from a full Islamic participation in the service of that vision. If it is the outsider who is more likely to see, and to state, that ultimate relevance of *islām* why should that circumstance matter? It remains Islam's significance.

Man, Suffering, Faith

We conclude with a final reflection about the Islamic capacity for tragedy. It is a faith which, historically, has lived in and by success. It is a religion of confident power. Since it sees itself as religion perfected, it believes it is destined always to succeed. The sympathetic observer is moved to wonder whether it is ever seriously afflicted or ill at ease in the world. Islam expects the believer to be free from *raibah,* doubtfulness, of which there is none in the Qur'ān. Yet a faith which never produces any loyal sceptics must seem to be "out of this world." Without inward doubters can any religion be safe even with itself? Do not all credal establishments need iconoclasts to call them into question? Was this not the ancient role of Abraham, of Muḥammad, according to Islam? Is it not necessary in respect of Islam itself, lest it should identify its own interests with God's and so become itself a kind of *Shirk*? Religious faith today must learn to comprise not only itself but doubt of itself. If there is an unexaminedness about belief, it means that there is a conspiracy of silence about latent, haunting questions. Islam has always been rigorous against apostasy, impatient with the doubtful.

Part of what makes for honest doubt is the mystery of suffering and evil. To these, in its normal attitudes, Sunnī Islam does less than justice. And this is where it may yet turn its most inquiring face toward other religions, especially Buddhism and Christianity.

Reflection quickly makes it plain that suffering is real, tragically real, in the house of Islam today. For that house shares in the pains and privations of "the third world," its pressures of population, its refugees, and sharpest of all, the deep enmities and passions created by the insertion and expansion of the state of Israel. Islam instinctively replies to suffering with the doggedness of endurance. As Surah 47:35 directs: "Do not falter or sue for peace; you will be the upper ones" —a verse quoted in a sermon in the Great Mosque in Mecca just after the June war with Israel in 1967. Hardship and adversity are seen as trials and tribulations on the way to their reversal. They are not in themselves the fabric of redemptive victory. Mastery must be sought and found only in their manifest requital.

Here lie the deepest themes in the religious life of man. Islam believes in the evident, the effectual, the undeniable, the successful. Yet history does not always go that way. Injustice may be irreducible by outward means. Suffering is often the only right option left to truth. Perhaps the answer here is present already in the Islamic conviction of the Divine sovereignty, if this can be seen, beyond eschatology and judgment, as more ultimate than the enigmas of sin and evil through the greater strength of love and mercy.

There have been passionate sceptics in Islam despite the sanctions tending against their emergence or their toleration. The name of ʿUmar al-Khayyām comes readily to mind. But of more radical intensity was the great blind poet Abū-l-ʿAlāʾ al-Maʿarrī of Maʿarrat al-Nuʿmān, a village in the Aleppo region of North Syria (973–1058 A.D.). Blind from the age of four because of smallpox, he became the most celebrated poet of his time and a legend after it. From beginnings as a panegyrist and a brief sojourn in intellectual circles in Baghdad, he returned to his native town on his mother's death, and developed a powerful criticism both of dogma and society, in poetry and letters, grim and unrelieved in their dark sense of tragedy, yet vividly human in their compassion. In his triple prison, "blindness, a narrow house, and a vile body," he considered all men blind where truth was at stake, preferring refuge in credulity or superstition, in dogma or authority. He wrote the most technically difficult verse in parable of the tedious strenuousness with which men engaged in life, artificial as it all was: *luzūm mā lam yalzam,* or "the necessity of the unnecessary," as it might be translated—

a notion not far removed from contemporary ideas of "the absurd." We acquiesce in the pointless task of existing. His couplet on "The gates of birth" runs:

> Here am I laid, my father's infamy,
> But never any child accuses me.

Yet he was not all misanthropy. His letters to friends, in bereavement, at childbirth, in counsel, breathe a warm humanity, and there was a wistfulness, akin to that of Thomas Hardy, about his incapacity to believe.

> Traditions have been handed down to me
> That would have had importance, would have had
> But for my powers of credulity
> Which are so bad.

Blindness and poetry are often allowed a liberty not readily available to the sighted and the prosaic. But the temper of Al-Ma'arrī and his kind, wherever it emerges, serves to keep the theism of Islam critical of its own confidence and, therefore, worthier in its ultimate quality. If we believe in God too readily, we surely believe in Him the less.

> The years have gone like water, and they sweep
> New populations to the shore of sleep.
> The kingdoms are not swayed by man alone,
> For God, in pity, dwells behind the throne.

But, with or without such chastening, what does the Islamic conviction mean in its final quality? What is it to "have" Allāh, to cry *Allāhu Akbar,* to live in the relevance of His prophets, His books, His religion and His judgment?

The answer must be as manifold as the house of Muslims. For the masses of ordinary believers it means a framework of belief and behavior, a preserving, demanding, encircling sense of God and duty. For the sophisticated it may mean only a habit of will, a cultural identity, a condition of life received from history. For the mystical it means "the shade of the wing of Gabriel," the abiding of the spirit under the remembrance of the Lord. To the activist it means the dynamism of a purposeful Heaven nurturing the ongoings of history. To the apostate in soul it is no more than the echo of a buried past. To the traditionalist it is a sacred trust to be served, with a steadfast fidelity both to the giveness of the Divine will and the hiddenness of the Divine knowledge. For the artists and builders, it is the inspirer of their forms, the indwelling of their domes, the cry from their minarets, the nurse of their skills.

Through all the diversities of its significance it is the invocation of the Name of the Merciful. "For all that is in the Qur'ān," declared Muḥammad, "is in the Opening Surah, and all that is in the Opening Surah is in the *Bismillah al-Raḥmān al-Raḥīm:*" *"In the Name of the merciful Lord of mercy."*

Questions for Further Study and Discussion

The first edition of *The House of Islam* suggested Quranic passages for reading in relation to each chapter, as well as themes for reflection. Some readers felt these to be superfluous; others found them valuable. Quranic passages will be presented in a parallel anthology. A few central question-issues are listed here for those who wish to use them.

Chapter 1. "Lord of the Worlds"

1. What is the meaning of *islām* (small 'i')?
2. How has Islam understood "the excellent Names" of God in its theology and devotion?
3. What, essentially, does the doctrine of the Divine unity mean for Islam? Why is it vital?
4. Muslims often take pride in the simplicity of their theology. Do they thereby reduce what theology should undertake?

Chapter 2. Muḥammad and the Rasūliyyah

1. Explain the call of Muḥammad and assess his personality.
2. What is the religious meaning of the "blessing" of Muḥammad?
3. Trace, around the pivot of the *Hijrah,* the sequence of vocation-opposition-impasse-power-success-vindication-statehood. What fundamental religious issue was at stake?

Chapter 3. Qur'ān

1. What, in broad terms, are the basic Quranic themes?
2. Does the Qur'ān *need* to be rearranged chronologically?
3. What part does Quranic recitation play in Muslim religious experience?
4. Consider the Qur'ān's view of its final place in a continuity of revelation through all the prophets.

Chapter 4. Law

1. What are the sources of law in Islam and how are they interrelated?
2. Explain the concept of *Zakāt* and its significance for social responsibility and economic obligation in Islam.
3. How has traditional Islam understood the institution of marriage, in the Qur'ān, in law and in practice?
4. What emphases in respect of character and conduct are to be found in Islamic *Sharī'ah*?
5. What, in your view, are the main problems of a theologically based ethics, as exemplified by Islam?

Chapter 5. Liturgy

1. What elements give Muslim prayer its unique character and quality?
2. Assess the Pilgrimage as a sacrament both of devotion and of unity.
3. How does *Ramaḍān,* in overall Muslim interpretation, compare with fasting as a general feature of the religious life of man?
4. Where in the history of Islam did Sufism take its rise? How would you analyze the fascination it holds for many western students?
5. Explain the tensions existing between Sufi, mystical theology and the doctrinal "orthodoxy" of Sunnī Islam. Is any reconciliation possible?

Chapter 6. Ummah

1. Consider the Sunnī/Shī'ah divergence in Islam as exemplifying basic problems of religion that have to do with authority, time, experience and community.
2. In theory, what was the Caliphate? What is the significance of its final demise?
3. Explain and assess the Islamic concept of toleration to minorities.
4. The *Ummah* in Islam is not a "chosen people," nor a church, nor a mere bond of belief. What, then, is it?
5. What problems were created for Islam by Western imperialism?
6. What savor of Islamic culture might a student derive from the travels of Ibn Baṭṭūṭa or the thought of Ibn Khaldūn?

Chapter 7. Questions of Modern Time

1. "Islam is, and will continue to be, what Muslims say it is." Comment and elaborate.
2. "God is not overtaken," observes the Qur'ān. How, then, do, or should, believers in Him cope with the flux of events?
3. What meaning can *Dār al-Islām* have in the contemporary world, for those in "the house" and for others?

Glossary

'*abd:* slave or servant—the status of man as doer of God's will, answering to *Rabb,* or "Lord," and linked with "worship," by the root verb.

adhān: the call to prayer made five times a day from every mosque.

'*ajamī:* foreign, i.e., non-Arabic, comparable to "barbarous" with the Greeks and to the original sense of "Wales" in English.

amānah: the trust of the earth given by God to man as having a delegated authority over nature.

amr: the word of command, the imperative by which the worlds came into being.

al-Amr bi-l-ma'rūf: the enjoining, in Islamic ethics, of what is right and sound and good, as conscience owns or knows it.

Asbāb al-Nuzūl: The "occasions of revelation." Situations or incidents with reference to which Muhammad's deliverances under inspiration are to be understood; the context, not the cause, of the Qur'ān.

balāgh: the content of Muhammad's preaching, as distinct from the sanctions or factors making for its acceptance or reacting to its rejection (see also *hisāb*).

Bismillāh: the phrase: "In the Name of the merciful Lord of Mercy," which prefaces every Surah save one (Surah 9); the general Islamic invocation of God.

Dār al-Harb: the areas of mankind as yet unsubdued to Islam; the house of war, or struggle unto Islamization.

Dār al-Islām: the house of Islam, the geographical realm and true domain of Muslim faith and practice; the territory in which Islam is in full devotional, political, and legal actuality.

dhikr: the practice of recollection of God by mention of His Names reciprocally to God's reminder to men which is the Qur'ān. Among mystics *dhikr* is the technique, or discipline, of absorption in God.

dhimmī: a non-Muslim subject under Islamic rule, in one of the tolerated minorities: subject to special taxes in lieu of *Zakāt.*

Dīn: religion in general and religious duties in particular: incorporates the five basic obligations of the Muslim. The word also means Divine judgment.

Fātihah: title of the opening Surah of the Qur'ān, being "the Opener" of the Book.

fatwā: a legal opinion given by a *muftī* (q.v.) by which the *Sharī'ah* is applied to cases or issues so that its authority and precedents may be upheld.

fiqh: jurisprudence, the legal order of Islam as exercised in courts and expounded by the several Schools of Law.

fitnah: originally trial or persecution borne by believers in the Prophet: then sedition or conspiracy against the Islamic state; a basic concept relative to hostility and in its evolution a term reflecting the movement of early Islam from minority to majority status.

fuqahā': pl. of *faqīh,* jurisprudents, those learned in *fiqh* or applied law.

furqān: mainly a title of the Qur'ān, meaning the distinguisher or the criterion.

al-ghaib: the unseen, the realm of Divine mystery and ineffability.

Hadīth: Tradition in Islam from the standpoint of its reporting and recording, thus yielding Tradition as *Sunnah,* or obligatory law.

Hajj: pilgrimage to Mecca and its environs in the sacred month; the fifth Pillar of religion.

ḥanīf: a seeker after true religion, descriptive of Abraham in the Qur'ān as an anti-idolater; a God-fearer before Islam.

ḥifẓ al-Qur'ān: keeping (i.e., in heart reciting) the Qur'ān; memorizing as the due participation of the believer in the God-given words of Muḥammad.

Hijrah: the emigration of Muḥammad and his community from Mecca to Medina in 622 A.D., from which the Islamic calendar dates; the definitive crisis of Muḥammad's career.

ḥisāb: the business of reckoning with, or requiting, the rejection of preaching (*balāgh*); vindication of the message as distinct from its simple predication; the Divine "arithmetic" with men in time and eternity.

'Id al-Fiṭr: the feast of the fast breaking, with which *Ramaḍān* terminates.

I'jāz: the quality of matchless eloquence attaching to the Qur'ān as revelation, whereby, for Islam, it constitutes a literary miracle; its style as evidence of its authenticity, Muḥammad being unlettered.

Ijmā': consensus, or converging, of approval; the means whereby the Muslim community in Sunnī Islam serves to identify loyal development in Islamic law and usage.

Ijtihād: the individual initiative of experts or pioneers whereby valid *Ijmā'* (previous term) is generated within the community, or (in Shī'ah Islam) is mediated to it.

Imām: the leader of mosque prayer: the spiritual Guide of Shī'ah Muslims by virtue of the "light of Muḥammad."

'Ilm: A term broadly covering all knowledge (especially in modern times, scientific knowledge), but used in medieval Islam for the competence in religious lore possessed by the *'Ulamā'* (q.v.).

Imān: faith, the activity of belief, correlative to *Dīn*, or practice; supposed in, but sometimes distinguished from, *islām*, as submission or allegiance.

Islām: the faith, obedience and practice of Muḥammad's people, the final, perfected religion of God. Uncapitalized it denotes the quality of surrender to the Divine word and will which long antedates Islam.

isnād: the attestation of a tradition of Muḥammad through a chain of vouchers for its truth going back to his companions; what the tradition leans on, as distinct from what it says.

Jāhiliyyah: the time of ignorance in Arabia, preceding Islam, sometimes over-darkened; the ignorance involves an element of unruliness or uncouthness. Cf. the Biblical "froward."

Jihād: the concept of militancy on behalf of Islam to bring *Dār-al-Ḥarb* (q.v.) into *Dār al-Islām;* also spiritualized as the mystic's struggle against evil within.

jinn: a generic plural in Arabic denoting the demons or spirits that operate in the human scene. They both aid and plague mortal existence and the Qur'ān assigns them many roles in mortal affairs.

jizyah: the tax payable by *dhimmīs* (q.v.).

kalām: lit. speech, the science of theology, the setting forth of the Divine attributes according to Islamic revelation.

Kalimah: the word or title given to the *Shahādah*, or confession: "There is no god but God; Muḥammad is the apostle of God."

kasb: acquisition: the view of a leading theologian, Al-Ash'arī, purporting to reconcile Divine disposition with human responsibility, through the formula: "God wills it *in* the will of the doer, who thus acquires the deed."

khilāfah: politically, the succession to the rule of Muḥammad from the first Caliph, Abu Bakr, down to 1924. ("Caliph" is the Anglicized form of *Khalīfah*, i.e., the possessor of *Khilāfah* or "caliphate.") Quranically the term means the status of Adam, or man, as trustee for God in the world.

khuṭbah: the mosque sermon, given by a *khaṭīb*, or preacher.

kufr: antithetical to *shukr* (q.v.): the ultimate evil, disbelief in God and His signs, rejection of revelation, thanklessness.

ma'rifah: knowledge, the mystical awareness of reality, as contrasted with the rational "findings" of *'ilm,* or intellection in the external world.

ma'rūf: the well-doing Islam enjoins: things acknowledged as good.

matn: the substance of a tradition, as distinct from its *isnād* (q.v.) or support.

maulid: the Prophet's birthday, or a saint's birthday, celebrated with festive songs and gifts.

mihrāb: the niche in the mosque which marks the *qiblah* (q.v.) of Mecca, the recess into which the *īmām,* or prayer-leader, prays.

minbar: the mosque pulpit, often retractable, and at right angles to the *mihrāb.*

mu'adhdhin (or *muezzin* in popular spelling): the mosque official, or individual, who gives the *adhān,* or call to prayer, five times daily.

muftī: a qualified legist able to give a *fatwā* (q.v.) for the guidance of a judge or in response to a question.

muhtasib: a superintendent, or inspector of ethical behavior; a spiritual accountant in the Muslim community.

mu'jizah: the miracle of the Qur'ān, its quality as possessing *I'jāz* (q.v.).

mujtahid: one capable of, or exercising, *Ijtihād* (q.v.).

mukhālafah: the difference, a technical term denoting the necessary distinction between a Name of God and the same adjective in human currency.

munkar: a thing vetoed or reproached, the ethically reprehensible.

muslim: one who believes in, belongs to, and performs *islām* (q.v.): the active participle of the verb to "islamize" or to "submit." (N.B. "Muhammadan" is never a proper descriptive. Muhammad's people are "Muslims.")

mutawwi': lit. the "obediencer," an official in (e.g., Wahhābī) Islam whose business is to ensure moral and religious conformity.

Mu'tazilah: a group and school of theologians, strongest in the ninth century A.D., who pressed speculative matters about the Qur'ān and human free-will far beyond the position which later (and largely in reaction against them) came to be the orthodox dogma.

al-nabī al-ummī: the unlettered prophet. Muhammad's role as the recipient of revelation without literary skill or personally gathered knowledge: or, the prophet to the Scriptureless.

al-Nahī 'an al-munkar: the prohibition of evil, false, and reprehensible behavior.

naql: lit. transmission, the delivery of truth via revelation and transmitted in faithful theology, as contrasted with *'aql* or investigative reason.

niyyah: intention, the conscious focus of purpose that must precede all ritual acts in Islam.

qadar: the Divine measure or determination of human events and actions; the decree, or power of God.

qiblah: the direction of prayer towards Mecca, by which every mosque is oriented and the house of Islam unified in *Salāt* (q.v.).

qiyās: analogy, a provision whereby the law of Islam may be extended to cover situations analogous to, but not explicitly in, the Qur'ān and tradition.

Qur'ān: the recital, or reading: name of the sacred Scripture of Islam, believed communicated *verbatim* to Muhammad and recited by him to his hearers and recorded, for their recitation, in 114 Surahs or chapters.

Rabb: Lord, the most frequent title of *Allāh,* often linked with ". . . of the worlds." See *'abd.*

Ramadān: name of the month of fasting during which there is complete abstinence from food and drink during the hours of daylight.

Rasūl: messenger or apostle; the title of Muhammad, though there are many *rusul,* (pl.) to a variety of peoples.

Rasūliyyah: the apostolate of Muḥammad, his dignity and duty both to proclaim and to vindicate the message from God.

ra'y: opinion or view (from the verb: to see) held or sponsored as a means to *Ijtihād* and *Ijmā'* (q.v.); a source, under conditions, of adaptation of law.

ṣadaqāt: voluntary alms, works of right-doing which show that faith is loyal.

Ṣalāt: ritual, or liturgical, prayer in Islam; the second Pillar of *Dīn,* performed five times daily.

Ṣaum: fasting, particularly during the month of Ramaḍan: the fourth Pillar of *Dīn;* lasts the whole lunar month during the daylight hours.

Shahādah: witness or confession, with intention, of the *Kalimah* (q.v.). The first Pillar of Islam.

Sharī'ah: the sacred law, grounded in the will of God, and given in the Qur'ān, tradition, *qiyās* and *Ijmā'* (q.v.): the path of duty, both ritual and general, for Muslims.

Shī'ah: the segment (lit. "sect") of Islam, in contradistinction to Sunnī Islam (q.v.), which originated in deep political, emotional and spiritual factors, in the first half century of Islam, and abides. Its themes of divergence are profound and elemental, relating to exegesis, eschatology, tradition, authority, and devotion.

Shirk: the cardinal sin of idolatry, or deification; any deviation from the sole worship of God; attribution of Divine power, knowledge, or will, to other than God.

shukr: gratitude or thankfulness, the proper human response to the Divine mercy; a favorite Quranic concern, contrasted with *kufr* (q.v.).

sūfī: the practicing mystic, often with ascetic attitudes. The term is derived from woollen (i.e., simple) dress characteristic of early Sufism. Sufis constitute a deep and vital element in Islamic life, history, and theology.

Sunnah: the path of tradition, the way of faith and conduct as followed by the (*Sunnī*) community of Islam.

Sunnī: the term denoting the broad mass of Islam from which the *Shī'ah* (q.v.) diverge. Sunnis reject the Shī'ah Imāms and rely on the Qur'ān, the Sunnah, and the community for the integrity and continuity of their Islam.

tafsīr: explanation, or exegesis, of the Qur'ān, involving Arabic grammar, study of *asbāb al-nuzūl* (q.v.) and erudition in tradition, allegory, abrogation, and commentary.

takbīr: the act of saying: *Allāhu Akbar*—"Great is God"; to magnify God.

taqlīd: hideboundness or authoritarianism in *tafsīr* (q.v.) of *fiqh* (q.v.); the state of adhering blindly to a traditional school; a frequent butt of modern reformers.

ṭarīqah: the Sufi way of discipline and initiation into Divine knowledge, through self-transcendence and self-mortification leading to the unitive state.

taslīm: the saying of "the peace of God be upon him," i.e., upon Muḥammad; the second half of the formula of benediction of the Prophet (see *taṣliyah*).

taṣliyah: the saying of "May God bless (lit. "pray upon") the Prophet" coupled always with *taslīm* (q.v.). This formula always follows mention of Muḥammad's name in orthodox speaking and writing.

tauḥīd: the assertion, or doctrine, of the Divine unity. God is One; let God be God alone; the driving motive and end of Islam.

ta'wīdh: the act of saying: "I seek refuge with God"—a frequent Quranic formula and one of the deepest themes of Islamic devotion.

'ulamā': (pl. of *'ālim*) doctors of theology or law, learned ones, the custodians of Islamic teachings.

Ummah: a very inclusive term—the community of Islam, the solidarity of faith and prayer, the political incorporation of the faith, the people of the allegiance.

ummī: unlettered, one of a people without Scriptures, or illiterate. See *al-nabī al-ummī.*

'urf: customary law, brought into Islam from the conquered peoples on condition of its compatibility with Islamic sources.

waḥy: the recipience of revelation by Muḥammad; the state of receptivity in which he received and communicated the Qur'ān; revelation and inspiration are not here distinguished.

Zakāt: almsgiving, the third Pillar of *Dīn;* property and possessions obligate men to society: what we pay validates what we own.

ẓulm: wrong-doing, or wrong dealing, the most fundamental Quranic term for sin.

Notes

Introduction

[1]Translated from Jamāl ʿAbd al-Nāṣir, *Falsafat al-Thaurah,* Cairo, 1953. An edition in English was published in Washington, D.C., by Public Affairs Press, in 1955, with the title: *Egypt's Liberation: The Philosophy of the Revolution.*

Chapter 1

[1]To add "submission" and "submitter" after the Arabic terms "Islam" and "Muslim" might be useful. But it would also distort, and possibly prejudice, the whole meaning which has to develop through an entire book. "Islam," of course, is the thing done and "Muslim" is the doer of it. The root contains the vital consonants: S-L-M and relates to "surrender," "peace," "safety," "salutation," "resignation," and "immunity." It would be sad to curtail so full a concept by a premature simplicity. In general, Arabic terms will be found elucidated in the immediate context of their first use. There is also the Glossary.

[2]*Kitāb al-Lumaʿ* (The Book of Insight), translated by R. J. McCarthy, Beirut, 1953, p. 56.

[3]*Ibid.,* pp. 99–100.

[4]Duncan B. Macdonald, *Development of Muslim Theology, Jurisprudence and Constitutional Theory,* New York, 1903, pp. 314–15.

[5]*Ibid.,* p. 303.

[6]*Ibid.,* pp. 303–04.

[7]*Ibid.,* pp. 304–08.

Chapter 2

[1]The early and deep schism among Muslims which gave rise to Shīʿah Islam will be explored in Chapter 6. The dominant and successful majority came to be known as "Sunnis," holding to the emerging political and legal "orthodoxy" of Islam against these unsuccessful schismatics—the "deviationists" or "sectarians."

Chapter 3

[1]Western orientalism has done much to foster the counterpart of an "Islamic orientalism." The former is seen by the latter as, in part, a worthy scholarship Muslims can emulate and, in part, the stranger's distortions or misinterpretations which Muslims must rectify. Quranic translation and study are the first of these fields. The leaders of the Aḥmadiyya Movements, for example, in the twentieth century, set themselves to give their own translations of the Qur'ān in the western languages.

[2]Arberry's fullest discussion of the issues in translation is found in his *The Holy Koran,* London, 1953, being selections appearing in advance of the complete edition.

[3]A. J. Arberry, *The Koran Interpreted,* New York, 1956. Surah 94.

[4]N. J. Dawood, *The Koran,* Baltimore, 2nd revised edition, 1966, p. 26. This translator follows his own chronological arrangement and uses no verse numberings.

[5]Translations from the Qur'ān in this work, save for the two noted in the two preceding footnotes, are by the author.

Chapter 4

[1]See F. W. Nietzsche, *The Birth of Tragedy,* translated by F. Golffing, New York, 1956, p. II.

[2]The canonical sources of the Sharī'ah are involved in the tensions belonging with the Sunnī/Shī'ah controversies, noted in their historical setting in Chapter 6.

[3]John Williams, *Islam,* New York, 1960, p. 96.

Chapter 5

[1]There are innumerable Arabic prayer manuals, containing such personal devotions for various occasions, intimate or mundane. Their more theological implications are studied in C. E. Padwick, *Muslim Devotions,* London, 1961. The Aḥmadiyyah in Islam published an English prayer book in 1955, at Lahore, with the title: *A Muslim Prayer Book.*

[2]"The accursed (lit. "the stoned") Satan" (*al Shaiṭān al-Rajīm*), is a recurrent Quranic phrase and may be understood in a sense close to the Biblical idea of "the accuser," the *diabolos,* who defies God in contesting the very creation of man, the creature, and his gift of the dominion over nature (see Surah 2:30 f.).

[3]Political unrest and theological questioning found sharp expression by the Kharijites (or *Khawārij*), a militant movement, based mainly on Basrah, from the middle of the seventh century A.D. Denouncing the excesses of the Umayyads, the Kharijites held that they were not true Muslims, since their "works" did not coroborate their profession of "faith." Not being valid Muslims they had no right to rule: allegiance to them must be withdrawn. The question of "faith" and "works" in turn excited the problem of human and Divine will. How was it that men could go counter to the Divine law?

[4]See *Readings from the Mystics of Islam,* by Margaret Smith, London, 1950, pp. 11, 12.

[5]Quoted from W. Montgomery Watt's translation of *Al-Munqidh min al-Ḍalāl,* in *The Faith and Practice of Al-Ghazali,* London, George Allen & Unwin Ltd., 1953, pp. 54, 56, and 58.

[6]Margaret Smith, *op.cit.,* pp. 8 and 97.

[7]Quoted by A. J. Arberry in *Cambridge History of Islam,* Vol. 2, Cambridge, 1970, p. 625.

Chapter 6

[1]The relation between the Islamic and the Christian calendars can be readily seen from the table of important parallel dates preceding the text. A complete table for the conversion of Muslim/Christian dates from the Hijrah to the year 2000 A.D. is given in G.S.P. Freeman-Grenville, *The Muslim and Christian Calendars,* London, 1963.

[2]See Nos. 438–461. There are very many editions of the classic.

[3]See A. J. Arberry in *Cambridge History of Islam,* Vol. 2, Cambridge, 1970, p. 624 f. Also R. A. Nicholson: *Studies in Islamic Mysticism,* London, 1921, p. 199f. The lines translated, by Nicholson, are 2280–2291.

[4]Translation by Bernard Lewis. See *Istanbul and the Civilization of the Ottoman Empire,* Norman, Oklahoma, 1963, p. 165.

[5]On Islam in the Soviet Union see the book with that title, by A. Bennigsen and Chantal Lemercier-Quelquejay, London, 1967. On the "socialist" implications of the Prophet's early biography much has been written by recent Muslim writers. They draw attention to Muḥammad's opposition from vested interests and to the fact that his first followers were mainly from among the poor. On the last point see W. M. Watt: *Muḥammad at Mecca,* Oxford, 1953.

[6]On Africa and Islam, in very broad terms, see: J. S. Trimingham, *The Influence of Islam on Africa,* London, 1966, and other more detailed surveys by the same author.

[7]The abridged translation by H. A. R. Gibb: *Travels in Asia and Africa, 1325–1354,* London, 1929. Extracts are from pp. 330, 331, 171–172 and 306 respectively.

[8]Franz Rosenthal, *The Muqaddimah: An Introduction to History,* translated from the Arabic, 3 vols., New York, 1958. Quotations are from Vol. 2, p. 436 and Vol. 3, pp. 36–38. The author sharply separates philosophy from theology and sees the former, at best, as of value only to certain individuals, and then only defensively in relation to faith. Cf. Vol. 3, pp. 52–55.

Chapter 7

[1]*Le Passé Simple,* Paris, 1962, English translation, London, 1972, under the title: *Heirs to the Past.*

[2]The first two volumes of *Al-Ayyām* appeared in English soon after the first Arabic edition. The third volume only appeared in Cairo in 1973. See E. Paxton: *An Egyptian Childhood,* London, 1932, and H. Wayment: *A Student at the Azhar,* London, 1948. Aḥmad Amīn's autobiography has not yet been translated.

[3]Published by René Guillard, Paris, 1962, English trans. *Ambiguous Adventure,* London, 1970.

[4]See his *Civilization on Trial,* New York, 1948, p. 188 f.

[5]English translation, by this author, London, 1965.

[6]These ideas are set forth in two Arabic publications, not yet available in English: *Al-Wādī al-Muqaddas* (The Hallowed Valley), Cairo, 1967, and *Al-Dhikr al-Ḥakīm* (The Wise Mentor), Cairo, 1972.

[7]Lahore, 1931.

[8]See *Soul: Black Experience,* edited by Lee Rainwater, New York, 1970, article by John Howard, pp. 77–92.

[9]*Autobiography of Malcolm X,* New York, 1964, pp. 338–347.

Bibliography

An invaluable tool for pursuing bibliographical questions in Islamic studies is: J. D. Pearson: *Index Islamicus, 1906–1955,* published at Cambridge, in 1958, and the same compiler's *Index Islamicus: Supplement, 1956–1960,* Cambridge, 1962. There was a *Second Supplement, 1961–1965,* Cambridge, 1967. See also: Charles Adams: *A Reader's Guide to the Great Religions,* pp. 287–337, New York, 1965.

Though the titles suggested below are arranged in line with the chapters of *The House of Islam,* many relate to all, or most, of the themes of this book.

1. Lord of the Worlds
Encyclopedia of Islam, 1913–1938, Leiden, Holland, and the Revised edition, begun in 1954. See article on Allah.

H. A. R. Gibb: *Muhammadanism: a Historical Survey,* revised edition, 1961, New York. A lucid and effective introductory presentation, with a useful book list.

K. W. Morgan, ed.: *Islam, the Straight Path,* New York, 1958. A collection of essays in confession of Islam by a number of Asian writers, and exposition from within.

Fazlur Rahman: *Islam,* London, 1961. Another work of thorough and competent scholarship from within Islam.

Alfred Guillaume: *Islam,* London, 1954. D. Sourdel: *Islam,* New York, 1962 (translated from French). John A. Williams: *Islam,* London, 1961. Three short, general surveys, presenting basic material. Williams annotates extracts from Muslim sources and there are several useful insights in Guillaume, coming from a long erudition which he does not obtrude.

Duncan B. Macdonald: *Development of Muslim Theology, Jurisprudence and Constitutional Theory,* New York, 1903. An older work, still to be consulted with profit.

W. Montgomery Watt: *Islamic Philosophy and Theology* (Islamic Surveys, No. 1), Edinburgh, 1962. A brief and sharply condensed summary of the main themes, schools, and figures, in classic Muslim thought about God, arranged in historical sequence, with very full bibliography.

———: *Freewill and Predestination in Early Islam,* London, 1948. A careful study of a theme prominent in the popular concepts held of Islam in the west.

A. J. Wensinck: *The Muslim Creed,* Cambridge, 1932. Daud Rahbar: *God of Justice: A Study of Ethical Doctrine of the Qur'an,* Leiden, 1960. Two exacting but representative works on Muslim theology. Rahbar breaks new ground in his exhaustive treatment of Quranic contexts in elucidating its teaching about Divine will and being.

M. M. Sharif, ed.: *History of Muslim Philosophy,* 2 vols. Wiesbaden, 1963.

H. A. Wolfson: *The Philosophy of the Kalam,* 2 vols, Cambridge, 1970. Two works of detailed analysis and assessment.

2. Muḥammad and the Rasūliyyah
Tor Andrae: *Muhammad, the Man and his Faith,* translated from the German, by T. Menzel, New York, 1960. Much the most vivid and adequate presentation of the genesis of the Prophet's mission and the psychology of his vocation in the pre-Hijrah period.

Arthur Jeffery: *Islam, Muhammad and his Religion,* New York, 1958. An anthology from
Muslim sources, covering all the main elements in the religious life of Islam, with
a valuable glossary and a very large number of Quranic citations.
W. Montgomery Watt: *Muhammad, Prophet and Statesman,* London, 1961. The best
single introduction to the biographical study of Muḥammad, condensing the same
author's two larger works on Muḥammad in Mecca and in Medina. A work of careful
scholarship.
Muhammad Ali: *The Living Thoughts of Muhammad,* London, 1950. Abd al-Rahman
Azzam: *The Eternal Message of Muhammad,* translated by C. E. Farah, New York,
1964. Two popular Muslim presentations of the meaning and significance of the
founder of Islam, in modern terms.
Richard Bell: *Origin of Islam in its Christian Environment,* London, 1926. C. C. Torrey:
Jewish Foundation of Islam, Yale, 1933. Two works by outstanding scholars, the one
giving the case for a general Christian, the other for a largely Jewish, indebtedness
of original Islam. Attempts to document the bearing of "the people of the Book" on
the antecedents of Muḥammad.
A. Guillaume, trans.: *Life of Muhammad,* Oxford, 1955. An English rendering of Ibn
Isḥāq's *Sīrat Rasūl Allāh,* one of the earliest full length biographies of the Prophet.
Invaluable for the atmosphere and authentic savor of what happened in the Qur'ān.
_____: *The Traditions of Islam,* London, 1954. A useful introduction to the vast field of
traditions, with some account of their development and examples.

3. *Qur'ān*

A. J. Arberry: *The Koran Interpreted,* New York, 1956. Much the best English rendering
of the Islamic Scripture, striving to match the meter and temper of the original
Arabic. (This is what is referred to in the word "Interpreted" in the title which,
otherwise, would be misleading. This is not a commentary.)
_____: *The Holy Koran, an Introduction with Selections,* London, 1953. The translation
is the same as the above, but this group of special passages is prefaced, as the full
work is not, with a detailed analysis of the problems of Arabic/English translation
and of how the translator has handled them.
N. A. Dawood: *The Koran,* New York, 1960. Another very useful translation, in places
even more intelligible than Arberry's. The drawback here is that the translator
rearranges the Qur'ān chronologically. But, in this laudable venture, he gives no
explanations or clues to his decisions, and the book is awkward to use, for lack of
these and for lack of verse numberings. Every passage has to be tracked down
laboriously, though by this means the user does get to know the Qur'ān.
Richard Bell: *Introduction to the Qur'ān,* Edinburgh, 1963. All that the general student
needs is here, about the technical problems and issues of Quranic study. This is an
indispensable tool.
W. Montgomery Watt: *Companion to the Qur'ān,* Edinburgh, 1968. A companion of
somewhat economical conversation, who does, however, offer brief, illuminating
comments and observations on every chapter, with useful wayside notes.

4. *Law*

N. J. Coulson: *A History of Islamic Law,* Edinburgh, 1964. (Islamic Surveys, No. 2).
Joseph Schacht: *Introduction to Islamic Law,* Oxford, 1964. Two competent manuals.
A. Jeffery: *A Reader on Islam,* 'S Gravenhage, 1962. An ample anthology of "Passages
from standard Arabic writings illustrative of the beliefs and practices of Muslims."
An invaluable source book of religious life, the gathering and editing of which
presents a lifetime of devoted Islamic scholarship.

Reuben Levy: *The Social Structure of Islam,* London, 1957. A revised edition of the author's *Sociology of Islam* (1933), with chapters on the status of women, of children, and of the Caliphate, in Islam, and moral sentiments and social customs among Muslims.

Abdul-Hakim Khalifa: *Islamic Ideology,* Lahore, 1951. M. R. Sharif: *Islamic Social Framework,* Lahore, 1954. Two representative Pakistani expositions of the themes of law, society, state and ethics, in Islam.

R. Roberts: *Social Laws of the Qur'ān,* London, 1925. An older, but serviceable, short presentation of the subject.

D. M. Donaldson: *Muslim Ethics,* London, 1953. May be consulted on particular themes, though some of its judgments are debatable.

I. Izutsu: *Ethical Doctrine of the Qur'ān,* Montreal, 1967. Through contextual study of certain basic moral terms and concepts in the Qur'ān, the Japanese scholar offers an original discussion of the mores of Islam.

T. Arnold and A. Guillaume, eds.: *The Legacy of Islam,* London 1931. A delightful volume with a variety of contributors and topics. Note especially Guillaume himself on Theology, and David de Santillana on Law and Society.

Joseph Schacht: *The Origins of Muhammadan Jurisprudence,* Oxford, 1950. A work of established scholarship by an expert in the field.

5. Liturgy and the Sufi Path

H. Lammens: *Islam, Beliefs and Practices,* translated from French by E. Denison Ross, London, 1929. A scholarly exposition.

G. E. von Grünebaum: *Muhammadan Festivals,* New York, 1951. Presents from several larger, authoritative sources, the rudiments of Muslim works of *Dīn,* or religion.

Ahmad Kamal: *The Sacred Journey,* New York, 1961. A popular, reverent manual of the pilgrimage rites with translations of prayers, and interpretation of participation.

Constance E. Padwick: *Muslim Devotions,* London, 1961. A careful, sensitive, and highly competent presentation of the major themes, phrases, attitudes and emphases of Islamic personal religion, drawn from a lifelong study of pocket manuals of prayer and praise, gathered through much loving converse with their users in markets and mosques across the Muslim world. A veritable treasure.

A. J. Arberry: *Sufism,* London, 1950. An introduction to a vast and exacting field of study.

R. A. Nicholson: *The Mystics of Islam,* London, 1914.

Margaret Smith: *Studies in Early Mysticism,* London, 1931. These two authors contributed greatly to the understanding and currency of Islamic mysticism in the west in this century. Their other works present material in greater detail.

J. Spencer Trimingham: *The Sufi Orders in Islam,* Oxford, 1970. A life work of scholarship and experience in the subject. Readers interested in Sufi influence within African Islam should refer to the same author's regional surveys: *Islam in the Sudan,* Oxford, 1949, *Islam in Ethiopia,* Oxford, 1952, and *Islam in West Africa,* 1959, *Islam in East Africa,* Oxford, 1964, and *The Influence of Islam upon Africa,* Oxford, 1968.

6. Ummah

A. J. Arberry, ed: *Aspects of Islamic Civilization,* Ann Arbor, 1967. A rich stimulus to the imagination and a comprehensive, expertly chosen, canvas of Islamic life, translated from original sources, Arabic and Persian.

R. Roolvink, et al.: *Historical Atlas of the Islamic Peoples,* Cambridge, Mass., 1957. Traces in competent color maps and charts the sequence of Islamic Caliphates and the territorial expression of Islam through fourteen centuries.

F. R. J. Verhoeven, *Islam: Its Origin and Spread in Words, Maps, and Pictures,* Amsterdam, 1962.

Carl Brockelmann: *History of the Islamic Peoples,* London, 1947. From the German original. The handiest and most utilized one-volume history of Islam.

Bernard Lewis: *The Middle East and the West,* New York, 1964. A useful, recent survey of the bearings of Arab Islam in the last two and a half centuries.

Sayyid Hosein Nasr: *Ideals and Realities of Islam,* London, 1967. A presentation of Islamic ethos from the standpoint of an alert and articulate Shī'ah Muslim of Persian nationality.

P. M. Holt *et al.: Cambridge History of Islam,* 2 vols. Cambridge, 1970. A valuable source-book of information and interpretation.

G. E. von Grünebaum: *Unity and Variety in Muslim Civilization,* Chicago, 1955. Chapters in the development of Islamic cultural self-expression.

Aziz Ahmad: *Islamic Culture in Its Indian Environment,* Oxford, 1964.

Clifford Geertz: *Islam Observed: Religious development in Morocco and Indonesia,* New Haven, 1968.

J. Kritzeck and W. Lewis: *Islam in Africa,* 1968.

W. Montgomery Watt and P. Cachia, *A History of Islamic Spain,* (Islamic Surveys, No. 4), Edinburgh, 1965.

The above are regional studies.

J. Kritzeck: *Anthology of Islamic Literature,* Princeton, 1962. A useful compendium of extracts and translations illuminating Muslim mores and society.

Eric Schroeder: *Muhammad's People,* Portland, Maine, 1955. Another intriguing anthology of life and letters, demonstrating the endless variety of the *Ummah* and its story.

7. *Questions of Modern Time*

W. C. Smith: *Islam in Modern History,* Princeton, 1957. Careful and penetrating reflection on the modern destiny and evolution of Islam, in the Arab, Pakistani, Indian, Turkish and African scene. A work of significance in intercultural interpretation.

E. I. J. Rosenthal: *Islam in the Modern Nation State,* Cambridge, 1965. Studies the contemporary expression of Islamic ideas and forms in terms of twentieth century nationalism.

A. J. Arberry, general ed.: *Religion in the Middle East: Concord and Conflict,* Cambridge, 1969, 2 vols. Volume 1 contains a comprehensive account of the Islamic aspects, under the subeditorship of C. F. Beckingham. An important major work.

J. H. Thompson and R. D. Reischauer, eds.: *Modernization in the Arab World,* Princeton, 1966. A symposium on the economic, political and social aspects of modernity and a useful measure of the current setting of religious obligation and challenge.

H. A. R. Gibb: *Modern Trends in Islam,* Chicago, 1946. Thirty years old and, therefore, factually in arrears, but still a penetrating analysis of the issues involved for Muslim faith and order in the new dimensions of the twentieth century.

G. S. Métraux and F. Crouzet, eds.: *The New Asia,* New York, 1965. A series of papers written in association with U.N.E.S.C.O. and *The Journal of World History.* Assesses Islam in Turkey and the Arab world.

A. A. A. Fyzee: *A Modern Approach to Islam,* Bombay, 1963. A short, but illuminating, example of the ventures of Islamic loyalty in reinterpretation and rapport with other faiths, in this case mainly with Hinduism.

Ibn Khaldūn: *The Muqaddimah,* translated by F. Rosenthal and abridged by N. A. Dawood, London, 1967. Brings the great classic of history within the reach of English readers.

J. N. D. Anderson: *Islamic Law in the Modern World,* New York, 1959. A brief review of major changes in Muslim jurisprudence this century.

G. E. von Grünebaum: *Modern Islam, the Search for Cultural Identity,* Berkeley, 1962.

Martin Lings: *A Muslim Saint of the 20th Century,* London. A revealing portrait of Shaikh Aḥmad ʿAlāwī, presented by an English Muslim.

Kenneth Cragg: *Counsels in Contemporary Islam,* Edinburgh, 1965 (Islamic Surveys, No. 3). Offers a very full bibliography of modern Muslim writing and a review of the major themes and movements of its inner debate.

_____: *The Call of the Minaret,* New York, 1956. The middle section is entitled: "Minaret and Muslim."

_____: *The Dome and the Rock,* London, 1964, and *The Privilege of Man,* London, 1968. Some account of the shape of religious life in Islam and a study of the Islamic concept of man the "caliph" of God and its relevance to our contemporary triumphs and dilemmas. See Preface.

Index

Quranic Quotations